YO-AFZ-591

FRANCE
A Geographical Study

FRANCE
A Geographical Study

PIERRE GEORGE
Translated by I. B. Thompson

BOOKS

10 East 53d St. New York 10022

(a division of Harper & Row Publishers, Inc.)

© Pierre George 1967
English translation © I. B. Thompson 1973

All rights reserved. No part of this publication may be reproduced,
stored in a retrieval system, or transmitted in any form or by any
means, electronic, mechanical, photocopying, or otherwise, without the
prior written permission of the copyright holder

French edition first published in 1967 by Presses Universitaires de
France, Paris
English edition first published in 1973 by Martin Robertson & Company
Ltd., 17 Quick Street, London, N1 8HL
Published in the U.S.A. 1974 by Harper & Row Publishers Inc. Barnes &
Noble Import Division

ISBN 06-492372-X (paperback)
ISBN 06-492371-1 (case edition)

Text set in 11/12 pt. Photon Times, printed by photolithography,
and bound in Great Britain at The Pitman Press, Bath

Contents

Translator's Preface

Professor George is one of France's most distinguished geographers and his analysis of that country is therefore endowed with exceptional authority. This translation is intended to make George's scholarship available to an English readership, since the original French edition is written in an individual style, rich in imagery, allusion and abstraction, demanding a high proficiency in the language on the part of the English reader. This translation adheres as closely as possible to the original but footnotes have been added to elucidate allusions which might otherwise have been ambiguous.

The book will serve best those who already have some background knowledge of France or who have read in advance some of the available books in English cited in the list of further reading. This applies particularly to Part One, which assumes some basic familiarity with the physical components of the nation and its cultural landscapes. Similarly, the value of the text will be greatly enhanced by constant reference to a detailed atlas of France and its regions.

The distinctive feature of the text is the blending of the traditional approach, with its emphasis on man in relation to his environment viewed through the perspective of history, with the current functional approach, which views regions as units of social and economic organisation, based on hierarchies of control from national, metropolitan, regional and sub-regional capitals. To read the book is to traverse the modern development of French geography from its foundation in the study of landscape as expressed in the distinctive *pays*, to its present emphasis on urban and regional systems, portraying the nation in a new light. To translate a book of such scope and sophistication has been a difficult task, particularly in terms of preserving as closely as possible the style of the original without sacrificing clarity. It is hoped that the result is a portrait of France as seen through the eyes of a scholarly and critical observer, in turn giving a new insight to the reader in English.

Southampton, 1973

Introduction

France in 1973 is a state with 551,000 square kilometres and 51 million inhabitants – 0.4 per cent of the world's continental area and 1.4 per cent of its population. It owes its rank and its international influence to the precious historical and cultural heritage which it has built up. There is no comparison in scale between its surface area and population totals and the weight of its history. Although the history of France owes something to geography through the effects of its position and its land over two thousand years, the reality of France as it is today seems to have been created by history. Its prestige is bound up with the projection into the present and the immediate future of its splendid history.

France ranks as a world power because of the spread of the French language, which is the mother tongue or language of communication for over 100 million people outside the national territory; because of the universal dissemination of French culture and technology; and because of France's economic and financial presence although its resources may seem slight in relation to this influence. It is true that during its history its position has often been more important than the extent of its territory; it has embarked on ventures with diverse consequences in distant places, which have constantly proved its world role. Moreover spiritual influence can be completely disassociated from the realities of space and location, and this is true to a remarkable extent of French influence.

Today, France belongs to the group of countries which have a high rate of output and national income. The average standard of living of its population classes it among the most prosperous nations. The per capita value of the gross national product, 10,000 francs, places it immediately after the richest nations – the United States, Canada, Sweden and Switzerland, among the states with high living standards in north west Europe and far ahead of its Mediterranean neighbours, Italy, with 6,000 francs per capita, and Spain with 3,500. It therefore shares the responsibilities of the industrial nations towards the underdeveloped countries. Its connections with other continents inherited from the past define preferential zones for action with technical and cultural aid.

1 A POSITION OF CONTACT

France's position is at the same time European, Atlantic and Mediterranean. The country is situated between the Rhine Triangle, the maritime area which provides contact with Britain and North America, and the Gulf of Lions. There are easy land and river links with the Rhinelands, the most concentrated industrial region in the world, by way of the Rhine and Moselle valleys to the east and the Belgian Basin to the north. The many invasion corridors of the past now form the important communications axes of the present: the Belfort Gap, the Saverne Gap, the Kaiserlautern Gap, the valleys of the Moselle and the Meuse, the Sambre and Scheldt routes, and the Plain of Flanders. Along each route are found place names recalling the battles of Louis XIV and the wars of 1870 and 1914; but there are also railways, motorways and canals, the most recently improved being the Moselle waterway. The entire frontier is simply a juridical line of over 600 kilometres, drawn without regard to physical geography from Lauterbourg to the North Sea and crossed daily by commuters. Although jealously preserving their regional and national character, the provinces of this frontier, Alsace, Lorraine and Flanders, are directly involved in everything European, while Strasbourg, the symbol of Alsace, is proud of its role as a European capital.

France has a coastline of approximately 5,000 kilometres on the Atlantic and the other seas, the North Sea and the Channel, which communicate with the ocean. From Flanders to Finistère it faces the south coast of the British Isles. The world's busiest flow of maritime navigation, linking North America with north west Europe, passes within a few miles of the French coast and reaches towards Le Havre, Rouen, Dieppe and Dunkerque. The attraction of the ocean has been felt ever since the time of the great discoveries; Saint-Malo,

Dunkerque and Dieppe have their history and legends of the sea; French vessels have, since the days of sail, cruised along the coasts of the two Americas carrying sugar from the Antilles and African slaves. Much later, when maritime navigation was relieved of some of its functions by aviation, France was among the first country to open up air routes across the doldrums towards Brazil and the Andes.

France is Mediterranean as well as Atlantic. Admittedly, the coastline of the *Midi** is less extensive, about 1,500 kilometres including the Corsican coastline, but for thousands of years there has been contact with other countries bordering the Mediterranean both by means of the rivieras and by sea. The French *Midi* is merely part of the great cultural zone of *Langue d'oc* which stretches from Catalonia to Italy. Since classical antiquity, the coast opposite has attracted the Mediterranean peoples of Europe and piracy forced the inhabitants of the littoral to huddle into fortified villages. The chequered course of Mediterranean history has drawn France in turn into the Crusades, surrender negotiations with the Sultan, the conquest of Algeria and the building of the Suez Canal.

With its many different areas of interest, France has taken a variety of initiatives which have made it at the same time an industrial state, a member of the North European group and a partner in the Common Market – although not as extensively industrialised as West Germany or Belgium – an Atlantic maritime power, drawn particularly towards the low latitudes although retaining lasting links with Canada, and a Mediterranean nation orientated towards Africa and the East. From all this, in the course of history, many contradictions have developed, resulting in a highly developed network of special relationships.

2   WORLD WIDE HISTORICAL CONTACTS

The most constant theme in French history is that of continental contacts in the course of which the national frontiers were established – not without bloodshed. These increasingly destructive conflicts have ended only with the formation of a west European economic complex. Modern France is now, not without certain difficulties, adapting itself to this new system of European relationships.

---

* The term *Midi* applies conventionally to the far south of the country. No precise limit exists but in general a line at the latitude of Bordeaux and Valence provides an approximate northern boundary.

A second theme concerns relations with the Orient. Throughout French history this has been a frequently recurring theme of eclipse: the Crusades, Bonaparte's expedition to Egypt, and the opening of a century of French influence in the eastern Mediterranean, the colonial adventure in the Far East. Different landmarks established at various times in distant places represent the centres of French influence in the Levant, Iran and South East Asia.

The third theme is that of relations between France and Africa, via the Maghreb, the Sahara and the Atlantic coast of Africa. More than the previous theme this is part of the colonial history of the nineteenth century. By imposing a language of communication and creating cultural and technical ties which have survived the colonial system with renewed vigour, this period – relatively short in terms of historical time – nevertheless still has the power to influence present-day events.

More subtle, but not negligible, are the Latin contacts maintained with Central and South America. Here, although it retains only the Antilles* and Guyana from the colonial phase of the eighteenth century, France benefits from the fact that the economies and cultures of Spain and Portugal are not inspiring examples for peoples who wish to develop in freedom and escape from North American tutelage.

3 THE GREAT CONTRADICTION OF THE END OF THE CENTURY

There is certainly a contradiction between the relationships with the rest of the world which France developed by the twentieth century and the technological conditions necessary for the realisation of power since the end of the Second World War. In that a state's authority depends on its possessing a nuclear arsenal or an aerospace fleet and its prospects of international economic competition imply a concentration of the means of production equal to those of the entire world in 1913 or in 1920, France can no longer claim the rank of a great power. The ambiguity of the French nuclear effort lies precisely in the fact that a great many sacrifices have been agreed to but have been ineffective as far as international competition is concerned – except of course in the field of technical expertise.

* Martinique and Guadeloupe, now overseas *départements* of France.

France has a unique world heritage which derives from its past as a great world power before the decisive turning point in the middle of this century. To retain its rank, it must become part of a greater continental grouping, and it is naturally towards Europe that it turns. However it is a matter of being European without losing its specifically French influence in the Third World. This obviously implies a certain reserve with regard to European integration, and also calls for considerable effort in developing what remains France's strength in international affairs – its culture and technological dynamism.

PART ONE

The Heritage: Over Two Thousand Years of Experiment

France is not the product of a unifying natural setting. It is characterised by its diversity and by the dispersion of its homelands far more than by any underlying unity. It is the product of historical events, in spite of the natural environment, as are almost all European states, with the exception of the United Kingdom which benefits from insular unity while still having great internal diversity. France is a more or less continuous aggregate of geographical regions so distinctive that one wonders if the geographical region, as usually defined by French geographers, is not essentially French, even if the term can by analogy be extended outside France, at least in Europe. Within a highly compartmentalised geomorphological whole, population groups were formed with a defensive organisation, in a protective natural setting which also provided the indispensable conditions for the life of the group, conditions supplied by groups of valleys or small interior basins. Between the groups more or less extensive expanses of forest unsuitable for defence or cultivation persisted for a relatively long time and formed protective ramparts as no-man's-lands separating the *pays*.* The unification of groups of *pays* in larger natural settings constituted the provinces of which the outlines have remained very stable for long periods of time. The provinces, corresponding to morphological and climatic units, constitute a basic type of geographical region, for example Brittany, Alsace, Franche-Comté, Auvergne and Provence. But the range of physical factors taken as a whole has not always governed the regions' historical evolution. A single element has in some instances been enough to

* This word is a sufficiently conventional term in geography to be left untranslated throughout, and indeed no single English word has quite the same connotations. Usually it refers to a small unit which is distinctive in terms of physical conditions and human response as expressed in its social organisation and landscape appearance.

1

polarise a unit; for example, the coastal position and the unity of the natural landscape of forests and humid valleys have clearly defined the unity of Normandy, which is constituted by differing rock types. Some regions seem to have escaped the framework outlined by the natural environment because they go far beyond the apparent physical boundaries. They have managed to unite two complementary natural zones, as for example the mountain and its foreland in Savoie and Dauphiné. The regions which seem most heterogeneous are those where this search for complementary elements and the exploitation of a crossroads location have been furthest developed, as in the case of the Lyon region. But unity has always been achieved by concerted action over a long period of time on the part of a dynasty or an urban bourgeoisie. Wars, partitions, arbitrations and administrative divisions have created boundaries which often are only conventional limits across frontier zones and which make little impression on the economic and political life of the *pays* they enclose. Nevertheless they have been the most bitterly disputed sectors, and those where the place names most clearly indicate attachment to the region. Tiny *pays* have retained their distinctive character on the borders of the great provinces, becoming geographical regions which are as it were traced over natural units, like Gâtinais, the Pays d'Othe, Minervois or the Corbières. The process of unification up to the present day has in some cases progressed as far as the level of major region and in others has stopped at the level of many distinctive *pays,* only weakly centralised with regional grouping and association as in the South West.

While the unification of the regions progressed at the slow pace of rural evolution, handicapped by the fragmentation into *départements,* the industrial revolution traced new power structures, calling into question the entire regional edifice inherited from the past. The regions of the North and North East – Flanders, northern Champagne and Lorraine – with their mineral resources, attracted basic industries founded essentially in the nineteenth century on coal and iron. The population in the surrounding areas was mobilised into diversified industrial activity using coal as a source of energy. Capital, labour, business contractors and skilled technicians poured into the industrial regions and the major transit centres – the seaports and main railway junctions which determined the location of some factories. At the same time, Paris, which until then had been only a political and administrative centre became the centre of financial and economic activity too. In contrast to developments in neighbouring countries, the greater part of the system of economic direction was transferred to Paris.

In the mid twentieth century, France seems to have far greater diversity than ever before. Running down of investment and the rise in the average age of the population affects central France, the South West and part of the Mediterranean South, especially its Alpine section. The distances which separate the southern regions from the zones of industrial development in northern and north-eastern France and north west Europe seem more and more prejudicial to the business conditions of firms in the remote and badly served regions, in spite of technical progress in transport methods. The system of rural territorial units formed over ten centuries has been abruptly dislocated by the shock of the industrial revolution and new processes of selective urbanisation.

CHAPTER ONE

The Natural and Historical Components

France has three major regional components differentiated by relief and situated around a central watershed which is a severe obstacle to communications – the Massif Central. To the north extend the *pays* of the Paris Basin, the northern plains and the intermediate mountains of the east, opening towards north west Europe and the Rhinelands generally. To the east and south lie the great Alpine mountains and the Mediterranean coastlands, bright, colourful *pays* facing Italy, the Orient and Africa. To the south west and west, plateaux and hills crossed by lines of trees and hedgerows, stretch as far as the Atlantic Ocean and the cul de sac of Spain.

The natural conditions prevalent in the uplands of the Massif Central are too severe for it to play a unifying role. The unification of France was achieved by by-passing it from a point in the heart of the Paris Basin, where the great natural routes converge from the Basque country, the lagoons of the Camargue, the upland basins of the Maurienne, Switzerland, the Germanic fringe and Flanders.

1   THE NORTH AND THE EAST

France has access to the most symbolic area of Western Europe, the Rhine Basin, by the regions of the north and the east, which were often battlefields where France fought over its very existence and its physical boundaries. After the disappearance of the Roman Empire, the first attempt at large scale territorial unification was the Empire of Charlemagne, which was a Rhenish empire. France became an individual entity after the Treaty of Verdun, as a younger son of the Empire. It proved more viable than the haughty Lotharingia extending from the shores of the Mediterranean as far as the Nordic seas. But

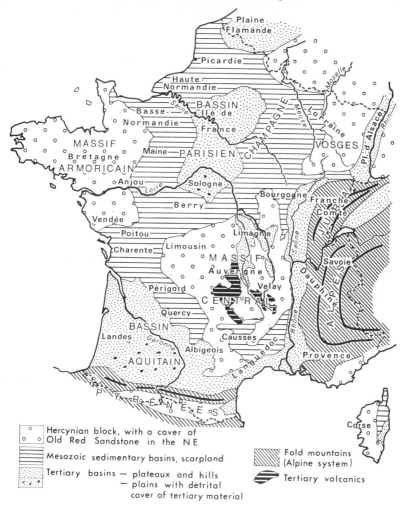

Hercynian block, with a cover of
Old Red Sandstone in the N E

Mesozoic sedimentary basins, scarpland

Tertiary basins — plateaux and hills
— plains with detrital
cover of tertiary material

Fold mountains
(Alpine system)

Tertiary volcanics

FIG. 1. The major structural units of France

very early on it had to face the imperial ambitions which followed the
relief of Lotharingia and of the Kingdom of Louis the German by the
German Holy Roman Empire and which it encountered simultaneously on all its frontiers at the most dramatic moments of its history. It
was, however, in the plains of Flanders, in the forests and marshes of
the east, that the decisive battles were fought. Until the nineteenth and

twentieth centuries, the outcome of wars was decided on the Yser, the Sambre, the Meuse and between the Vosges and Ardennes. The place names are historical rather than geographical. The names of provinces and the names of towns and villages are a memorial to the building of the nation – so that when the enemy was the English, the symbol of national resistance, Joan of Arc, came from Lorraine. The *pays* of the north and east are a museum of military archaeology, combining medieval fortifications, the town walls built by Vauban, the fortresses of the nineteenth century and the beginning of the twentieth, and Verdun, with memories of the Maginot Line, set among scattered garrison towns. The essential characteristic of these *pays*, therefore, is their openness.

To the north, the opening is towards the Belgian Basin which is extended by the mouths of the Rhine and Meuse and by Holland. After the barely perceptible threshold of Artois the drainage is towards the North Sea by the Aa, Yser and Scheldt. The climate is the same as that of the outflow plains of the Rhine Basin: frosty, icy but not excessively cold winters, often overcast skies and summers which on the rich soil produce the continent's most abundant crop yields. Stone is rare, the soils are clay and *limon*,* and the houses are built of brick. On this rich soil, the population has withstood the ups and downs of history and has proved to be more fertile than elsewhere. Even before industry attracted great concentrations of workers, there was a dense and hardworking population in a compact grouping of villages, small towns and market centres mingling with fortresses. The coast is inhospitable, but the least difficult site, protected by a deep sea trench, had of necessity to be used for an artificial port excavated from the dunes. This is Dunkerque, which after one of the most dramatic episodes in its history, has today become an industrial growth sector on the new basis of steelmaking.

The distinctive feature of the Nord† region, with its long insecure frontier without natural barriers, is the constant search for new sources of wealth and new types of work. An agricultural system, ingenious rather than skilled, has exploited the varying potential of the *pays* which only very close scrutiny can discover. On a basement of permeable chalk covered by *limon,* as in Picardy, Hainaut and Cam-

---

* The term 'limon' has no one-word equivalent. It is loessic material which has often been reworked by water action. It yields loams of high natural fertility.

† The Nord region generally implies the two heavily industrialised *départements* of Nord and Pas-de-Calais.

brésis, wheat is cultivated, with sugar-beet, potatoes and fodder crops, combining stock rearing on the farm with field crops. The Flemish Plain introduces the grassland and market garden landscapes of Belgian Flanders and Holland. Interior Flanders is a transitional region. The heavy but better drained soils have encouraged speculation in sugar-beet production. Several generations of artisan and industrial experience have been superimposed on this agricultural basis, which is one of the best balanced in France; these include the working of thread and cloth, from linen to cotton as well as wool and flax, and the exploitation of coal, which gave a new form to traditional activities and opened up new perspectives for metallurgy and chemicals. Today industrial raw materials come from overseas and from across the frontier to supply the region's industries by substituting for local resources materials from abroad such as petroleum from the Middle East and the Sahara, iron ore from Mauritania and natural gas from Groningen. Three million inhabitants live in an area of less than 1,200 square kilometres, a combination of industrial, urban and agricultural landscapes, with interminable lines of brick houses, spoil heaps, railways, canals and roads, burdened by the problems of all old industrial regions in search of constant renewal: part of industrial Europe, but also a chapter in the history of France.

Another chapter opens with the approach to the plateaux and great forests of the East. The term 'slope' is totally applicable here. Two natural bastions intercept circulation – the Ardennes and the Vosges. The Ardennes are the terminus in France of the high plateaux of the Belgian Ardennes and the Rhine schist massif, high tablelands levelling off the primary folds and drastically deforming the beds of sandstones, schists and the hard or marmorised* limestones. Although the altitude is only just over 500 metres, the Ardennes is characterised by a severe climate, with long cold winters which prolong the snow cover. There is little soil to attract agriculture on this slab of old Primary material; the rubble is covered by forests. Clearings are rare and the settlements huddle in the valleys; in the Meuse valley which dissects the massif from south to north and in the valleys of its tributaries which have cut through the less resistant outcrops forming a discordant Appalachian type of topography in the Semois area. The unity of the Vosges, like that of the Ardennes, is based on the forest, which covers both the crystalline and sandstone Vosges. The core area is an intrusion of granite which bulged and cracked open the

* Converted into marble by metamorphism.

sedimentary cover and fractured to form the rift valley of Alsace and Baden, separating the Vosges from the Black Forest. Deprived of its outer cover of Permian and Triassic sandstone, the granite reaches its highest points at between 1,200 and 1,400 metres along the *route des crêtes,* which link together the *ballons.** The valleys, which rapidly become entrenched, dissect this hard mass so that it forms domes ringed with forests and bare on the summits. They are narrower on the western, Lorraine slope than on the eastern slope, where the proximity of the Rhine trench stimulated erosion by fluvial action and the Quaternary glaciation. To the north, the crystalline rocks plunge underneath Permian conglomerates and the Old Red Sandstones of the Trias. The summits become tabular, as exemplified by the Donon, and have ruiniform slopes. The forest extends everywhere. It dominates the sandstone Vosges and throughout the gap which separates the Vosges from the Ardennes, in the Hardt, and bordering the Saar, in the coalfield area of Forbach, Hombourg and Saint-Avold. It is only interrupted along the Moselle furrow and in the Gutland of Luxembourg.† The relief is composed of huge sloping surfaces fringed with wooded ledges. The same arrangement is found to the south of the Vosges, between the Vosges and the Jura, on the plateaux of the Belfort Gap and in Alsace, where the forest is still important on the sandstones and limestones in the spaces between the honeycomb of clay where grassland and crops have been established in the vicinity of Luxeuil, Lure and Vesoul.

Behind this great mountainous and forested crescent, where bastions alternate with passes, from Sedan and Forbach to Belfort, begin the scarplands, the *pays des côtes.* Geomorphologists prefer the term *cuesta* to *côtes* to avoid any ambiguity, but in this area the terms 'côtes de Moselle' and 'côtes de Meuse' are used. The infilling of the huge bowl of the Paris Basin alternated spreads of clay and marl with the deposition of hard reef or shelly limestones. The calcareous masses form major slopes turning their scalloped scarp fronts to the east and north, while inclining gently towards the west-south-west to plunge underneath the sheets of clay and clay marl which form the plains, for example the Lorraine Plain and the Plain of the Woëvre. Towards the south the plateaux vice closes, the plains are now only valleys, furrows

---

* The term applied to the rounded summits of the crystalline Vosges, of which the highest are the Ballon de Guebviller, 1,426 metres, the Hohneck, 1,362 metres, and the Ballon d'Alsace, 1,247 metres.

† The Gutland, or Bon Pays, occupies the southern two-thirds of Luxembourg.

gouged in a predominantly limestone upland, which between the sources of the Marne and the Seine make the transition from Lorraine to Burgundy.

Lorraine is a historical province, a region of contact with intersecting communications which have given it a military function as a frontier province protecting east-west and north-south routes. It occupies the western edge of the Vosges, faces the Saar and Luxembourg to the north, borders on the Ardennes along the Meuse valley and is subdivided into alternating bands of vales with heavy soils, wooded slopes, rows of *buttes** and limestone plateaux. The drainage network, which has played an important role in the distribution of population, is partially secant and partially tangential in relation to the pattern of major relief features. The strong points, like Metz, Nancy and Toul, guard north-south or east-west routes, and often both at the same time. For centuries the military function was more important here than productive activity. The agriculture consisted of poor subsistence farming of which the only good points were some well drained scarps where vines and fruit trees introduced a note of gaiety and well-being into a grey landscape with low cereal yields, where sheep grazings were more extensive than rich pasture. It was a hard *pays,* of long misty winters, with towns which were destroyed several times over and rebuilt without style to facilitate the billeting and transit of armies. Industry developed late here, in the nineteenth century, in the gaps between the nodes and axes of settlement born of agriculture and the control of routes for defence and commerce. It called into being technical complexes rather than new towns, which attracted new inhabitants from elsewhere. It hunted for a capital town which would be a compromise between the need to serve industry and the historic heritage. However, there is already some anxiety about the future of industries which were at times in the past believed to guarantee French power and independence.

After the sloping relief of Lorraine and in contrast to its austere appearance, comes Alsace, one of France's openings on to the Rhine and a region in contact with Switzerland, Germany and Holland. It is profoundly European, while remaining the most deliberately distinctive French province. Mountainous by virtue of the Vosges valleys, the Thur, Fecht, Liepvrette and Bruche, and the narrow massifs which separate them, it is primarily a *pays* of hills, with vineyards surrounding huge villages which have the atmosphere of stylish little towns,

* For the most part formed by outliers of limestone on the clay vales.

and of the great Rhine plain where cereal fields give way in places to forests and to the *ried** landscape of pasture and marshes. An exceptionally high fragmentation of the land into narrow elongated strips, the many villages with their pointed roofs, gables facing the street and walls half-timbered in geometrical designs with solid wooden beams, the conservation of the dialect, the adherence to traditions which have survived in spite of change, make Alsace an historical rather than a geographical region, although it is so well defined and has such clearly drawn natural units. However, as in Lorraine, the province is controlled in varying degrees by urban centres: Strasbourg does not have total control over Alsace although it is in every sense the capital; Mulhouse still has its own individuality and functions; and Colmar considers itself the most Alsatian of Alsatian towns.

The alternation of mountains and bleak plateaux forming eastern France is continued to the south of Lorraine and Alsace with the plateaux of Burgundy and Franche-Comté and the Jura mountains. Here a major north-south breach links up with the Rhine trough, but in terms of the general structure of natural units rather than in terms of historical events or even present day activities. Its orientation is more European than French and, for a thousand years, France moulded its frontier at the expense of its European neighbours. As much from an economic standpoint as because of its original geomorphological features, the Saône depression functioned as an enclosed basin until the present day, and its opening to the north by appropriate civil engineering works has still not been decided. As a communications axis, it forms an annexe to the Lyon crossroads and a link between the Midi and the Paris Basin. It is part of the internal pattern of French circulation intersected by east-west routes leading to the frontiers. The eastern frontier between the Belfort Gap and the French section of the Rhône valley is formed by the Jura, the least historic of French frontiers since for a very long time relations between France and Switzerland have been untroubled. It is nevertheless clearly defined physically, more effectively by the high limestone plateaux which are very little dissected by valleys, than by the height and continuity of the chains which succeed each other to the south, reaching 1,700 metres and blocking the passage between the Swiss lowland and the Saône plain. Formed by quite tightly packed folds in the south and by broad plateaux fifty kilometres wide

* The *ried* refers to the depressed zone of alluvium corresponding with the former flood plains of the Rhine and Ill.

in the north, and in large part coinciding with the former province of Comté or Franche-Comté, the Jura is an enclosed environment whose population has managed to organise a varied economy, with many complementary features, offering its services to neighbouring regions. Because of their long standing determination to live in the mountains and by means of mountain resources the Jura offers a variety of activities which keep a relatively numerous and hard working population living there in picturesque if harsh surroundings.

Opposite the plateaux of Comté, those of Burgundy have evolved in a quite different way. At an early stage they became involved in the gradual concentration of activities and population towards the centre of the Paris Basin and they were gradually depopulated in favour of Dijon and above all the Paris region. At the same time they have become part of the retirement and recreational zone of the Paris agglomeration. An elderly population is gradually leaving the plateaux's infertile soils and the countryside is assuming a tertiary function as it is transformed into a refuge for retirement and a setting for children's holiday hostels and for second homes. The valleys form uninterrupted chains of renovated villages from the harsh plateaux of the Montagne* of Burgundy and from the Morvan, as far as the Forêt d'Othe, the Senonais and Gâtinais. This is the most frequented transit area in France between the central Paris Basin and the regions of the South East; the route to the Mediterranean which the Italians would probably have called the 'sunshine road'.

II   THE LYON CROSSROADS

The Lyon crossroads is also France's opening to Italy. The city, which was founded as the capital of the Gauls in the time of Augustus, remains one of the great centres of internal communications in France and it is a staging post towards the Mediterranean and across the Alps to Northern Italy. Lyon is a point of convergence and of contact, situated at the confluence of the major valleys of the Saône and Rhône and opening up three natural routes towards Germany, Switzerland and the Mediterranean. It is a point of contact between regions with radically different structures and vocations; the Saône trough, the

---

* The name 'Montagne' is applied to the series of high limestone plateaux, north of Dijon, which form part of the major structure of the Plateau de Langres.

chains and *cluses** of the southern Jura, the compact but indented uplands of the eastern Massif Central, the great Alpine mountains and
the Rhône furrow.

Between the Burgundy plateaux, the Vosges, the Jura plateaux and
the crystalline bosses which show how near the Massif Central is to
Lyon, the great Saône depression extends 250 kilometres north-south
with a width of 80 kilometres. A Tertiary tectonic trench, occupied by
lakes during the Pliocene, it is in the form of a huge keel-shaped
ellipse, composed of tiny geographical units, each different from the
others, which disputed control over the adjoining provinces; they
include the hillslopes of Franche-Comté, the forests of the *pays* of Dole
and Citeaux, the Dijon lowlands, Bresse, Dombe, the ribbon of flood-
prone lowlands of the Saône, the vineyards on limestone to the north
(Côte Dijonnais, Côte de Nuits, Côte de Beaune) and on granite to the
south (Mâçonnais, Beaujolais). It is a region with a centuries-old
reputation and with solidly based wealth, in spite of its wooded
wilderness scattered with lakes. The productive lands are found along
the Côte, the Saône valley, Bresse and parts of the Jura margin. To the
south, the Saône depression seems to close up, precisely at the approach
to the major crossroads, which is protected to the north, between
Villefranche and Lyon, by the granitic mass of Mont d'Or.

The Jura makes contact with the crossroads zone by means of its
southern chains and the lowland embayments recessed between their
extremities. There is no clear-cut boundary between the Jura and the
Alps. The Jurassic chains merge into the foreland of Savoie, and the
old province of Savoie encompassed Bresse and Bugey. The Rhône
cuts across the limestone folds of the Jura, swinging round in hairpin
bends. Its valley, confined in a succession of *cluses,* such as the Crêt
d'Eau or Bellegarde-Génissiat, does not represent a continuous
historical or geographical frontier and it is even less a route between
Geneva and the approaches to Lyon. The main roads and railways cut
through the folds to the north, via the Albarine valley, Culoz and Aix-
les-Bains, and to the south, via Bourgoin, La Tour-du-Pin and
Chambéry.

The eastern margin of the Massif Central to the west forms an
obstacle between the *pays* of the Saône and Rhône and those of Velay
and Auvergne which is difficult to cross. However, the herring bone
arrangement of the massifs favours approach through the gaps, for

* The term *cluse* is applied to the transverse breaching of the Jura folds, and by
extension to similar structures elsewhere, notably in the Pre Alps.

example the furrow of Montchanin-Montceau-les-Mines, the Grosne and Gier valleys. The wall only becomes really continuous from the massif of Pilat, in Vivarais and as far as the Cévennes. Two of the passages, those of Montceau-les-Mines and the Gier valley, coincide with old industrial zones based on the exploitation of coal. Between the two, the mountains of Beaujolais and Lyon which since the fourteenth century have exploited the water power of their rivers to run the silk-spinning and weaving industries are like faded pictures of old provincial France, now facing problems of conversion.

To the east, the Alps are higher, more impressive, easier to penetrate and more modern. These mountains, the mightiest in France and in Europe, are very diversified and have a very uneven resource base. The most marked contrast is between the structural and geographical complex of the Northern Alps, and the very different unit of the Southern Alps, which nevertheless belong to the same orogenic system. The Northern Alps are higher, with large, famous massifs, great glaciers and a substantial snow cover throughout the winter. This is a mountain tourist area par excellence, where investment in the infrastructure of cableways, hotels and winter sports resorts is guaranteed to be profitable – as, for instance, in the massif of Mont Blanc and the Arve valley, the massifs of Belledonne, Tarentaise and Vanoise, the valleys of the Isère in Tarentaise and of the Arc in Maurienne and the massifs of Pelvoux and Oisans. However, these mountains are also the easiest to penetrate and cross. They are scarcely an obstacle between France and Northern Italy. The great schemes completed, from the building of the Fréjus railway tunnel at Mont Cenis to the road tunnel under Mont Blanc, successfully combine two attractions – the appeal of the highest mountains with the advantages of the fastest and most heavily used routes. The Sub-Alpine trench and the *cluses* which cut through the limestone ramparts of the Pre Alps, to the west of frontier and interior massifs, make movement within the mountains easier. Together with Chambéry and Annecy, Grenoble controls this mountain traffic, and the functions of a mountain capital are concentrated in it. Merely listing its activities reveals that industry is one of its most important functions. In fact, the climate gives the Northern Alps a powerful renewal of its water resources, stored as snow and ice and redistributed by means of the many cascades, torrents and large rivers which have made these mountains a test bed for hydro-electric generation and one of the important energy resources of the national economy. This natural wealth meant that industry was established in the mountains before it was known how to transfer electricity over long distances, and this industry still survives there.

The Southern Alps are completely different. They are drier, more compact, wilder and less open to the exterior except by way of the Durance valley. Above all they are less accessible to Italy, less favourable for winter sports, less suitable for either an agricultural or an industrial economy and more effective than the Northern Alps as a natural obstacle. The mountains continue with no embayment except the gap of the Lower Durance between the Luberon and Alpilles, which are in fact heights outside the Alpine range, as far as the Rhône corridor, dominated successively by the limestone battlements of the Dents du Diois and the Barronnies, and the huge inclined surface of Mont Ventoux and the Monts de Vaucluse.

The Rhône valley, which played a frontier role throughout the Middle Ages, is not well suited physically to be the routeway between Central Europe and the Mediterranean which at first glance it appears to be on a large scale map. The breach between the Massif Central and the Alps opens out in a discontinuous way, the river remained a violent, irregular torrent until the improvement carried out between 1945 and 1965 by the Compagnie Nationale du Rhône. The geological furrow which effectively separates the old uplifted and fractured block of the Massif Central, the margin of which is uplifted to 1,500 metres in the Vivarais and the Cévennes, from the Pre Alps of Dauphiné and Provence, is plugged by detrital material piled up during the Tertiary and at the beginning of the Quaternary, and above Montelimar is cut across by transverse ridges. This results topographically in a succession of basins and very narrow defiles, entrenched in granite or pierced through east-west running bands of hard limestone – for example, the defiles at Les Roches de Condrieu, Saint-Vallier, Tain-Tournon and Donzère. Upstream, between Lyon and the approaches to the Valence plain, the slopes of debris torn from the Alps form long spines which the roads cross by climbing steeply. Only with the achievements of modern technology – the electrification of the railway, the improvement of the river which still only offers limited possibilities for inland navigation, the construction of the motorway and the laying of the Berre-Strasbourg pipeline – was it possible to realise the recurrent dream of the last hundred years, the inauguration of a major trans-European axis from the Mediterranean to the Rhineland. Even now the links between the Saône plain and the Rhine basin have still to be improved: Although the routeway has not been fully exploited, the Lyon crossroads has shown its vitality whenever historical circumstances have not been against it. Since the fifteenth century, the city has developed its dual function as an industrial and regional centre, and in all respects, in terms of population size as well as by the national and international spread of its influence, it has acquired the rank of a major regional metropolis on a European scale.

III   THE MEDITERRANEAN MIDI

France is a Mediterranean country by virtue of its extensive and varied coastline, 600 kilometres in length from the Spanish frontier and the end of the Pyrenees, of which the eastern parts, Albères, Canigou and Corbières, are essentially Mediterranean mountains, as far as the imperceptible transition from the Côte d'Azur of Nice to the Italian Riviera di Ponente.

This long chain of contrasting *pays* which owes its unity entirely to the climate and the coastal position is barred from the interior except

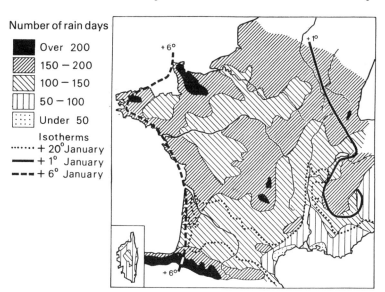

Number of rain days

Over 200
150 – 200
100 – 150
50 – 100
Under 50
Isotherms
+ 20° January
+ 1° January
+ 6° January

FIG. 2. Climatic indices

for the outlet of the Rhône furrow. It is shaped like an amphitheatre, the highest points of which form an interior aureola over 1,500 metres high in the Maritime Alps, the Pre Alps of Grasse and Digne, the mountains of Lure and Ventoux, the Cévennes and the Montagne Noire, and the eastern Pyrenees. In front the lower tiers are formed by the crystalline massifs of Esterel and Maures, the Plans de Provence, the Gras du Vivarais and the Garrigues of Nîmes and Montpellier. The lowlands are at the centre of the amphitheatre in the basins of Basse-Provence, still framed by lofty ridges over 1,000 metres high, in the plains of the Rhône outflow and those of Bas-Languedoc and Roussillon.

History has destroyed the unity which this amphitheatre achieved as the Roman province of Narbonne. Tourism is in the process of recreating the unity, but there are still strong contrasts between all aspects of provincial and regional realities – physiographic, economic and demographic. The staircase of plateaux and plains in Bas-Languedoc, its Spanish and Catalonian affinities particularly and its polarisation by a viticultural economy make it a completely different region from Provence, which is compartmentalised, more intimate, more mountainous, more diversified as regards its economy and which is influenced by neighbouring Italy.

Today the coastline is like a huge fringe of summer tourism. Holiday making and seaside activities were initially attracted to the two rocky sections of the coast, the short Pyrenean section from Collioure to Port-Vendres and, above all, the coast of Provence, from the *calanques** of the Marseille and Toulon region, the Maures and Esterel, to the broad sunny bays of the Côte d'Azur, Antibes and Menton. However now even the flat coasts, the lagoon coasts of the Camargue and Languedoc, are being developed to receive millions of visitors each year. The tourist role, which has so transformed the landscapes of the Provence coast and the Côte d'Azur in the last fifty years, is not the only economic wealth of the Mediterranean Midi. The climate, with its sunny hot dry summers, in spite of its harshness, its torrential downpours in autumn and the cold violent winds of the *tramonte* and *mistral,* favours the cultivation of valuable crops, trees and bushes. Pride of place goes to the vine and to irrigated market garden crops sheltered by windbreaks of cypresses or reed screens. In the last hundred years delicate specialised crops have replaced the

---

* The term is applied to towering precipitous cliffs heavily dissected by marine erosion.

former cereals and sheepgrazing on the plains and in the interior basins. The hills and the dry bare mountains have gradually been depopulated. Even the high mountains are almost entirely without inhabitants except for several humid furrows where cattle rearing persists and where tourist resorts have been built at the limit for possible exploitation as winter sports stations, as in the valleys of the Tinée, Vésubie and, particularly, the upper Durance. If one excludes Nice, which by virtue of its eccentric location and its year-round tourist function, stands out as a major town with its own specific activities, the whole of the Mediterranean region is centred on Marseille and the Rhône outflow of the European north-south axis. However, this is a recent situation. Provence and Languedoc have lived for centuries as hostile and jealous neighbours, covering the river banks with fortifications which crown all the rocky eminences of the valley. Marseilles' wealth as a colonial port between 1830 and the Second World War linked it to Paris and the rest of France rather than to the Mediterranean region with which it had little contact. Each town in Provence and, even more, in Languedoc controlled a larger or smaller part of the region, not to mention Avignon which controlled the former Papal province of Comtat, now the *département* of Vaucluse; examples are Aix-en-Provence, Toulon and Draguignan in Provence, Nîmes, Montpellier, Béziers, Narbonne in Languedoc and Perpignan in Roussillon. The unifying framework was on the one hand Catalan and Languedoc speech, on the other Provençal. Even today, in spite of the attraction of the Marseille-Rhône axis which acts as one of the new backbones of the French economy, the towns of Languedoc and Provence defend their independence and eagerly launch out into economic and technological competition to consolidate and guarantee this independence. Nevertheless, the industrial economy is above all attracted towards the Rhône Valley and the complex of Marseille-Berre-Gulf of Fos, while the problems of viticulture and the markets for vegetables in Bas-Languedoc, as in the Comtat, still occupy the lowland plains.

IV   THE CENTRE AND THE WEST

The Centre and the West form a major unit of 230,000 square kilometres looking towards the Atlantic and the Channel and almost entirely drained by the Loire and Garonne basins. In spite of their extent and their differences, the *pays* which constitute this grouping have certain unifying characteristics. First, certainly, comes the climate. While it is true that from the Channel coasts to the Basque country and from Finistère to Central Limousin or Cantal, the temperatures, rainfall amounts and proportion of snowfall in the precipitation vary quite clearly, all the facts indicate that the area belongs to the same major climatic division of heavy precipitation, especially in the cold seasons, distributed over many days, high levels of atmospheric humidity and a limited temperature range. They are all green *pays,* where grassland, heath and forest still occupy a high proportion of the land and where the landscapes are dissected by lines of trees. The population is scattered in these secretive and misty landscapes. There is nothing resembling the large Mediterranean villages which look like little towns, or the villages of the East, huddled around their church steeples or in long lines of connected houses.

The uplands are differentiated. Major breaks of relief compartmentalise them and give them distinctive volcanic landforms, as in Cantal, Mont-Dore and the Chaîne des Puys. Except on the floors of basins deep in the heart of the crystalline mass, as the Limagnes, Velay and Forez, the granitic gneiss rock type and the extension of the oceanic climate give the same landscapes of plateaux and blunted massifs, covered by bracken, forest or summer pasture. The same massive buildings built in huge stones of granite or dark coloured lava are found everywhere. Everywhere too the water, darkened by black mica from the granite, flows over small cascades between rounded blocks towards the peripheral lowlands. And everywhere there is the same desertion by man. In a hundred years the population of the Massif Central has declined by over 600,000, dropping from 8 per cent of the total population to 5 per cent. The proportion of the gross national product achieved by the *départements* of the Centre reaches less than 5 per cent including the Puy-de-Dôme, 2 per cent if the Puy-de-Dôme is excluded, and yet this 'water tower' furnishes 20 per cent of the hydro-electric power and roughly 10 per cent of the total electric energy consumed in France.

To the south, the Massif Central is affected by southern structural and climatic influences, and it encompasses the huge limestone mass of the Causses, where the permeable rock, riddled with caverns and pierced by karstic depressions, makes the nearness of the Mediterranean more apparent through its bare whiteness and pockets of red soil.

However, as with the south of the Massif Central, the Causses open out towards the west and the south west and not towards the Mediterranean.

The South West shares several features of the Massif Central, at least from a human standpoint. The soils, wrongly criticised as being unsuitable for agricultural progress, have for a long time depended for their exploitation on social structures which sterilised them, and there has been a shortage of investment; the soils have discouraged the peasant population, who are, however, as niggardly with their savings as they are with the number of children they produce. Here, not counting the agglomerations of Toulouse and Bordeaux, the loss of population in a hundred years has been 700,000; equal to 22 per cent of the population in 1861. In 1861 the population of the South West represented almost 9 per cent of the French total. In 1962 it constituted no more than 5.3 per cent. Nevertheless, apart from the Landes area, which has not really advanced with successive changes in its activities, the region is pleasant and promising, in the undulating, tree-lined Albi area, Luaraguais, Armagnac, the Chalosse or the Basque country, and in the rich valleys of Périgord and Quercy, so full of history and prehistory.

The natural gas deposits have not been sufficient to reverse the downward trend from which the urban complexes now increasing in numbers, such as Pau, Toulouse and Bordeaux, have had difficulty in escaping. The two rival metropolises watch each other jealously; recently they have indulged in a certain amount of copying from each other in terms of growth and development. Bordeaux is scoring points but Toulouse is getting ready to lay its cards on the table. The competition concerns especially the rank of the two towns in relation to advanced technology industries dependent on scientific research, such as the aeronautical industry, chemicals, nuclear and ballistic research and manufacture. Unlike the rural population, that of the towns has markedly increased, especially during the last decades.

The *pays* most heavily affected by the last exodus of the rural population are the plateaux and hills of the north and east of the basin. Périgord has lost 25 per cent and Albigeois 20 per cent. The valleys have proved more resistant than the chalk or limestone plateaux of Périgord and Quercy, but the manor houses of earlier times today reign over fallow land. Tourism and the acquisition by town dwellers of old manors and huge fortified farmhouses as second homes save these *pays*, with their charm or grandeur, from complete decline.

To the south of the Garonne, *terreforts* and *boulbènes** share the same state of abandonment. Attempts at an agricultural revolution, intended to retain a population which was being renewed more by immigration than by natural increase, have proved disappointing on several occasions. The improvement of livestock rearing, tree cultivation and mechanisation have all increased the yield of land and labour and the investment made by Algerian repatriates has brought to the area new methods of production, but the future remains uncertain, in Luaraguais as well as in Armagnac and Chalosse.

The *pays* of the Middle Garonne and of the Bordelais escape the unhappy fate of the South West. The specialised crops, like tomatoes, market garden produce, fruit (the growing of Ente plums for example) and tobacco, grown on the alluvium and on the Tertiary hills overlooking the valley and the lowland embayments, save them from mediocrity and even make it possible to describe them as prosperous. This is especially true of the Bordelais vineyard which supplies the largest quantity of fine and superior quality wine in France. Apart from the vineyard area and the market gardening zones, the only region which still has a relatively dense population is the Pyrenean foreland. The Basques form a solid core of population which refuses to migrate to other regions of France although it is extremely enterprising in maritime affairs and overseas. The Pyrenean piedmont, especially to the west of Lannemezan, is dotted with small or medium sized towns, like Mauléon, Oloron and Tarbes, which are adept at maintaining or converting their traditional manufacturing activities. Pau benefits from the nearby natural gas deposits. The first great field to be exploited, Lacq, has given rise to a new town, Mourenx, which houses the work force of the extraction plant operated by the S.N.P.A.,† and the enterprises using the gas as a source of energy or chemical raw material, such as Pechiney and Aquitaine-Chimie. However, it is the town of Pau, with its 110,000 inhabitants, which is profiting most from new industrial plants, although they are rather limited, and it gives the appearance of being both a tourist centre and a regional capital.

The Pyrenean mountains, which are never more than 40 kilometres wide within French territory with maximum elevations of 3,000 to 3,300 metres, support only 350,000 inhabitants in the transverse

---

* Literally the best and worst soils. The *terreforts* are fertile soils suitable for grain whereas the *boulbènes* are gravelly soils.

† Société Nationale des Pétroles d'Aquitaine.

valleys which form such distinctive *pays* as Bigorre, Comminges, Couserans and Capcir, or in the longitudinal basins of the east, such as Cerdagne, Conflent and Vallespir.

The essential features of western France are the humid and variable climate, the prominence of grasslands and woodland in the vegetation cover and in the rural economy, and the small importance of industry. Between the *pays* of Charente and Poitevin and the former northern frontier of Normandy on the river Bresle, the range in temperature between the January mean and the July mean exceeds 15° only well inland. The atmosphere is always humid and the average precipitation is 700 to 1,200 millimetres, falling on 150 to 200 days in the year. This mild, damp climate is well suited to oak and beech forests and, on land that has been cleared or is too stony to be easily reafforested, to heathlands of heather, bracken, broom and gorse. On the rich deep soils it is suitable for pasture and also for cereal growing. Under the changeable, often rain-laden skies generations of peasants have developed an enclosed landscape with hedgerows of trees and bushes adorning the low granite walls and shading the meadows. The *bocage** encourages isolation and the homely coming and going of people and livestock along sunken lanes beneath a vault of greenery. It is an archaic heritage, ill-suited to present day conditions of rural life and gradually disappearing. The population of the *bocage* areas has for a long time maintained high fertility levels, and it is still clearly distinguished from the South West, the Centre and the Midi by a rate of natural increase above the national average. Over the generations during the nineteenth century, the rural family farmholdings became smaller and smaller. The artisan activities, which not long ago guaranteed the prosperity of worker-peasants – the processing of hemp and then cotton in the Cholet area, leather in Haute-Bretagne,† the small forges in Normandy – were severely disrupted by industrial products. However, industrial production has not taken root in the West, or hardly at all. Only the ports, and in general terms, the estuaries, have combined diverse industries and transit trade, with shipbuilding as the main industry. Rouen has added to this the textile in-

---

* The term *'bocage'* is applied to the enclosed landscape with dense hedgerows and tree-lined, rectangular field patterns, and access along sunken lanes which characterises much of western and north-western France. Further definition is to be found on page 33.

† There is a distinction between Haute-Bretagne, corresponding with the eastern portion of the peninsula, centred on Rennes, and Basse-Bretagne, the western portion, which has retained the indigenous culture of Brittany to a greater degree.

dustry. However, these industries have never been extensive enough to absorb the entire work force of the western regions and they now find themselves in a critical situation. The West has served mainly as a pool of labour for the major industrial regions, most especially for the Paris region and each generation has lost a large number of its young people and its most talented members. Now in danger of falling behind the times, it is bracing itself against decline and demanding industrial development and the creation of new types of employment. There are four distinct major regional units within western France; the 'warm' areas to the south of the Loire, Britanny, the hinterlands of Angers and Le Mans, and Normandy.

Charente and Vendée are the 'warm' *pays* of the West, with an Atlantic vegetation marking the transition between the vegetation of the cold oceanic regions of Brittany and Normandy and that of the Basque country. Charente is mainly a *pays* of open plains. The vine has lost ground there but is cultivated for the production of cognac and remains as evidence of the southern character of this part of the West. The vine is also found as far as the northern limit of this group of *pays* in the Muscadet area south of Nantes. The Vendée may be divided into two parts. The Vendée plain is simply a prolongation of the Charente and Poitevin plain, the *bocage* covering the primary rocks and the granites of the old massif. It is an enclosed *pays* which, in spite of appearances and while retaining the essential features of its rural landscape which was the setting for the Chouan partisan war,* has accomplished an agricultural revolution in the last twenty years after a long period of stagnation and traditionalism. On the other hand, the coast, which in the past was active only at the points which were suitable for fishing, maritime trade, naval warfare and coastal livestock rearing, such as Marennes, Rochefort, La Rochelle, the Marais Vendéen and Les Sables d'Olonne, has today become a tourist zone. The large offshore islands of Ré, Noirmoutier and Yeu, are among the most popular spots.

Brittany is certainly the most representative *pays* of the West. It has the most oceanic climate, especially to the west, and its people make it a distinctive province which clings to its gaelic speech. Here the coast has pride of place but it is unevenly exploited. In the north the minute subdivision of the granitic-gneissic material by faults and the combined or successive work of rivers and the sea, makes for a great dis-

* Partisan bands in western France who resisted the Republic and First Empire after 1793 in favour of the Bourbon cause.

persion of maritime activity. Apart from Saint-Malo, the gradations between the various fishing ports are scarcely perceptible. Rural life on the loess of the coastal hinterland and naval service were more important than life on the coast itself, until the coming of tourism which gradually created an increasingly active seasonal economy. However, this is not enough to counterbalance the economy of small, often very small, farms whose market garden crops allow them to employ all their labour reserves without guaranteeing regular sales and stable prices. The west coast, directly exposed to the Atlantic storms, is the wildest, but the roadstead of Brest sheltered the principal French naval base and arsenal on the Atlantic coast until the Second World War. Douarnenez and Audierne belong to a different type of littoral and coastal life, with larger physical units resulting from major structural movements, producing the Appalachian bays of the west and the small drowned basins of the south coast. This coast has the most varied fishing, especially deep sea fishing, from Concarneau, Etel and Lorient, and also shellfish culture in Morbihan and at Le Croisic. Tourism has reached here, but it is more concentrated, especially on the major centre of La Baule. The western and southern coasts have their industries. Brest and Lorient have converted their arsenals to other functions. The Loire estuary has over 100,000 workers, but the shrinking market for shipbuilding and the weak and irregular market for food processing have made this one of the crisis regions of French industry. The interior of Brittany is divided into two parts which have contrasting natural conditions and which have changed in different ways. In interior Basse-Bretagne, represented by the Rohan plateau and the Châteaulin basin, with its typical oceanic climate and varied soils, the *bocage* has been thinned out in the last twenty years, making room for specialised crop growing and animal rearing, for example seed potatoes and poultry farming. The Rennes basin, on the other hand, is good grain-farming land; it contains the provincial capital where in the last twenty years new industries have developed, eagerly encouraged by this town, which clings to its rights as an historical capital.

Anjou and Maine constitute the hinterland of the maritime West of Vendée and Brittany. The climate becomes gradually more continental, but the *bocage* is still the most common landscape type. The two former provinces are situated astride the Armorican massif and the sedimentary areas bordering it. Certain persistent features distinguish the landscapes, the forms of social organisation and the psychology of the *pays* of the massif, in the Cholet area and Bas-Maine for example, from those of the Gâtines, the plains and valleys of the sedimentary *pays,* Haut-Maine and Baugeois. The drainage network has traced the communications lines in relation to the major axis of the lower Loire valley from Touraine to Brittany.

The fourth unit of the West is Normandy, an historical province which occupies the shores of the Channel from the bay of Mont-Saint-Michel to beyond the Pays de Bray. This is the cold variant of oceanic France, with mean annual temperatures 4° to 5° below those of the Aquitaine coast. The variation in landforms and soils is greater than in the other provinces of the West, except perhaps for Maine; there is the old massif* with its varied rock outcrops of marble, quartzitic sandstone and schists; the tightly packed Mesozoic sedimentary series which extend for 100 kilometres in Normandy and which continue in the east and in the eastern portions of the Paris Basin for almost 300 kilometres; the variation in the superficial material covering the Cretaceous, grouped together under the name of Clay-with-Flints. As a result the landscapes are very diversified, but *bocage pays* with a grassland economy predominate except in two parts of the region, the Plain of Caen and Alençon, and the plains situated here and there in the Lower Seine like Lieuvin, Roumois, Vexin normand and the Pays de Caux. Modern industry is represented in two places; at Caen where it is connected with the presence of the iron ore deposit of the Orne Valley and with the port, and on the estuary of the Lower Seine, where the traditional industries of Rouen are joined immediately upstream by the outlying industries of Paris; Le Havre is still the leading French port of the western coast.

V   THE PARIS BASIN

20 per cent of the surface of France is taken up by all the lowlands and low plateaux which together form the Paris Basin. The Paris Basin is certainly a geological unit but the drainage pattern subdivides it into several river basins. The Seine drains only the central part of the Basin, while to the south the Loire, to the west the small coastal rivers of Normandy and Picardy, and to the east the Meuse and Moselle drain large portions of it. Communications between the different

---

* In the Cotentin peninsula and the extreme west of Normandy.

drainage units are easy and the Seine basin, with its huge radiating river axes, acts as a zone of polarisation, both by convergence and divergence; convergence with respect to waterways and trade routes, divergence in the case of the flows of organisation and the power of command.

As well as having easy communications throughout the interior of the Basin which give Paris, at the point of confluence of the Seine, Marne and Oise, centripetal and centrifugal powers, the Basin communicates with other French and European regions by means of easy natural passageways. These thresholds on its periphery are: to the north, Artois which allows communication with the Nord region; to the north east, the Ardennes threshold of Thiérache and the Sambre valley leading to Belgium; to the east, the gaps of Saverne and Belfort which make it possible to skirt the Vosges in the direction of Alsace and Germany; to the south east, the Burgundy threshold which provides the link with the major European trading axis of the Saône-Rhône furrow; and in the south west, the Poitou threshold which opens the way to Aquitaine. These thresholds were invasion routes, but they were also strongholds during the great efforts towards the territorial unification of the nation undertaken by the kings, whose domain initially did not even include the whole of the Ile-de-France, but who benefited from Paris's geographical role as a catalysing centre.

The diversity, which is more or less imposed by the geological substratum, is expressed as aureolas around the Tertiary basin of the Ile-de-France where the limon-covered beds of limestone succeed each other in layers.* These aureolas are constituted by the Cretaceous *pays* of Haute-Normandie,† Picardy, Champagne, and Senonais, and beyond the annexe of the Sologne Tertiary basin, by Touraine, the Jurassic *pays* of the Lorraine plateaux, Auxerrois, Nivernais, Berry, Poitou, Bas-Maine and the plain of Caen. Continuity of landscapes and economies is, however, far from the rule all along the aureola of a given rock type. The nature of the superficial deposits, the extent of forestlands or heaths, the systems of land ownership and farming, the impact of events like the First World War in Picardy, the varying degrees of financial speculation, the leisure activities of urban dwellers and the specific characteristics of major valleys like the Loire, all serve

---

* In order of geological succession from the top to the base these form the *pays* of Beauce, Brie, Valois, Soissonais and Vexin.

† Haute-Normandie refers to the *départements* of Seine-Maritime and Eure, as opposed to Basse-Normandie, the *bocage* dairy region of central and western Normandy, west of the Seine Valley.

to differentiate the regions or *pays,* which may be demarcated according to their position on radials drawn from Paris. The Paris Basin is
in fact a mosaic based on a concentric radial network, in which certain
radials are strong lines because they lend themselves to the smooth
running of certain types of flow. These include the axis of the Basse-
Seine from Paris to the sea, the valley of the Oise, which is the principal axis of contacts with the Nord region, the routeways to the south
west and south east which lead to the thresholds of Poitou and
Burgundy and the east-west routeway reaching Lorraine and Alsace
via the Marne.

Determinist theory apart, it remains true that the physical
characteristics of the Paris Basin in relation to the rest of France have
favoured Paris's centralising role.

VI   The Renewal and Relative Weakness
of the Demographic Situation

France is a relatively sparsely populated nation in the West European
group of countries. Its population is less than a quarter of the total
population of the six original countries of the European Economic
Community, although it occupies half the area. It is also the least urbanised country; the rural population still represents nearly 40 per
cent of the total population, while it is between a quarter and a third in
Germany, Belgium and Holland, and France has only one agglomeration of over a million inhabitants, the capital, while there are ten in the
other countries of the original European Community. This means that
for several years to come a characteristic of France will be a high
pressure of rural population. At present 20 million persons live in
communes of less than 5,000 inhabitants. In fact the population
pattern in France is very disparate. The population is very unevenly
distributed over the nation's territory, so that the development
prospects of certain regions are compromised by labour shortages.
The present population distribution results on the one hand from
longstanding differences in demographic growth rates between the
various regions, and on the other hand from internal migrations which
have transferred the vital forces of several regions to the Paris
agglomeration.

There have been two distinct major regional units for several decades. These are a northern crescent with high fertility levels and natural increase rates above the national average which runs from Vendée, encompassing the Paris region to the north, skirting Brittany to the west and reaching the Swiss frontier in the Jura, and a central and southern nucleus with low fertility, an aged population structure and low rates of natural increase. For twenty years from 1945 the nation's crude birth rate was maintained at four or five points above the pre-war level; 18 to 19 per 1,000 instead of 14 to 15 per 1,000. It declined by at least two points from 1966 to 1971. The death rate has declined during the last two decades, from 15 to 11 per 1,000 approximately. Natural increase has therefore moved from a level tending towards zero before the Second World War, to levels of 5 to 6 per 1,000. For the whole inter-census period 1954–68, natural increase was above 5 per cent in thirty-two *départements,* of which thirty belonged to the northern crescent and only two, Haute-Savoie and Isère, to the southern half of the nation. Twenty-one *départements* had a natural increase of below 2 per cent or even a natural decrease, all of them in the centre and south of France. This situation results from the permanent mobility of the population inside the country which means that young people from the countryside in the Centre and South gravitate towards the industrial regions of the North, the North East and the Paris region, and a proportion of elderly people move towards the rural regions.

The greatest concentrations of population, apart from the Paris urban region with over 8 million inhabitants, are the Nord region (3.8 million), the region of Lyon-Saint Etienne-Grenoble (4.5 million), the Lorraine industrial region (1.6 million), Alsace (1.4 million), the urban and industrial region of Marseille (over 1 million) and the estuaries of the Seine, Loire and Gironde* (each with almost 1 million inhabitants), giving a total of over 23 million, or 45 per cent of the national population. The population of small communes with less than 2,000 inhabitants is slightly more than 15 million, or roughly 30 per cent of the national total. The urban proportion has noticeably increased during the last fifteen years and is continuing to increase. From 52.4 per cent in 1936 and 57.5 per cent in 1954 it exceeded 60 per cent in 1962, and according to certain criteria for defining urban and industrial regions exceeded 70 per cent in 1968. This urban population is not, however, evenly distributed throughout the country.

---

* The urban industrial region of Bordeaux.

The regions with high rates of urbanisation are offset by regions which have remained rural and which are usually in process of ageing demographically. In fact the rural regions have retained their populations to varying extents. The West still has rural densities above thirty-five per square kilometre. The Centre, the eastern plateaux and the Midi have densities of less than twenty-five. The replacement of generations is precarious and often uncertain.

Like all industrial countries, and the more so since it is the least populous industrial nation in north west Europe, France has resorted to immigration. For almost half a century, France has combined the need for permanent immigrants with the use of temporary immigration, whether seasonal, annual or for periods of several years, for heavy labour. In the twentieth century it has made extensive use of Latin resources to make up for the nation's low fertility level, assimilating Italians and then Spaniards, especially in the South West. It has also absorbed a proportion of immigrants from the Slavonic countries of Central Europe, especially Poles, often arriving without intending to stay permanently. North Africa, Spain, Portugal and, as in Germany, Turkey, supply temporary workers. The total number of foreigners in France in 1971 was estimated at 3 million or 6 per cent of the total population. Between the two world wars France was exceptional in Europe in that it was a country with heavy immigration and this has been correlated with the depression of natural population growth. In spite of a clear demographic revival in Europe, France, like the other industrial countries, is experiencing increasing difficulty in recruiting inside the country unskilled labour for unpleasant, dangerous and badly paid jobs. In this respect it is in the same position as Germany, Belgium, Holland and Britain, and it draws on the same sources as them – the countries with surplus rural population and the countries of the Third World, including Black Africa. The largest number of workers come from the Iberian Peninsula (33 per cent of the total) and North Africa (25 per cent), while the whole of the original European Economic Community, especially Italy, account for 25 per cent.

CHAPTER TWO

The Major Stages of the Nation's Organisation

The present distribution of all types of activities in the nation seems highly mobile, to such a degree that it is not always easy to distinguish between locations which have been established for a long time and which depend on permanent factors and more or less long-term trial locations. The idea of gradual occupation ending in a permanent state of equilibrium is no longer valid. The factors influencing location and development which were initially strongest now seem to be of only relative importance and their value and effectiveness is weighed against other factors resulting from technological changes and the preference for particular systems of organisation and directional control. Establishing basic facts has never been so far removed from simple straightforward mechanisms governed by natural laws. Only a few economic laws, based on a quantification of profitability, take into account the impulses which affect geographical relationships formerly considered immutable. The counter proof can be seen in the way certain political events have an obliterating effect on economic mechanisms by modifying the geographical framework of the circulation of goods and the elaboration of local, regional or national prices. The appearance of new technological systems can have the same effects.

In fact, what is now happening is the questioning of all the geographical values which were taken for granted thirty years ago. Some of them were consecrated by centuries of elaboration and consolidation, others appear to have acquired their permanent status in the course of the nineteenth century as a result of the industrial revolution. Today no one dares any longer to describe as irreversible an evolution which has created situations which apparently cannot change any more. People are more than ever aware of how relative notions of regional or local wealth and poverty are, and realise that

29

what had been taken to be the application of an intangible law was in fact merely an episode in a dialectic evolution in which contradictions multiply as it proceeds. The effect, however, survives the action which produced it. It is an obstacle to the creation of new forms out of the mass of the national territory. The mould survives the organism which secreted and fashioned it, and for a period of time it inhibits the progress or insertion of new organisms. Technological and economic cycles do not succeed each other, they overlap; landscapes, environments, urban or rural societies are profoundly affected by these overlaps. In each location vanishing ways of life, production and contact coexist with others which are being born and whose exact destiny is not yet clear.

A simplified presentation of the overlaps and contradictions which make up the visual expression of the present day geography of France now follows, adopting three successive approaches. Firstly, by studying the formation of the natural landscape and the major historical units which determined the foundation of major towns. Secondly, by analysing the disturbance of a rural and provincial geographical structure brought about by the industrial revolution born of coal, steel and railways. Thirdly, by examining the present crises of the inherited structures, the questioning of respective regional values and the search for a necessary compromise between the contradictory effects of on the one hand the pressure of new technologies on economic mechanisms and on the other the opposition of vested interests calculated on a different scale.

I THE FORMATION OF RURAL LANDSCAPES AND PROVINCES

The occupation of the national territory took place slowly and irregularly, punctuated by wars and epidemics. The main and often the only objective was to secure the population's food supply and the simple raw materials used by the family or village for the manufacture of clothing and work implements and for the preparation of food. For at least two thousand years the value of the nation's land depended on the extent to which it could easily provide the simple necessities of daily life for a relatively sparse population with a low or non-existent rate of increase from century to century. Productive land was reclaimed from forests and occasionally marshlands; larger numbers of clearings were made during periods of high population increase in peacetime. Since the possession of men was the source of power, the people who took over an area or received the right of temporary possession were the first to be concerned with mobilising resources to secure a basis for settlement. The monastic clearers were, intentionally or not, their best helpers. The process of clearing revealed soils of very variable quality beneath the forests. Until the nineteenth century the types of agricultural implements were not very varied or efficient, and it was in this context that the *terroirs* were defined. It is convenient to follow old texts on farming and apply the term *terroirs* to natural units within a small region of one or two parishes with the same agricultural aptitudes. It is thus possible to speak of *limon terroirs*, suitable for cereal growing, *terroirs* of pasture, scarp *terroirs* with orchards or vineyards, and *terroirs* of heavy or light soil. The peasant groups learned with experience the different qualities of their lands,* and also the unsuitability for continuous cultivation of certain parts, which reverted to heath, *garrigue* or forest according to the region. They developed their lands using a small number of simple techniques which were the same throughout quite extensive regions. This development was achieved by means of certain types of farm and work organisation, in a given context of general conditions or mental attitudes which were produced by the continued existence of the general conditions – insecurity, a permanent physical and social grouping of population, or a dispersion of settlement in small family households. This process resulted in the rural landscapes whose origins are sometimes difficult to define now that the vital factors underlying these forms of spatial organisation have disappeared. Gradually these inherited features are giving way in the face of modern techniques when they are by their nature an obstacle to the latter. At this stage it is easier to measure the elements which result from permanent factors, such as relief, hydrology, climatic conditions and soil characteristics, and which are connected with social and technical circumstances. The universal social and economic fact is the defining of the piece of land allotted to each household for work and upkeep, even where obligatory collective working by the village community persisted longest. In fact this holding is usually subdivided into several parcels. The basic visible rural unit is thus the field, meaning every exploited parcel of land, whether under grass or planted. The field is a specific unit

* The area of a settlement's land on which *finage,* the working of a specified area, could be practised was defined either by law or by custom.

of cultivation within a *terroir* and within a farm holding. Geographically speaking, the first question is how the field becomes an individual unit and this leads on to the definition of rural landscape and the differentiation between rural landscapes.

The work of historians under the impetus of Marc Bloch, and of geographers after the publication of *An Essay on the Formation of the French Rural Landscape* by Roger Dion,* has revealed several fundamental differences in the development of the landscape by successive generations of peasants. The first is the contrast between enclosed and open fields. The latter constitute the wide expanses of the *campagnes.*† In most cases these *campagnes* are treeless. Trees have been retained and planted only around the villages, the best example being the villages of the Pays de Caux set among the greenery and the hedgerows of the pastures in the middle of completely bare *campagnes.* However, although the *campagnes* of Picardy, the Ile-de-France, Nord and Champagne fit this definition exactly, the open fields of Lorraine, Lower Burgundy and of part of Berry still have walnut trees, which recall the planted fields or open fields with walnut trees of former times. Mechanisation and land reform are managing to make the *campagnes* in all of the northern half of France uniform. This rural landscape of open fields is associated with a traditional rural habitat of various kinds of nucleated villages, for example the street villages of Lorraine and the concentrated villages of the Ile-de-France, between which there are only large isolated farms, relics of the presence in each territory of one or two large seigneurial or monastic properties. This concentration of the population has been explained in terms of agricultural customs rather than a concern for defence. Communal grazing and the collective rotations of the three field system maintained the custom of group living. The village today, which is merely a shadow of its former self, preserves traces of earlier rural life and it faithfully reflects a vanished society. One can pick out the houses of major landowners, the prosperous farms, the former presbytery and the little one or two-roomed houses with tiny outbuildings which formerly sheltered the hired casual farm workers. Sometimes these workers were to some extent artisans who by clearing the steep slopes outside the rotational fields carved out a bit of land on which by dint of unrewarding effort grain and, particularly,

* Dion, R., *Essai sur la formation du paysage rural français,* Arrault, 1934.
† Alternatively termed *champagnes* or *champeignes,* referring to level or undulating plains of open fields as found in Champagne or Picardy.

fruit trees and vines could be grown. The marginal character of this small scale rural economy, in both an economic and a geographical sense, helps to explain the distinctive appearance of the rural landscapes of the *campagnes*. Dissected by valleys, their valley bottom and scarp front *terroirs* lay outside the open fields and today often support only fallow or form a terrain with a changed function resulting from new tourist activities. Observation, made easier by aerial photography, shows that the open fields are also elongated fields, and the shape of the fields is the second element of differentiation between French rural landscapes. Massive shaped fields are almost always enclosed, marked off by definite boundaries; hedges, stone walls, banks or wire fences. Probably these are fields which were originally worked manually as opposed to the elongated fields which were ploughed and the pastures used for grazing livestock. Throughout the West, the enclosed field is accompanied by a dispersed settlement pattern, indicating rural colonisation by small working units, share croppings and small farms, subordinate to the dividing up of the land by the châteaux and the abbeys. There are many variations and it is not always easy to define precisely the terms which describe them. It is convenient to restrict the term *bocage* to groupings of enclosed fields clearly defined by thick hedges, often planted, and reached by sunken lanes. These are found in the greater part of Basse-Normandie with the exception of the Plain of Caen, Bas-Maine, Anjou, Vendée and Brittany where they give way occasionally to fields bordered by granite walls with clinging clumps of broom, gorse and bracken. Brittany has occasional islands of open fields.* Similar *bocage* landscapes cover the lower slopes of the Massif Central in Bas-Limousin and the uplands of Charentes. However in the South West another variation of the enclosed field takes the place of the true *bocage*. The fields are separated from each other by thinner hedgerows, increasingly replaced by artificial enclosures, and the sunken lane is unusual. Some writers have suggested the term *bocage clair* to describe this landscape. There is even greater variety as regards building types — the granite farmhouses with muddy yards in Brittany, the light coloured houses of limestone with external staircases in the Charentes and Poitevin areas, brick-built houses with open outbuildings in Aquitaine and the house types of the Basque country and the Landes. The South

---

* These patches of open field landscape surrounded by *bocage* are termed *méchoux* or *gaigneries*.

East combines square fields, often enclosed by stone walls, with a defensive hilltop settlement form. Here the enclosure is a terrace and a bank of cleared stones rather than a boundary, although the fields, especially cropland, must be protected from goats and sheep. The lowland is generally unenclosed, even when planted with vines as in Bas-Languedoc and in some of the basins and interior lowlands of Provence. The enclosure reappears in areas of market gardening, but it is a technical feature acting as a wind break, made up, for example, of quickset cypress hedge, clumps of reeds or a dead hedge of canes. In established horticultural areas like the Comtat and the lowlands of the lower Durance, there was scattered settlement in the spaces between the old villages when irrigation and market garden crops were introduced at the end of the nineteenth and beginning of the twentieth century.

The mountains have their characteristic landscapes resulting from the layering of vegetation and land use zones. In the days when the valleys or high mountain areas lived in economic isolation complementary systems were organised combining the crops of the valley floors, woodlands on the slopes and seasonal high altitude pastures. In the Mediterranean zone, livestock migrations linked the mountain and its foreland, as in the Cévennes and the Southern Alps.

These rural landscapes are the product of a long process of evolution leading from the village subsistence economy to the market economy. Before the eighteenth century, the universal concern was to produce the bread necessary for food. Everything centred on this preoccupation which was really a concern to ward off lean years or famine. Even the rearing of cattle was in many regions limited to raising draught animals and beasts of burden and the production of wool, flax and hemp, nuts and fruit, played only an accessory role in the context of the small domestic family economy. Moreover yields were very low, only six to eight quintals of grain per hectare, and a large part of the land remained unproductive as two or three year fallow. In the course of just over a century, agriculture acquired the means of increasing its yields and productivity with the gradual development of the so-called agricultural revolution which involved the replacement of physiocratic ideals* by modern technical studies; at the same time it had to meet the needs of a market suddenly

---

* The eighteenth century school of thought which held the soil to be the only source of wealth in an inherent natural order of society.

exposed to international competition. The rapid increase of urban population and the resultant change in consumption patterns increased
the demand for animal produce, market garden crops and fruit. This
led to the development of specialised agricultural regions taking into
account their own aptitudes which was a feature of the second half of
the nineteenth century, although the trend had been in existence since
the development of road haulage and since the Turgot laws* on the
free circulation of wheat. Differences in climate, relief and soils
acquired previously unknown importance. Physical geography dic-
tated choices which had been impossible before when each village
group, or anyway each province, had to provide its own subsistence.
Thus a distinct area of cereal and sugar-beet production with the
rearing of stall fed livestock developed throughout the *limon* covered
plains of the northern half of France and a large part of Brittany,
where yields were gradually increased to reach twenty quintals per
hectare at the outbreak of the Second World War and over thirty
today. On the other hand, the humid *bocage* regions of the West and
certain cool terrains for example in Bray, Boulonnais, Thiérache,
Nivernais and Charolais, specialised in cattle rearing for meat or dairy
produce. The value of grazing land for cattle fattening equals or
exceeds that of the best cereal land. Marketing on a national and international scale allowed specialisation in viticultural regions which
produced fine wines, ordinary wines and wines which are now termed
superior quality and in market gardening regions. The railway played
a decisive role in these specialisations, supplying the means of taking
products to different markets. It helped to concentrate commercial
transactions and consumption at various stages. However in most
cases it confirmed already existing hierarchies of centres of power,
decision and communication. It also consolidated the provincial structures which by then had become regional structures stronger than the
département administrative structures created by the administrations
of the Revolution and the Empire. By the modern device of
proclaiming the former provincial capitals regional metropolises,
hierarchies inherited from the political and administrative structures of
the *ancien régime* survive up to the present day (Fig. 3). They had no
administrative prerogatives until the Second World War. However,

* Turgot was Controller-General to Louis XVI, and introduced laws in 1774
enabling the free circulation of corn, aimed at easing the problem of regional shortages.

FIG. 3. Provincial divisions of France in 1789

the *département* structures that the Constituent Assembly* wished to substitute for the provincial framework were gradually found to be too small for the needs of economic and political life. The former provincial system has turned out to have more life in it than the *département* and it is now a candidate for new regional responsibilities.

* The National Assembly which in 1789 drew up a new constitution after the Revolution.

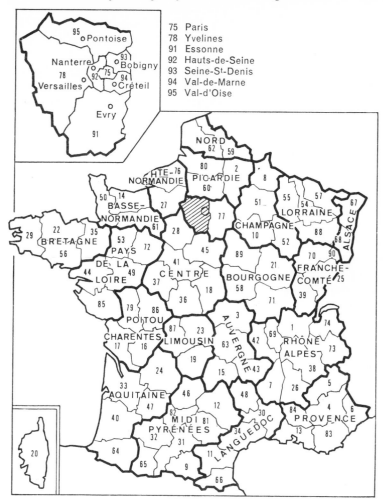

FIG. 4. The *départements* and planning regions

The provincial capitals are towns which had experience of political and administrative responsibility and now hope to recover it. They have remained regional marketing centres, and to the extent that new regulators of services and distribution systems have developed, they have polarised these services. They would have formed the essential links in the national spatial organisation if industrial development had not introduced new disparities.

II INDUSTRIALISATION AND REGIONAL INEQUALITY

As in all Western Europe, the industrial revolution brought to the fore
the coalfield regions and the major crossroads of heavy transport,
seaports and transit zones of canal and railway transport, which
sometimes coincided with the urban concentrations called upon to act
as regional metropolises or capitals. The result was a concentration of
new activities in a few restricted areas of the nation which have drawn
production forces, young workers, managers, entrepreneurs and
capital investment from the entire country. The power of decision, especially in economic matters, was gradually concentrated in several
major centres of development, headquarters of banking, commercial
and industrial operations, and ultimately in Paris. The regions have
reacted differently to these continual appropriations. Some of them
have been stripped of their resources, and the way in which all those
by-passed by the industrial revolution evolved has been adversely
affected. Even when they have not declined in terms of absolute
numbers, they have declined relatively; their contribution to the gross
national product has declined, their average income levels are lower
than those of industrial regions and their towns decline compared with
the industrial towns. However just when it seemed that an irreversible
stage of evolution had been reached two phenomena have called into
question the concentration of activities in a very small number of
privileged centres; the demographic revival and the changed
technology of the industrial activities which were created in the
nineteenth century and up until 1950 in relation to their international
competitive position. The proudest industrial regions of the first half of
the twentieth century are today problem regions.

1 Nineteenth Century Concentrations

The industrial revolution may be summarised under technological
headings: the primacy of coal as a source of energy through the intermediary of the steam engine; the arrival of iron and steel as the raw
material for the construction of all kinds of production machinery and
modern transport; the simultaneous occurrence of changes in the
character of industrial activity and an enormous leap forward in the
volume of output which called into existence new methods of
transport and ensured the monopoly of the railway and steam

navigation; and the circulation at the same time of amounts of money unparalleled in the transactions of the preceding period. As well as these trends, a new social class of financiers, contractors and businessmen made itself felt and another numerically much more important class was formed – the industrial proletariat of miners and labourers in major construction works and large scale industry.

The geographical effects appeared immediately. Population and capital, productive machinery and finished goods became concentrated in regions possessing coal and minerals or whose location allowed them to administer the new economy, establish manufacturing industries or receive overseas products. This favoured the major sea ports, the intersections of continental circulation and political capitals, like the major estuarine ports, Marseille, the Lyon crossroads and above all Paris, which already had systems of direction, a transport infrastructure and facilities for external contacts. The comparative evolution of population between 1850 and 1900 for the industrial and agricultural *départements* and for France as a whole shows the importance of this phenomenon (Table One).

TABLE ONE

THE COMPARATIVE EVOLUTION OF THE POPULATION OF SELECTED
AGRICULTURAL *DÉPARTEMENTS* AND THE PRINCIPAL HEAVILY
INDUSTRIALISED AND URBANISED *DÉPARTEMENTS*, BETWEEN 1851
AND 1901 IN THOUSANDS

Agricultural *Départements*	1851	1901	Industrial and Urban *Départements*	1851	1901
Côtes-du-Nord	632	609	Nord	1,158	1,866
Ille-et-Vilaine	574	613	Pas-de-Calais	692	955
Sarthe	473	422	Meurthe-et-Moselle	365*	484
Manche	600	491	Rhône	574	843
Creuse	287	277	Loire	472	647
Corrèze	320	318	Bouches-du-Rhône	428	734
Lot	296	226	Seine	1,422	3,670
Gers	307	238	Seine-et-Oise	472	707
Yonne	381	321	Seine-Maritime	762	853

* In 1872.

Two regions seemed particularly privileged at the end of the nineteenth century, the coalfield of Nord-Pas-de-Calais and the Paris region, each with several million inhabitants. Concentrations of workers grew up and factories were built everywhere to exploit coal. The map of population density exactly coincided with the map of the distribution of industrial activity. Away from the coalfield regions, the iron ore mines and the steelworks of Longwy-Briey, the map highlights the seaports and the major canal and rail intersections (Fig. 5). The ports became more important and their power of attraction increased with the development of maritime and colonial enterprises. The period 1880–1925, interrupted by the First World War, witnessed a great expansion of the port complexes. Marseille, the 'gateway to the East', developed port contacts with North Africa and by way of the Suez Canal with the Indian Ocean and the Far East; the Basse-Seine became the gateway to the Atlantic Ocean; Bordeaux, and to a lesser extent the port complex of the Loire estuary, turned towards tropical America and West Africa. The destiny of many places was also determined by railway development and the new organisation of overland transport. For example, in spite of delay in carrying out the works planned in the Freycinet Act* the canal system was reorganised, with the gradual disappearance of navigation on the Loire and the decline of Orleans, and the expansion of the Nord canal system. Above all, however, there were distinctions between different railway lines, with certain towns favoured by main line services and major marshalling yards, like Dijon, while other towns were downgraded, like Bourges, because they were by-passed by rail traffic. The sense of frustration about new methods of production and business was one of the causes of internal migration of businessmen and capital. But this migration was accelerated at the close of the nineteenth century and the beginning of the twentieth century by the transition from structures based on family-owned businesses to company structures with shareholders and banking capital which accompanied changes in the size of companies. At this stage of evolution the power of attraction of the Paris agglomeration increased very rapidly.

2 *France During the Decade 1920–30*

The presence of a capital market and a market for all kinds of products, State protection and the placing of government orders, the

---

* The Freycinet Act of 1879 was a blueprint for the national transport system establishing the alignments and construction norms for canals and railways.

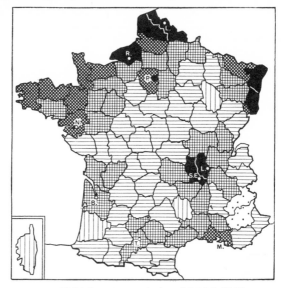

1860 (total population 37,386,000)

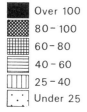

Over 100
80 – 100
60 – 80
40 – 60
25 – 40
Under 25

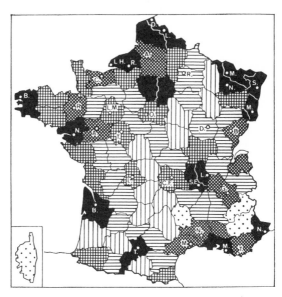

1968 (total population 50,000,000)

FIG. 5. Population density by *départements* and towns of over 100,000 inhabitants

concentration of infrastructures which initially at least reduced production costs, the presence particularly of training facilities for all kinds of workers and managers and the build up of population supplying a diversified pool of labour for all sectors attracted many industries. The availability of transport, initially organised for political rather than economic motives, became an instrument of excessive concentration. It was as though the shortest distance between any two points in the nation passed through Paris. After the decade 1920–30 not only industries directly related to the life of a great developing capital were to be found there, like the building industry, furniture making, food industries, clothing and luxury and prestige goods of international reputation, but also the greater part of the engineering industry, motor construction, aircraft building, electrical engineering and a large proportion of the chemicals and chemical derivative industries. The Paris agglomeration became the greatest concentration of workers in France and it has suffered socially and politically as a result. The transfer of the head offices of all businesses over a certain size made it the centre for massive financial operations. Alongside the head offices, banks, insurance societies and transport companies, service activities proliferated, gradually entering into competition in the labour market with the demand for industrial workers. Paris is both the largest city of office and professional workers in France and the largest working class agglomeration.

Its population has grown from three million at the end of the nineteenth century to almost six million at the outbreak of the Second World War and almost ten in the mid 1960s. This uninterrupted expansion has meant that all the basic facts of urbanisation have been magnified and in all respects this gigantic scale is an anomaly with many worrying effects. Imperceptibly but steadily all production and service costs increase. Firms are forced to pass on the increased cost of public services, road maintenance, construction of public housing, urban transport, hospital services, education and professional training and sports facilities. Paris is becoming a parasite on the gross national product. The increase in building costs, inflated by speculation in land and buildings, and the increased cost of all services are such that the State shrinks more and more from investment and financing. There is no longer a balance between needs and the injection of funds, so that everyday living· conditions are gradually deteriorating. It appears that the average standard of living is higher in the Paris region than in the remainder of France, but nevertheless living conditions there are deteriorating and circumstances are becoming more and more trying for the human constitution.

With this hypertrophied capital city, the whole nation has lost any dynamic structure. Only a few industrial regions retained relative vitality and a modicum of leadership until the Second World War; the Nord region, the Lyon region and to a lesser extent Lorraine, although this region is too specialised in iron and steel to form a harmonious and balanced region. Apart from these some urban centres had established and kept various industrial activities. In addition to the ports, there were industrial towns based on technological links, like Strasbourg, Clermont-Ferrand, Grenoble and Toulouse. There were also small towns, maintaining to the bitter end activities springing from the artisan activities and manufactured products of bygone days, like the towns of the Pyrenean piedmont zone, the Cévennes and Bas-Dauphiné, and a handful of towns in the West, the Centre West and the Centre, like Fougères or Cholet, Châteauroux or Vierzon. Between the two world wars, decentralisation gave an impetus to some towns which until then had only had the functions of regional centres of agricultural regions, like Le Mans or Pau. A small number of towns are in a better position through their ability to focus regional commercial activity – for example Tours or Poitiers and the towns of Languedoc. But the entire urban network seems disjointed. At the beginning of this century geographers invented the 'geographical regions' which became the basis for the description of France in secondary and higher education. Since they were not describing a nation structured by productive activity and overlaid with completely diverse agricultural regions, they built up a picture of homogeneous regions based on a distinctive characteristic, sometimes the geology, sometimes relief, climate, history or rural landscape, sometimes the organisational influence of a town, sometimes the choice of a particular cropping system or industrial installation. Examples are Limousin, Vosges, Jura, Burgundy, Anjou, the Lyon region, Bas-Languedoc and the Nord region. From a strictly economic point of view, this division hides enormous regional variations. A few spatial units, which are moreover poorly defined because their outlines vary according to the intensity and strength of their economic effects over a given regional area, deserve to be called economic regions. This status stems from the fact that they are involved in the growth process through possessing industrial plant and production and as centres for organising transport and distribution and collecting agricultural products. Such regions also influence the systems of crops and livestock, both as a function of their consumption demands and through investment in agriculture leading to an increase in yields and productivity. The Nord region, as a result of coal, has become both a major industrial region and one of the most advanced agricultural regions. The Lyon region is a model of the unification, from the highest point of development, of disparate natural elements, each one with a distinctive potential and all bound together by the influence of Lyon as distributor of work, absorber of surplus labour and consumer of agricultural produce, creating tourist centres and guaranteeing the capital investment necessary for regional development. The case of Lorraine is more ambiguous. The centres of specialised industries, coal and carbo-chemicals, iron and steel, salt and chemicals, and the textile industries of the Vosges, are not enough to support a regional organisation on a provincial scale. Agriculture is dying, because the countryside has supplied its labour to industry. It even had to draw extensively on immigrants for its labour needs in the years 1940–50.

On the eve of the Second World War most of France seemed to be devoid of any creative energy, except for a few large towns which could not at that time have been accurately described as 'regional metropolises' since they had only a weak and irregular influence on their surroundings. The Aquitaine region of the Midi, Bas-Languedoc, Provence, the lowlands and basins of the middle and lower Rhône, like Champagne, Jura or Brittany, were in fact geographical regions, in some cases coinciding with former provinces, but the innovations and the extension of influence which create regions had forsaken them and were concentrated in Paris. France was thus made up of a centre, combining almost all the power of economic decision and a large proportion of the productive activity; a small number of regions benefiting from a certain degree of economic unity and retaining some element of control, especially where they had distinctive, specialised features, such as the coalfield North, the Lorraine iron and steel industry, and also Alsace and the Lyon region; and, finally, geographical regions, with no real economic unity, characterised by shared natural or rural landscapes and directly linked by various economic currents to the Paris agglomeration – for example Brittany, the Aquitaine Midi, Bas-Languedoc or the Alps of Dauphiné and Savoie. The commercial currents were initially differentiated according to the particular productive aptitudes of the region in question, but ultimately they were made uniform by the systematic nature of consumption, tourist influxes or demographic movements. Several centres, in isolation, benefited from their specialised function as links between Paris and foreign countries, for example Marseille, Bordeaux, the Loire estuary and, especially, the Seine estuary. The provinces were dismantled, the *départements* were ill-suited to evolve into economic units on an appropriate contemporary scale, true regions were still to be born, and yet the centralisation of Paris, far from making a contribution, was the principal obstacle preventing the realisation of the potential of the various regions. In their sterilised condition, the geographical regions allowed young people to leave for the Paris agglomeration, the handful of leading economic regions, the ports and the few regions with industrial and commercial installations which guaranteed labour demand and a certain local influence.

3   New Perspectives?

The close of the Second World War coincided with profound and rapid changes in the technology and structure of productive output. After a short period of less than ten years, during which the objectives were in the nature of a reconstruction effort, important changes suddenly called into question situations which had only recently been created and opened up new perspectives for development, allowing possible new locations and the revitalising of areas. The 1950s and 1960s were characterised by the struggle between trends towards innovation and the momentum acquired by the growth processes inherited from the earlier period which had slowed down considerably but still continued to impose constraints and at times to deflect new initiatives.

The principal new features are the diversification of output, the relatively diminished importance of the size of the work force involved in the productive processes, the reduced constraints of bulk weight in locating and organising firms and the more important role of management and research. The number of end products offered by industry has increased astonishingly in a very short time in all sectors, from metal industries to textile products, chemical and chemical derived industries, food processing and so on. If one compares the range of domestic products in use in the household of the 1960s with those of a family in the '20s and '30s, one can appreciate the increased demand for industrial products. The result of this increased volume has been a general modification of industrial structures, which distinguishes more clearly than in the past between two kinds of industry: basic industries which supply semi-finished products, where location still obeys quite powerful laws even if they are not the same as laws which governed pre-war installation; and industries which produce goods delivered directly to users and consumers, which can be very diversified and dispersed because they require little in the way of bulk transport, can find the necessary supplies of energy and water almost anywhere, and have easy access, wherever they are, to the network of storage and distribution centres through the closely interconnected system of light and medium transport. The road system fills the role for these new manufacturing and finishing industries that the railway filled for the predominantly heavy industries of the nineteenth and early twentieth centuries. These industries employ comparatively small numbers of workers and wages usually represent less of the cost price than the machinery, the financing of research laboratories and offices, and the purchasing of raw materials or ancillary components. In fact a second technical and geographical separation tends to occur between the production factory and the offices and technical services. Heavy industry is still tied to the regions producing raw materials or to the points where these enter – the coal and iron ore mining regions and the ports importing foreign minerals, petroleum and coke. The finishing industries to an increasing degree seek vacant land close to the major transport arteries and especially to the motorways, in places provided with public services and housing, and particularly in regions which still have large enough population resources to permit the training and recruitment of labour which can adapt to modern types of industrial work and be retrained easily when necessary. These locations in certain circumstances are able to fulfill the needs of industrial decentralisation. Administrative, commercial and technical offices are specifically urban features. They require a location in a major town with all the infrastructures springing from both private initiative and public services, in a regional metropolis if not in the capital city. A page has been turned in industrial geography, but before the next the difficulties of accommodating the technical and organic legacies of two generations must be resolved. This is one of the reasons why the most liberal minded are resigned to State intervention or to mixed economy organisations in order to define the general outlines of a long term national development through the application of planning techniques.

PART TWO

A Time of Structural Change

In 1935, with 42 million inhabitants, France had slightly less than 22 million employed persons, of whom 8 million were employed in agriculture, roughly the same number in industry, 4 million in commerce, banks and insurance and less than 2 million in administration, public services and the professions. In 1970, with 51 million inhabitants, France had only 2.7 million persons employed in agriculture, the industrial work force amounted to 8 million, including 1 million technical and managerial directors, and 9.8 million people were employed in commerce, services and administration; in all 21 million people including the 356,000 seeking employment. In the space of thirty-five years the character of occupational activity has fundamentally changed. The active* population is diminishing in relation to the total population because of the evolution of the nation's age structure, the reduction of employment in agriculture especially in the case of female workers, the extension of schooling and higher education, and the lowering of the retirement age in certain professions. The distribution between sectors has completely changed. The economy no longer requires the same kinds of work, an indication of very important technological and structural changes calling for an examination, sector by sector, of the nation's activities before turning to a projection of these changes on regional life.

Although one might question the use of the term 'agricultural revolution' to describe a series of transformations occurring over 150 years, one can today apply it unhesitatingly to the rapid and even brutal changes, accompanied by social conflicts, which are driving this

---

* The term 'active' is used to denote persons in the potential labour force, excluding those retired, below the age of employment or not seeking employment. It includes persons unemployed or changing jobs or seeking employment and thus does not equate with the actual employed labour force.

sector from traditional patterns of family work to industrial methods of land exploitation. While retaining its individual characteristics, the countryside is undergoing a transformation – villages are disappearing, the field pattern is changing and the number of genuine farm operators is falling dizzily. In the fifteen years from 1954 to 1970, the number of persons employed in agriculture declined by over 2.5 million, that is by half, which corresponds to an occupational and geographical change in the order of 5 million people. In fact the average annual rate of transfer from the agricultural sector to other branches of activity between 1965 and 1970 was 120,000 active persons. This shift naturally accompanied a technical revolution and fundamental changes in the productive and commercial structures and runs the risk of causing more or less long-term distortions in the labour market.

Industry is on the threshold of major technological changes – for instance the introduction of nuclear power in the energy production and consumption cycle or the substitution of natural gas for coke as a reducing agent in the steel industry. The chemical industry has already affected certain branches of production by supplying new raw materials, such as synthetic fibres, resins and glues, plastics and detergents. But with the prospect of the systematic and economic mobilisation of nuclear energy, it is certainly the advances in production methods which have the most varied consequences. Automation, the widespread use of remote control processes and the possibilities opened up by electronic methods of calculation and research, call for new types of professional qualification, upset the systems and scales of remuneration and increase productivity at such a rate that it seems both possible and necessary to reduce employment time gradually. Imperatives regarding location are changing and generally becoming weaker. Human factors, and especially the factors of services, play an ever more important role, while natural and material factors are losing importance. A new geography of production is developing which takes into account considerations stemming more from social and psychosocial facts than from natural impositions, while the economic element obviously remains essential.

The increasing amount of free time demands new forms of organisation and use of leisure during retirement, holidays, weekly or daily leisure time. The use of time is inevitably superimposed on the use of space. The national land area takes on a new and original appearance in the face of these new needs. In response, specialised

B9-0630

France;: A geographical
study

regional and local characteristics assert themselves. They call for the creation of appropriate systems of circulation. It is apparent that the national territory is only a fragment of a European area, even of the European Economic Community. According to whether it is receptive or repellent, it can attract part of the foreign gross national product or witness the flight of part of the French gross national product. The transition from a liability to an asset is a political operation and an involvement in physical development. The exploitation of the potential of tourism is a complex economic enterprise, which involves both a large private economic sector and State responsibilities. Once again special interests and national interests overlap and often conflict, as between general government policy and regional development. However in the end it is the region which is both the test bed and the setting for achievement.

CHAPTER THREE

Active Population and Employment

In recent decades the French population has been characterised by two apparently contradictory trends; rejuvenation and ageing. The rejuvenation followed the upturn in the birth rate by three to four points for twenty years compared with the period preceding the Second World War, while ageing is linked to an equivalent reduction in the death rate. By European standards, the population is growing relatively rapidly, as a result of the increasing proportion of young people, children, and elderly persons. In 1931 children under 15 years old constituted 23 per cent of the total population, in 1946 21.8 per

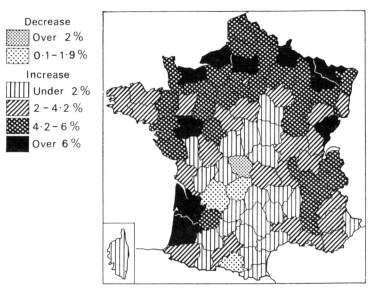

Decrease
Over 2 %
0·1–1·9 %
Increase
Under 2 %
2–4·2 %
4·2–6 %
Over 6 %

FIG. 6. Rate of natural increase 1962–68 (national average 4.2 per cent)

cent, in 1965 25.4 per cent and in 1971 24.5 per cent. The proportion of elderly people over 60 years old has increased regularly from 13.9 per cent to 15.9, 17.5 and 17.7 per cent at these same dates.

TABLE TWO

THE COMPOSITION OF THE FRENCH POPULATION BY AGE GROUPS
IN 1962, 1965 AND 1970

Age group	Total in thousands			Total as a percentage of the entire population		
	1962	1965	1970	1962	1965	1970
0–4 years	4,078	4,141	4,277	8.7	8.5	8.3
5–14	8,240	8,255	8,353	17.5	16.9	16.3
15–19	3,227	4,140	4,169	7.1	8.5	8.1
20–59	23,305	23,853	25,205	49.6	48.6	49.2
60–64	2,506	2,634	2,658	5.3	5.4	5.2
Over 65	5,544	5,927	6,628	11.8	12.1	12.9
Total	47,000	48,950	51,290	100.0	100.0	100.0

(Source: Parliamentary papers for the Fifth Plan, Assemblée Nationale. No. 1638, annexe
25 October 1965, p. 8)

TABLE THREE

TOTAL POPULATION PROJECTIONS BY AGE GROUPS
(in millions)

	1975		1980		1985	
	Max.	Min.	Max.	Min.	Max.	Min.
0–14 years	12.7	12.5	13.5	12.6	14.2	13.0
15–39	18.3	18.0	19.2	19.3	20.4	20.4
40–59	11.3	11.5	12.4	12.3	11.9	11.9
Over 59	9.7	9.7	9.1	9.3	10.0	9.7
Total	52.1	51.7	54.2	53.5	56.5	55.1

(Source: I.N.S.E.E., D6, March 1970.)

The active population has remained stable in France in spite of the increase in total population numbers, as a result of the ageing and the extension of education. It has remained curiously stationary between

20 and 22 million since the beginning of the century, while the total population has increased by over 10 millions.

TABLE FOUR

TOTAL AND ACTIVE POPULATION IN FRANCE

(in millions)

	Total population	Active population
1906	38.8	20.7
1921	38.8	21.7
1931	41.2	21.6
1954	42.0	20.7
1962	46.4	20.3
1971	51.0	20.7
1975 (Forecast)	52.0	20.8
1985 (Forecast)	55.0	22.5

Today the demand for work is being affected by pressure from groups reaching the employment age which are 25 to 30 per cent larger than the groups of that age born before and during the Second World War. This results from the upturn of the birth rate from 14 to 15 per thousand to 18 to 20 per thousand during the twenty-year period from 1946 to 1966.

If the essential condition of full employment is a numerical balance between supply and demand in the labour market, then this condition also requires that the jobs available are balanced by the skills available.

Until recently, the relatively minor distortions between these two sets of circumstances have been responsible for a certain amount of technical unemployment. This was estimated, at the beginning of 1972, at approximately 600,000 persons, including young people seeking their first jobs. At the same time the number of job opportunities open to the work force (which includes a rather high proportion of foreign workers) was 1.5 million.

However, although unskilled work can be entrusted to immigrants who are largely temporary, it is a fact that the failure of the school and university system to adjust to the needs of the economy threatens the French economy with a scarcity of managerial and skilled workers and an excess of unemployed graduates.

TABLE FIVE

THE COMPOSITION OF THE ACTIVE POPULATION IN FRANCE BY
EMPLOYMENT CATEGORY IN 1954, 1962 AND 1970

(in thousands)

	1954	1962	1970
Farming and forestry	5,175	3,878	2,929
Fishing	80	76	55
Qualified labourers, artisans and foremen }	6,685	3,475	3,953
Specialised workers and machinists }			
Scientific and technical personnel	460	622	939
Administrative personnel	1,507	1,850	2,351
Commercial personnel	1,664	1,627	1,695
Managerial employees	304	378	503
Health services	250	346	468
Teaching and literary professions	361	506	656
Transport workers	1,616	2,008	2,043
Personal services	106	129	159
Legal professions	62	56	63
Artistic professions	49	47	49
Army, diverse categories	624	593	549
Total	18,944	18,955	20,165

(Source: Documents for the Fifth Plan, p. 49.)

The present major trend is towards saturation of employment in services, which will not continue to expand at the same rate as in preceding years unless there is an upsurge in productive activities. The reflation of building and public works and of certain other industries through government orders and the granting of financial inducements were among the stimulants in use at the beginning of 1972. The orders being taken by several branches of industry encourage a certain amount of optimism. However, France will not be able to escape from the difficulties which generally beset the labour market in Europe and industrial nations as a whole. Fundamental and difficult changes must be made in the economic systems and employment structures to achieve new kinds of balance in the present decade.

As a consequence of the concentration of economic activity during the first phase of industrialisation, the distribution of population in France has been considerably disturbed as compared with the situation before the industrial revolution. The previous relatively uniform distribution over the whole of the land area, slightly weighted by variation in natural conditions, especially relief, has been succeeded by a

TABLE SIX

CHANGE IN EMPLOYMENT BY DETAILED BRANCH FROM 1 JANUARY
1970 TO 1 JANUARY 1971 IN FRANCE

Title of branch	Total labour force 1 January 1971 (provisional figures)	Change 1971/70 as per cent
Agriculture	2,802.7	−4.1
Agricultural and food industries	659.9	−0.1
Coal industry	121.9	−8.0
Production and distribution of electricity, gas, water	165.2	0.7
Refining and distribution of petroleum	105.2	2.6
Iron ore mining, iron and steel industry	198.3	3.1
Mining and metallurgy of non-ferrous metals	30.2	0.0
Primary processing and working of metals	449.1	2.7
Engineering industries	763.1	3.7
Electrical and electronic industries	428.5	4.3
Vehicle industry	402.2	6.0
Ship and aircraft construction, armaments	200.2	2.8
Glass industry	68.9	1.2
Chemicals and rubber industry	465.0	4.8
Textiles industry	425.4	−5.4
Clothing industry	332.2	−5.9
Leather industry	155.1	−5.0
Wood industry	269.7	−3.4
Paper industry	135.0	0.2
Printing, newspaper and publishing	280.1	3.6
Plastics processing and diverse industries	222.8	−0.9
Extraction and manufacture of building materials, ceramics	219.8	1.1
Building and public works	1,964.9	0.3
Transport	823.3	0.2
Telecommunications	379.8	1.4
Housing business	97.3	4.4
Other services*	2,663.1	4.3
Commerce	2,443.6	1.2
Banks, insurance, financial institutions	411.2	11.4
Administration	2,647.7	0.5
Total employment	20,702.7	0.7

* 'Other services' include alf private services offered to firms, such as research offices, accounting, legal ser-vices, and to private individuals, such as medical care, leisure, and health.

(Source: I.N.S.E.E., *Economie et Statistique,* no. 23, 1971.)

TABLE SEVEN

THE COMPOSITION OF NON-AGRICULTURAL EMPLOYMENT CREATED IN FRANCE BETWEEN 1962 AND 1970 BY MAJOR SECTORS

	1962 Change in thousands	Per cent	1963 Change in thousands	Per cent	1964 Change in thousands	Per cent
Industry	100.7	28.8	143.2	30.7	31.3	9.0
Building, public works	51.9	14.9	96.1	20.6	104.6	30.0
Services	196.7	56.3	226.9	48.7	212.5	61.0
Total	349.3	100.0	466.2	100.0	348.4	100.0

	1965		1966	Per cent	1967	
Industry	−41.3		46.7	15.8	−111.1	
Building, public works	53.3		26.8	9.1	18.4	
Services	175.7		221.6	75.1	176.6	
Total	187.7		295.1	100.0	83.9	

	1968		1969	Per cent	1970	Per cent
Industry	−27.0		179.1	30.6	53.6	20.6
Building, public works	41.9		55.8	9.5	6.7	2.6
Services	256.3		350.0	59.9	199.3	76.8
Total	271.2		584.9	100.0	259.6	100.0

(Source: Centre d'Etudes de l'Emploi, Bulletin d'Information, no. 1, September 1971.)

very uneven distribution. The dense concentrations correspond with regions industrialised during the nineteenth and early twentieth centuries; the mining regions, the port agglomerations, the major centres of business and industry like the Paris and Lyon regions. The age-structure distribution has changed in the course of the last decades. Until the Second World War, the rural areas of the West, the North and the East constituted a reservoir of youthful population, with a pronounced positive natural increase rate connected with the continuing high fertility levels. This reserve of population began to be seriously undermined by the ageing of population resulting from constant emigration, especially in the case of Brittany (Fig. 6). A slight reversal of these facts may be observed today. The internal migration of the working population has had the effect of rejuvenating the reception areas and of ageing the areas of departure. Since they are frequently accompanied by a migration of retired persons in the opposite direction, the migratory movements are responsible for aggravating regional contrasts which were originally provoked by the industrial revolution.

The map of net migration between 1962 and 1968 shows that at present, the old industrial regions, like the industrial North and Lorraine, which must undergo difficult processes of renewal, have

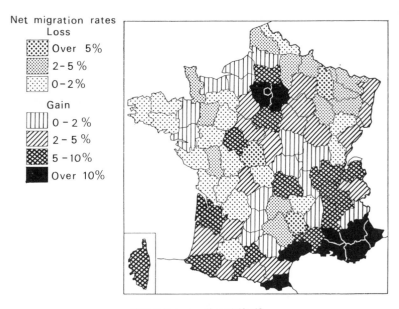

Net migration rates
Loss
Over 5%
2-5 %
0-2%
Gain
0 - 2 %
2 - 5 %
5 - 10%
Over 10%

F IG. 7. Net migration 1962–68

become zones of exodus. The attractive areas are the regions of specialised industry and those where tertiary service employment is expanding, the Paris region and, generally speaking, the Rhône-Alpes region. Another important fact shown by this map is the extent of the resettlement of Algerian repatriates in the Mediterranean *départements*.

Four industrial regions account for almost 40 per cent of the French population; the Paris region with 18.5 per cent, the Nord with 7.6 per cent the Greater Lyon region with 8.7 per cent and Lorraine with 4 per cent. The addition of the urbanised port regions of the Lower Seine, the Gironde, Marseille and the Lower Loire makes up half of the nation's population on approximately one-tenth of the national land area, concentrated into urban agglomerations or in the urbanised terrain of the *cités industrielles*.* The four regions cited above account for almost half the nation's natural increase, and this 48 per cent is increased to 58 per cent with the addition of the port regions. The major traditional rural regions have lost both their population and their youth, and have rates of natural increase markedly below the national average, the more so as the natural increase rates of the urban industrial regions continue to benefit from the migration of young people and the return of a proportion of their elderly to the countryside.

Two types of rural regions must be distinguished. Firstly there are those which have still retained both a large agricultural and a large total population, even though supplying large migratory movements – such as in the West (Normandy, Maine, Anjou, Brittany, Vendée, Poitou and Charentes) with nearly 9 million inhabitants or 18 per cent of the national total. Secondly, there are those regions which have been very largely emptied of population. These are the South West and the Mediterranean Midi, with the exception of their major urban agglomerations, the Alps, except for the surrounding fringe of towns, the rural East, Central France and even the plateaux and plains of the Paris Basin. In all, these regions account for only 15 million inhabitants, a third of the national total, on over two-thirds of the land area. There is a strong contrast between the models of internal demographic evolution appertaining to each of these two types. The West maintains annual average rates of natural increase equal to or above the national average at 7 per thousand. The other rural regions have noticeably aged demographically and their rates of natural increase fall below 4 per thousand throughout Central France, the South West and Languedoc (Fig. 6).

The regions with prominent reserves of active population are obviously the most attractive for the location of new firms, especially where it seems possible to recruit locally the excess rural population released by the technical evolution of agriculture. On the other hand some regions seem beyond help in the context of a modern economy for anything other than recreation, since it is not possible to provide a permanent and profitable economy with satisfactory living standards, and even less possible to recolonise in order to replace the indigenous population that has emigrated. More light is thrown on these problems

* High density housing concentrations related to mines or very large factories, often dependent on a single activity, which, while not having the administrative status or services of towns, nevertheless often have many thousands of inhabitants.

by the close study of agriculture and of the spontaneous location of new industrial firms – subjects which are dealt with in the two following chapters.

TABLE EIGHT

TOTAL AND ACTIVE POPULATION IN THE PLANNING REGIONS

Region	Total population (1000s)		Active population (1000s)	
	1962	1968	1962	1970*
Paris Region	8,454	9,250	4,098	4,876
Rhône-Alpes	3,991	4,422	1,773	1,999
Nord	3,655	3,815	1,362	1,519
Lorraine	2,201	2,274	859	956
Haute-Normandie	1,373	1,497	574	648
Brittany	2,417	2,468	1,032	1,007
Pays-de-la-Loire	2,454	2,582	1,037	1,075
Poitou-Charentes	1,453	1,481	579	600
Basse-Normandie	1,217	1,260	531	549
Limousin	723	736	325	306
Aquitaine	2,313	2,460	988	1,001
Midi-Pyrenées	2,044	2,185	866	931
Languedoc	1,538	1,707	563	612
Provence-Côte d'Azur	2,830	3,299	1,122	1,273
Corsica	181	—	51	49
Franche-Comté	920	992	385	429
Bourgogne	1,440	1,502	586	623
Champagne	1,196	1,279	490	548
Alsace	1,311	1,412	550	594
Picardie	1,465	1,579	575	661
Centre	1,880	1,990	799	856
Auvergne	1,262	1,312	528	535

* Estimate

CHAPTER FOUR

Agriculture Sheds Ballast

Twentieth century France has inherited a rural social structure which gradually evolved from the society of the *ancien régime,* in the course of the nineteenth century. In many regions aristocratic land-ownership is still considerable and this casts doubt on the effectiveness of the confiscation of land under the Revolution. However the predominant type of farm operation is the family farm, either tenanted or owner-operated. Share-cropping has gradually lost ground with the legislation improving the cropper's conditions of contract. The two major categories of farm operators in France are owner operators and farmers renting land under tenancy.* They were a constant feature in social and political life throughout the nineteenth century and up until the First World War. In 1913 the peasantry comprised 58 per cent of the French population. Between the two world wars it still formed an important section of the electorate and so it seemed opportune to certain politicians to keep in existence a society which had ceased to have an economic basis. Change was therefore delayed and the distortion between rural economy and rural society was increased. This explains the present strains, the critical situation in some regions and the acceleration of often contradictory processes, posing serious problems in the medium term for the stability of the agricultural economy.

I The Crisis of the Traditional Family Farm and Rural Exodus

The farm holding considered as the economic and social optimum at

---

* Although regulated to the advantage of the cropper, the practice of sharecropping is in process of disappearing and accounts for only 3 per cent of farms.

the beginning of the century was one capable of supporting a family and at the same time fully occupying its total working capacity, taking into account the seasonal variations in activity during the agricultural year. The relatively small size of the national urban market of only 7 million persons in 1851, 15 million in 1913 and 20 million approximately between the two world wars, within which there was competition from imported produce, went well with the retention of a large self-sufficient sector involving over three-quarters of the French population in 1851, two-thirds in 1911 and a half between 1920 and 1940. The stereotype French farm was a holding providing for the family food supply and the sale of wheat, milk, the natural increase of the livestock herd and *basse-cour** produce, which covered expenses payable in cash; the payment of rent in the case of tenants, taxes and public services, the purchase of groceries, clothing and household goods, work implements, doctors' bills and so on.

The holdings which seemed best balanced were those which, by practising a system of *polyculture†* and animal rearing, yielded the widest possible range of produce for family consumption, as for example in the West and South West, the plains of the Rhône and Saône, Central France and the East.

Life was particularly hard for those who did not own a farm and as a consequence were deprived of a family subsistence economy. Miserly wages, paid for 100 to 150 days of agricultural labour per annum, were generally supplemented by earnings from fruit picking, artisan work, labouring in quarries, forests, transport and building. Sometimes the agricultural labourers obtained the right to clear parcels of common land, to plant trees and vines, to sow vegetables, and to graze a goat, a few ewes or a donkey.

This was a society of misery. The small family holding extracted only meagre yields in spite of ceaseless effort. The surpluses sold were small and produced little income. This society also felt particularly bitter when it was necessary to work for other people. The apologists for peasant society nevertheless did not fail to praise its frugality, and the wisdom of the peasant in knowing how to be content with so little.

The realisation that there was a discrepancy in earnings as

---

* *Basse-cour* products refers to the miscellany of animals and poultry raised almost at random in the farmyard, ranging from hens, ducks, geese and turkeys to pigs and rabbits, the rearing of which was normally the concern of the farmer's wife and children.
† The growing of a wide range of crops.

expressed in cash terms between agricultural work and work in industry or administrative employment gradually precipitated the social
crisis in rural areas. The first affected were the landless peasants, daily
and casually hired labourers, who witnessed the disappearance of their
non-agricultural means of support in artisan activities in competition
with industrial production and who were attracted by the new construction works opened up by the industrial revolution, the building of
railways, building works, and then employment in factories. The
exodus epidemic came nearer to the small farmers, who also had to
supplement meagre farm incomes by outside work, the younger sons
in particular having no land to work. An extensive literature which
mingles observation with moralising and reiterated banalities has
described this rural exodus, the first phase of the ballast-shedding
operation from an agricultural sector which was undoubtedly
overloaded at the beginning of the industrial revolution, especially in
relation to the low productivity of farming. Moreover, rural exodus
suited the labour demands of industry and all the activities engendered
by industrialisation, urban development and the increase in government
responsibilities. The intensity of the exodus and its effects on rural life
varied.

In a few extreme cases it resulted in a real run-down of human
resources on a regional scale. Once the majority of the young adult
population had left, the ageing of the population structure soon
sterilised the regions of exodus, as in the Southern Alps, certain parts
of the Massif Central and the Aquitaine Midi. On the other hand some
regions with high demographic fertility spread their exodus over a
longer period and continued to increase their population slightly, the
exodus acting as a demographic regulator. This applied to the majority of the West until the period 1940 to 1950. The Ile-de-France, and in
general terms the broad plains of the Paris Basin, underwent an intermediate evolution. Losing their hired rural population and a
proportion of their small scale farmers because of the direct effect of
the Paris labour market, these *pays* were the first to succeed in
rebuilding their economic structures. The indigenous agricultural
workers, after being temporarily replaced by immigrant labourers,
notably Poles and Italians, were finally replaced by intensive
mechanisation. Farm holdings were consolidated. A new agricultural
economy and society was built up after 1920 and completed after the
Second World War. These regions had moved ahead in relation to the
second phase of manpower shedding, which might be termed the

technical and accounting* stage, which has taken place since the end of the Second World War.

II THE NEW AGRICULTURAL ECONOMY

French agriculture must adapt to the new circumstances of a market economy. In the first instance this means the national market, and in the future the European market, where the importance and relevance of the self-sufficient sector disappears. This adaptation is taking place through a marked increase in productivity and yields and the transition implies profound structural changes which currently means the departure of peasants again.

Since the beginning of the twentieth century certain sectors of production and certain regions especially favourable for the expansion of these sectors have been completely integrated into a commercial economy while benefiting from the growth and the specialisation of urban consumption demands, for example the increased demand for animal products, fruit, vegetables and wine. They have also benefited from the wider availability of fast transport. The first areas to experience this phenomenon were the outskirts of towns, which for a while enjoyed an almost competition-free market for delicate and perishable produce. The land was used with meticulous care, the steep slopes being covered with orchards, the valley floors improved as market gardening zones, the cool valleys devoted to pasture, dairy produce and nurseries, the latter supplying ornamental plants for the gardens of suburban detached houses and municipal parks. The first example was the rural-urban fringe of Paris in the late nineteenth and early twentieth century. Here market gardening covered the alluvial terraces and flood plains of the convex lobes of the Seine, Marne and Oise meanders, and the small valleys of the Bièvre, Yvette, Orge, Essonne and the Yerres. Orchards were planted on the scarps of Montreuil, Montmorency, Sceaux and Fontenay-aux-Roses. Nurseries stretched along the Seine Valley, in the Yerres valley and in the Bièvre and Yvette valleys. Milk was produced in the lower Marne valley in western Brie, in the *pays* of Yvelines between Rambouillet and the Chevreuse valley, and further off in the *pays* of Bray. Each village or

---

* In the sense of farming as a strict financial business operation as opposed to the *ad hoc* and largely uncosted commercial operations of the past.

group of villages had its speciality: Clamart for peas, Argenteuil for asparagus, Palaiseau for strawberries and Arpajon for beans. This system was destroyed by the development of a national market based on the rail network, the competition of industrial and urban employment depriving the suburban agriculture of its labour force and above all by urban expansion, which was preceded spatially and chronologically by land and building speculation. In the inner suburbs nurseries and flower cultivation resisted these trends better than food growing and dairy farming which gravitated by stages to the periphery. Each transfer was accompanied by a sound profit from the sale of land. The evolution was slower in the agricultural suburbs of Lyon, Lille, Bordeaux or Strasbourg, but the competition of a nationally organised market, based on specialised regions of production, weighed more and more heavily on local markets, which have tended in turn to become specialised in order to resist this competition better.

In fact the second form of agricultural specialisation was regional specialisation for the national market, taking the maximum advantage of local productive capacity in order to sell throughout France and if possible to export.

Over and above the traditional wheat growing, now using modern methods and concentrated in the northern half of the country, especially in the Paris Basin, Alsace and Brittany, and in combination with sugar-beet in Flanders, Picardy and the Ile-de-France, farmers engaged in four main enterprises.

Firstly, dairy farming and meat production, carried on outdoors on natural pasture, in Normandy, Charentes and a few intermediate mountain zones.

Secondly, the fattening of livestock, usually born in mountainous areas, on natural pasture to some extent enriched by using liquid manure and fertilisers and by periodic resowing, as in the regions of Charolais, Nivernais, Bazois and Marquenterre.

Thirdly, viticulture, devoted either to mass production of ordinary wines, as in Bas-Languedoc, or the production of superior and fine wines, wholesaled after maturing in cellars, as mainly in Bordelais, Burgundy, the Rhône valley, Alsace and Anjou, or as, after special processing, in Champagne and the Vouvray district.

Finally, market gardening and fruit growing was concentrated around the collection and distribution centres linked to the major consumption areas by rail or road, and was practised by high yielding methods, by irrigation or under shelter, as in the Comtat Venaissin, the plains of the lower Durance, in the zones irrigated by the canal of Bas Rhône-Languedoc, in the Vaunage and Costière areas and Roussillon. The same enterprises took place without irrigation in regions favoured by a damp, mild climate and limon soils, as in north west Brittany, the confluence zones of the Garonne basin around Marmande and Moissac, and the Loire valley. Or again, in the case of orchards, cultivation took place in valleys with favourably exposed slopes, like those of the Doux and the Erieux for peach growing in Ardèche, the slopes of the Vaucluse and Luberon hills for apple growing.

The transition to a market economy in all the regions involved in these agricultural specialisations took place after the first decades of the twentieth century. The farmer bought all the commodities needed for consumption. The farm produced practically nothing for its own consumption, except any surplus output. The peasant was confronted at an early stage by the middleman who undertook the difficult operations of the geographical distribution of produce and the regulation of the market. The very real element of risk which burdens all wholesaling of perishable produce justified high profit margins, against which the producer's reactions have been frequent and prompt. But attempts by the producers at organising direct marketing have always been doomed to failure, except in the case of dairy produce in the Charentes and Jura. Forecasting is too difficult and the vested interests entrenched in the markets too strong to tolerate a parallel cooperative market or short circuit. Only the wine producers of the Midi succeeded in commanding respect for their interests by organising strong pressure groups beginning with the 1907 movement, and they obtained by various successive systems the guarantee of a minimum price for the total sale of the annual output.

The market economy has affected all sectors of agricultural production, nibbling away progressively at the self-sufficient sector and introducing everywhere the notion of rural accounting, at first empirically, then methodically in the last fifteen years with the creation of regional offices for rural accounting. The costing of agricultural operations inexorably reveals the wastage, underemployment and low yields of both land and labour. It gives a merciless diagnosis of the archaic nature of the small traditional family farm and helps to define the sizes and forms of farm holding suited to modern production techniques. Increased productivity achieved by the introduction of machinery and increased yields through the application of fertilisers, the use of selected seed, the artificial insemination of cattle from pure stock and the treatment of crops against insects and mildew, represent high medium term investments and operating costs in relation to specific and relatively unfavourable conditions of profitability; the cost of equipment must be amortised in a relatively few years and with a small number of hours' usage for each agricultural year. Farm units must be defined in relation to their ability to make these investments and to engage in high operation costs, taking into account the best possible utilisation of the equipment employed. The creation of working capital and optimum profitability from this investment can only be achieved above a certain size threshold which has continued to rise in the last twenty years, because of the increased working capacity of agricultural machinery and its diversification according to the particular work to be done. In 1938 it was thought that a representative average size for a family farm should be 12 to 15 hectares; the actual figure being weighted according to the regions and to the system of cropping and livestock rearing. In 1950 the threshold was established by experts at approximately 25 hectares or even at 50 to 60, and in regions of specialised grain farming at 80 to 100 hectares. Maximum productivity is reached in cereal farming without cattle or root crops in the Ile-de-France or in Picardy on 250 to 400 hectare units with three or four permanent workers including the farm operator. Naturally the threshold falls to much lower levels in the case of specialised crops or fattening, and the price of land varies in the opposite direction. The idea of a threshold of viability is valid essentially in the case of predominantly grain farming, where a tractor, modern machinery and a reasonable use of fertilisers make it possible to attain yields of 30 q/ha;* or in the case of grassland farming, rearing about forty head excluding the lesser livestock associated with cattle rearing. At the census of 1959 75 per cent of the agricultural area consisted of farms of less than 50 hectares. In 1968, in spite of a clear reduction in the number of farm operators especially in the East, where the reduction was over 25 per cent in ten years, central France and the South West, holdings of less than 50 hectares still occupied over two-thirds of the farmed area.

An arithmetical calculation would no doubt make it possible to estimate, for each agricultural region, the number of holdings which will have to disappear and the number of rural inhabitants who will have

* Quintals per hectare.

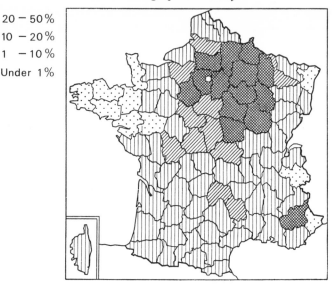

▓	20 – 50%
▨	10 – 20%
▥	1 – 10%
⸬	Under 1%

FIG. 8. Proportion of farms of over 50 hectares as a percentage of the total number of farms, by *départements*

to abandon the land. It would eliminate the possibility of maintaining smallholdings by devoting them to specialised activities with high labour productivity on small areas. There are many if not always successful attempts; market and fruit gardening, flower growing, poultry and pig rearing, and the planting of vines to produce superior wines. They conflict with the limited size of the national market and uncertainty about the possibilities of absorption by the European market, but they are able to retain locally a higher rural density than would result from simply applying a 'norm' calculated according to the viability of standard farm units for a given agricultural region. In fact the evolution is much more complex and full of contradictions. The concentration of farm holdings is generally accompanied by or preceded by land consolidations* which strengthen the supremacy of the large land owners. The stabilisation of the redistributed field pattern makes it impossible – and in any case it would be pointless – to increase the size of small holdings by acquiring adjacent parcels of land. The hierarchy of land ownership, if not of farm operation,

* The process of *remembrement*, the consolidation of scattered individual parcels of land into more compact and generally larger holdings.

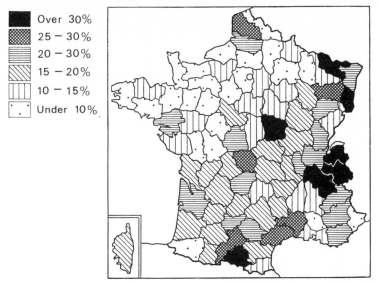

FIG. 9a. Decrease in the number of farm holdings between 1955 and 1963 by *départements*

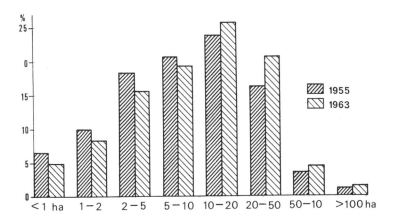

FIG. 9b. Farm size, based on productive land area, as a percentage of the number of farm holdings

appears to be permanently established and this makes the small farmers acutely aware of their comparatively small scale. As a result the exodus is accelerated and the concentration of land is made easier. However, very often there is no balance between the migration of rural population and the transition to a profitable economic structure. Even tenants or title holders of viable farms are discouraged. In this case a factor other than optimum size comes into play, the method of handing down farms. The fact that farmers retain the responsibility for running farms while their grown-up children are still subordinate encourages the departure of the young people who would normally be the inheritors of highly viable farms, but who do not want to wait for this inheritance until they are over forty; moreover present legislation allows the farmer to have only one heir apparent so as to avoid the splitting up of holdings. Concentration is therefore not a solution to the technical problem of agriculture. If it operates in favour of farmers without inheritors able to engage in agriculture it leads to a dead end situation. In some cases land is taken over by foreigners, Dutch or Germans in the Paris Basin for example, who have acquired the ownership or tenancy of farms without successors. North African repatriates have also taken over farms which were about to be abandoned in the South West and the Mediterranean Midi. These are chance solutions which do not resolve the whole problem of the breakdown of traditional mechanisms of agriculture and rural society and the lack of integration between the technical concentration of working the land and the demographic run-down of rural areas. The numerical man-land ratio appears to be approaching the optimum, but this appearance is deceptive in that the active rural population is ageing without the young generation being ready to take its place.

Since the Second World War the agricultural problem has concerned young people because the faster evolution of production methods and farm structures can only be followed and promoted by young people. It was young farmers who encouraged the quite successful formation of cooperatives for the use of agricultural machinery (C.U.M.A.).* It was to keep young farmers on the land that the Decree of 1963 guaranteed elderly farm operators who agreed to retire a supplementary pension in the form of a life annuity on stopping work. It was to increase the area available for younger farmers that the State thought of the compulsory purchase of fallow land for

---

* Coopératives d'Utilisation du Matériel Agricole.

those wishing to work it, and gave S.A.F.E.R.* the task of supervising, in the interest of the agricultural community, land which had fallen vacant while awaiting reallocation. It was also the young who were most involved in the creation of agricultural technical training centres (C.E.T.A.).† In some regions they do not hesitate to introduce entirely new methods of administering cropland, invoking the law of 8 August 1962 to form farming companies which are in fact, if not in name, commodity cooperatives; a nice solution to the problem created by the non-replacement of generations in regions with elderly populations. There remains the problem that agriculture is not always capable of employing satisfactorily the young people who ten or fifteen years after their entry into the work force may be called on to direct a farm. It is therefore desirable for the countryside to offer temporary employment without people being uprooted. Industrial decentralisation, extending as far as the level of *canton* capital or important village, is a means of stabilising a rural population density sufficient to assure the changeover of generations on farms. However it runs into so many obstacles that it is perhaps an illusory solution.

The activities of the Regional Development Companies‡ appear more substantial and seem to be more immediately translated into solid achievements. The most typical is the Company of Bas Rhône-Languedoc, whose purpose is to convert an area of extensive farming in the Costière area to a high productivity economy and thus to increase rural densities, by creating farms of a size appropriate to modern techniques of production and management, much larger than the traditional early vegetable and market garden holdings of the left bank of the Rhône for example. They also aim to renew the economy of the viticultural region, providing more employment here too, and to create the basis for a new rural society better integrated into the modern regional economy.

Where concentration or association has taken place to produce a size of holding that is profitable and progressive, production methods

---

* The Sociétés d'Aménagement Foncier et d'Equipement Rural are government-financed regional bodies; they can intervene by pre-emption and directly in the land market to create reserves of land for reallocation primarily in order to enlarge small farms to viable proportions.

† Centres d'Enseignement des Techniques Agricoles sprang up spontaneously after 1945 as a self-help movement towards farm modernisation.

‡ Major government-sponsored development companies which have a regional sphere of action and an integrated approach to resource use; they were set up to solve the physical, economic and social problems of specific areas.

are markedly different from those of the traditional family farm. The use of fertilisers, the more effective working of the land with tractors and suitable machinery, the introduction of techniques of crop treatment and livestock husbandry perfected in laboratories and on experimental farms all mean that the most advanced farms obtain yields per unit area at least double those of the small farms. The tractor has markedly increased agricultural output by permitting more rapid and effective working of the land at the right times, and by freeing the area devoted to feedstuffs for draught animals. It was calculated in 1965 that if all the arable land of France was worked by tractor 2,500,000 hectares could then be given over to commercial crops by the elimination of a million working horses and 500,000 draught oxen. Each concentration of farm work by the use of suitable machinery makes possible a double increase – in yields and productivity. For example, it has been pointed out that in modern poultry farming, a single worker can fatten 100,000 chickens in a year or manage 10,000 laying hens; his productivity has increased ten-fold in ten years;* and it is about a thousand times higher than that of the farmer's wife raising poultry in the farmyard. The gap is thus inexorably widening between the income of the small farmer and that of the large scale operator, inevitably reducing the possibility of investment to enlarge and modernise the small farms, especially at a time of inflation. The palliatives, such as the possibility of acquiring abandoned land or the redistribution to smallholders by the S.A.F.E.R. of land put up for sale, especially because farmers are leaving, have little effect, and as a result 150,000 peasants continue to leave the land every year. Rural society is changing and the agricultural economy is taking on a new style. The fundamental paradox is the apparently direct correlation between the reduction in the number of peasants and the increase in agricultural output. However, with the exception of a few regions entirely given over to large scale farming, the clash of interests between small and large holdings exists everywhere and the bitterness of the small farmers is a source of permanent unrest.

Taken together the changes in the agricultural economy are disturbing the basic structure of traditional rural society. In a good many regions the numerical majority of the rural population is now not the farming community but trades people, the representatives of various industrial branches and retired persons. The farming villages are

---

* M. Gervais, C. Servolin and J. Weil, *Une France Sans Paysans*, Seuil, 1965, p. 106–8.

emptying, with two or three farms replacing twenty or thirty smallholdings. There are some elderly people, usually peasants, who have retired to their smallholdings, or people who migrated thirty or forty years previously and have now returned to their family home, or people who are spending their declining years in what were secondary homes during their active life. Services, business and artisan activities related to the distribution of manufactured goods, such as cars, agricultural machinery, electrical machinery, domestic equipment and television, are concentrated in a small number of villages; these are former capitals of *cantons* or crossroad villages which have attracted the functions of local control and are the terminal points of flows emanating from the urban network, and thus from the structure of the industrial system. The traditional relationship between the major landowner, whether he actually resided on his estate or was a town dweller, and the tenants or smallholders dependent on him in various ways, and the authority of the rural gentry, solicitors, country doctors, veterinary surgeons, wholesale dealers and small scale manufacturers are being replaced by relationships between producer and retailer, consumer and distributor, in other words the relationships characteristic of a market and industrial economy. The aristocracy and the gentry now have no contact with the peasantry apart from subscribing to their protests against the retailer's profit margins, the parasitic nature of marketing through middlemen, the discrepancy between the agricultural prices paid to the producer and the prices of industrial products for which they are consumers, and against the State. They join in the action of unions and agricultural associations and often direct them. Defending favourable prices for people who earn little is by no means displeasing for people who are equipped to make larger profits. On the whole, however, contacts of a personal nature which were characteristic of the predominantly peasant traditional rural society have been replaced by impersonal institutional and monetary contacts which are hardly any different from those of the urban and industrial society. The standardisation of information levels and of entertainment succeeds in destroying the distinctive character of rural society. It is a society of small and medium sized enterprises which have a particular job to do and whose income is doubly uncertain because of the risk of bad weather and because of the fluctuations of a market with which it is practically impossible to coordinate variations in output. Apart from these entirely negative characteristics, the economic and social structure differs less and less from that of the industrial economy and urban society. However, this evolution has not reached the same level in all regions.

III AN INCREASING OUTPUT WHICH IS STILL BELOW ITS POTENTIAL

The last twenty years have witnessed a considerable increase in agricultural production in France, in spite of a marked decline in the area cultivated and in the agricultural labour force. In 1851 arable land occupied 26 million hectares. In 1910 it had already fallen to 23 million hectares and it stabilised at approximately 19 million hectares in the 1960s. An increase in the area devoted to grass by no means accounts for the difference, having only increased by two million hectares between 1910 and 1965. Nor have specialised crops increased in area very much. The vine has disappeared from 500,000 hectares, while market garden crops, fruit and flowers have gained approximately an equivalent area. The male agricultural labour force has declined from 8 million at the beginning of the nineteenth century to a little over 5 million in 1913, 3.5 million in 1952 and 2.7 million in 1970.

The major items of production, however, have continued to increase. In spite of a large reduction in the area under grain, in the years 1961–70 the output of wheat was twice that at the beginning of the century with three times the yields. The production of barley and maize has also doubled. The sugar-beet and potato crops have tripled. The total number of cattle has increased from 14 to 22 million head. Only the sheep population has declined markedly, from 17 to 10 million head. Milk and meat yields have increased considerably, by at least 100 per cent. The output of milk has increased to over 300 million hectolitres and that of meat to 3.2 million tons, of which 1.5 million tons are beef and veal and 1.5 million tons pork. Market garden production shot up after the First World War and has only been slowed down by the size of the market. The viticultural economy has surmounted the difficulties of the overproduction of ordinary wines by increasing the supply of superior wines. The total output of wine averaged 65 million hectolitres during the period 1959–70.

In terms of the volume of production French agriculture is the most important in Europe except for the U.S.S.R. France produces 4 per cent of the world output of wheat, 5.6 per cent of milk, 5.5 per cent of world beef production, 4.2 per cent of the pork, 3 per cent of the mutton and 10 per cent of world sugar-beet production. However the yields in weight remain below those of other European nations, except for Italy, and the income per cultivated hectare is the lowest of the six original countries of the Common Market.* This overall backwardness is explained in part by the diversity of natural conditions and in part by the persistence of considerable differences in efficiency between the entirely modernised farms with high productivity and high yields, like those found in the Ile-de-France with one employed person to every 60 to 80 hectares and yields of 40 quintals of wheat per hectare, and the small residual farms in the West, South West and Massif Central with one employed person per 10 hectares or less and wheat yields of less than 20 quintals per hectare.

The proportion of agricultural revenue in the gross national product is still very small; scarcely more than 10 per cent for 18 per cent of the active population. The agricultural sector therefore still appears weak and has the lowest productivity and remuneration for time worked. It has not completed its transformation and, far more quickly than the industrial sector, it comes up against the limits of a market which is much less elastic than that for manufactured goods, in the internal market as well as in the European framework. The position of France in Europe, which has often been described as a crossroads location and ideal environment, means that French agriculture is in no sense specific and thus is in competition in all respects with neighbouring countries as well as with overseas imports. It meets competition in the market for dairy produce from Holland, for fruit, vegetables and wine from Italy and it has difficulty in international trade competition because of high production costs. This explains the Malthusian spirit of the agricultural economy in which, too often, farmers have preferred to produce a small amount to be certain of maintaining prices, and in which adaptation to the European Economic Community produces the greatest confusion. Thus one finds poor maintenance of pasture, under-stocking of pasture, under-production of milk by comparison with the norms achieved by the major livestock rearing neighbours, especially Holland, and uncertainty in the expansion of market gardening and fruit production and the creation of a national fruit and vegetable processing and conserving industry.

* Expressing French income per cultivated hectare as an index of 100, that of Italy is 130, West Germany 180, and Belgium and Holland between 280 and 300.

IV REGIONAL DIVERSITY

In spite of the need for specialisation, with its reduced production costs, French agriculture remains one of *polyculture* integrated with livestock rearing in the great majority of the regions. Practically everywhere the tradition of subsistence *polyculture* is still strong. The small scale variations in land resources encourage a diversification of land usage even within the farm unit. The instability of the market, although regulated by numerous measures guaranteeing minimum prices, and the varying susceptibility of different crops and animal rearing to unpredictable changes in climate, are both important factors underlying the persistence of *polyculture*. With the exception of livestock rearing on mountain or *bocage* pasture, specialised and large scale viticulture and market gardening, French agriculture is characterised by the varying proportions of the diverse elements in the *polyculture* and livestock rearing system rather than by real specialisation. However, in the course of the last decades, specialisation has gained ground.

The land use map of France, drawn by M. J. Klatzmann*, shows a number of major variations, both from the point of view of crop combinations and economic value, and it makes it possible to distinguish homogeneous units.

The first unit corresponds with the *limon* covered plains dominated by grain farming, which extend from the Belgian frontier to Orléans, over the *départements* of Nord, Pas-de-Calais, Somme, Aisne, Oise, Marne, Aube, Seine-et-Marne, Yvelines, Essonne, Val d'Oise, Loiret and part of Yonne, Eure-et-Loire and most of Eure. This encompasses the regions of Nord, Picardy, the Ile-de-France, Dry Champagne and part of Normandy. It occupies 15 per cent of the national land area, 20 per cent of the arable land and 50 per cent of the wheat crop, with average yields of between 35 and 45 quintals per hectare.† It produces 87 per cent of the sugar-beet crop, with yields of 300 to over 400 quintals per hectare, and 23 per cent of the potato crop. Cattle rearing by stall-feeding, which at the beginning of the century was a widespread feature of intensive farming on the best soils, has declined on the most heavily mechanised plains like Beauce and Champagne, where the

* J. Klatzmann, *La Localisation des Cultures et des Productions Animales en France*, 1955, INSEE.

† Yields exceed 40 quintals per hectare in the *départements* of Nord, Oise, Seine-et-Marne, Essonne, Yvelines, Somme, Aisne, Eure and Pas-de-Calais.

climate and the tendency for the soils to be dry are less suitable for the production of fodder crops and root feedstuffs. Nevertheless this unit supplies 20 per cent of the national production of milk, although as an activity it is only visible within the farms themselves. Only in the neighbouring *département* of Seine-Maritime, which in any case is related to the group described previously, does milk production occupy a more important and conspicuous position. With 1.15 per cent of the national land area and 1.25 per cent of the arable acreage, Seine-Maritime produces 2.5 per cent of the wheat crop, with yields of 44 quintals per hectare, 4 per cent of the sugar-beet, with yields of 450 quintals per hectare, but also 2 per cent of the nation's milk output. The *limon* plains of northern France and especially the northern Paris Basin possess the most concentrated farm land in France, with 30,000 farms of over 50 hectares out of a national total of 95,000. Altogether there are 255,000 farmers on 2,341,600 hectares, or a little over 10 per cent of French farmers for approximately 35 per cent by value of the national agricultural output. Some privileged branches of agriculture obtain even higher levels of productivity and yields, as for example in the market garden and dairying valleys of the Oise, Marne, Seine and their small tributaries, in the viticultural area of Champagne on the scarp of the Ile-de-France between Reims and the Saint-Gond marshes, and in the Loire valley with market gardens, fruit growing, nurseries and flower growing in the Orléans area.

The East, from the Ardennes to the Jura inclusive, combines low-yielding cereal growing with unimpressive livestock farming. Lorraine, Wet Champagne, Lower Burgundy, the plateaux of the Upper Saône, the plateaux of the Jura and the region of Bresse, represent a cultivated area of 1,700,000 hectares and 2 million hectares of grassland; 9 per cent and 15 per cent respectively of the corresponding national totals. The level of output is much lower than the areal proportions, with 7.6 per cent of the nation's wheat production and 13 per cent of the milk. The mountains are divided between forest and pasture, meadows and fodder crops in the valleys and summer pasture on the plateaux and summits. The three *départements* of Vosges, Doubs and Jura have a cattle population of 600,000 head and produce 9.5 million hectolitres of milk, 4.5 per cent of the national total. The plateaux have cereals and fodder crops with low yields, which in the case of wheat generally falls below 30 quintals per hectare. In spite of a heavy rural exodus since the beginning of the century, small farms are still numerous, but fallow has gained heavily at the expense of cultivated land and it is in the *départements* of the East that the biggest effort at fallow reclamation is being undertaken. In spite of the severity of the climate, the Jura makes a better showing than the plateaux of Lorraine and Burgundy, because of the organisation of livestock rearing and the persistence of a high rural population, helped by small scale manufacturing and cottage industry. The struggle of the cheese cooperatives, the *fruitières,* against the major dairy companies shows the vitality of a social structure with no wish to give up. The other regions of the East, however, offer a picture of a countryside drained of its blood, with villages for the most part empty, where the relative consolidation of farmland gives an appearance of wealth to farmers who are still far from achieving the maximum productive capacity of these lands, which in fact are not very fertile with the exception of Bresse and the Dijon lowland.

The Burgundy vineyard area, occupying a very small space along the front delimited by the fault scarps separating the Burgundy plateau from the Saône plain, and to the south, along the escarpment of the first of the crystalline massifs overlooking the Saône, is one of the high productivity regions of French agriculture. An output of a million hectolitres of fine and superior wine is achieved from 25,000 hectares and the value of exports totals over 50 million francs.

Alsace is a completely distinctive agricultural region in eastern France. The plain of Alsace is one of the main cereal farming regions, producing 1.2 million quintals of wheat with average yields of over 25 quintals per hectare, and 800,000 quintals of barley with similar yields. The farms are highly fragmented, with 500,000 holdings of from 1 to 10 hectares and only a hundred of over 60 hectares. Cattle rearing, integrated with crop growing, supplies 4 million hectolitres of milk. Market gardening in the *ried* zone, industrial crops and hops complete a very wide range of high quality production based on an intensive economy. The Vosges foothills of central Alsace are the domain of viticulture, producing 900,000 hectolitres of quality wine, and orchards. Overall in the province 400,000 hectares of agricultural land are worked by 50,000 persons employed in farming; a ratio of 8 hectares per worker as compared with the national average of 15. The farms are impecunious, but tiny and well cared for and their occupants often seek a supplementary income in industry.

At the opposite extreme, the massive area of the West is characterised by the importance of grassland and cattle rearing, but with the exception of Lower Normandy, cereal cultivation is never absent and throughout most of Brittany it is the essential element in the farm economy. The five regions of Lower Normandy, Maine, Anjou, Brittany and Vendée, rear approximately a third of French cattle and a quarter of the pigs on 2.6 million hectares of grassland and pasture amounting to 13 per cent of the national land area, and they yield 28 per cent of French milk production. In addition they have 3.3 million hectares of cropland, some 17 per cent of the national total, but produce only 14 per cent of the cereal crop, with 15 million quintals of wheat. In northern and central Brittany the grain farming region forms an uninterrupted mass, giving way to field production of market garden crops, early potatoes, cauliflowers, onions, artichokes, peas and beans, and strawberries on the coastal plateaux of western Côtes-du-Nord and northern Finistère, and to the production of seed potatoes in the Basin of Châteaulin. With the exception of the open plain of Caen, Lower Normandy is entirely pastoral. The three *départements* of Calvados, Orne and Manche have a tenth of the French cattle population and produce a tenth of commercial milk supplies. It is here that the traditional *bocage* rural landscape is best preserved and still has its functional character. Maine, the western half of Brittany, Anjou and Vendée have an agricultural economy between that of central and northern Brittany and that of Lower Normandy, combining cereals and fodder crops with a system of livestock rearing which is making great technical progress. As in eastern Brittany, the *bocage* is being cleared, under the pressure of modern techniques and mechanisation. Nevertheless, it is still dense in Vendée and in southern Loire-Atlantique. Relatively densely populated by the standards of the French countryside, the western regions are characterised by small farms, if not always smallholdings. The four Breton *départements* of Côtes-du-Nord, Finistère, Ille-et-Vilaine and Morbihan have a total of only 844 farms of over 50 hectares, but in contrast they have 100,000 farms of from 1 to 10 hectares of which only a small proportion are located in the market gardening zone. Moreover the market for market garden produce is irregular, the dispatching conditions are difficult and costly, the prices paid to the producer are considered too low, and the intensive market garden smallholdings, which might be expected to lower the size threshold necessary for profitable operation, are in difficulty. Brittany is one of the hotbeds of peasant unrest, especially in the market garden zone of Trégorrois and Léon.

The western part of the Loire valley in Anjou and Brittany forms a small and distinctive agricultural region. It benefits from a southern variant of the Atlantic climate which makes it possible to grow delicate crops. Pride of place goes to the vine, grown from the Saumur area as far as the estuary in the vineyards of Saumur, Vouvray and Anjou in the Loire valley and in the small tributary valleys such as the Côteau du Layon, and the Muscadet area around Nantes. Vegetable growing, flower cultivation and nurseries are also important, especially around Angers.

To the south of the major regional unit of the West, made up of Lower Normandy, Brittany, Anjou and Vendée, the Central West, coinciding with the *départements* of Indre-et-Loire (Touraine), Vienne, Deux-Sèvres (Poitou), Charente, Charente-Maritime, and to the south, Vendée,* is again a grain-farming region with pasture of secondary importance. In favourable locations market garden produce and fruit crops are grown as is the vine, above all in Charente-Maritime where, on the edge of the Bordeaux wine-producing area, viticulture has fallen back at the present time on the production of spirits with Cognac as the main centre. The Central West region has 1.8 million hectares of arable land, 8 per cent of the French total, and only 450,000 hectares of grassland, a little over 3 per cent of the national total; 1.3 million cattle are reared, 5.5 per cent of the national total and roughly 6 million quintals of wheat are produced, 7 per cent of French output. The distinctive feature of the Central West is the achievement of a better yield from the grassland than from the arable, even though twice as much land is devoted to arable as to meadows and grassland. The ratio of farmers to arable land is lower than that of the western regions, with 1 person employed in agriculture per 16 hectares compared to Brittany with 1 person per 8.8 hectares, but higher than that of the major cereal farming regions of the Paris Basin with 1 per 31 hectares.

The South West is clearly divided into two units – a heterogeneous unit corresponding to the planning region of Aquitaine and a homogeneous unit, the Toulouse area. The first unit combines two very distinctive regions by means of an intermediary link, the Landes area, which from an agricultural standpoint is almost empty. To the north, the Bordelais is one of the richest viticultural regions of France, while to the south, Béarn and the Basque country are *pays* with traditional *polyculture* with a southern flavour and a high proportion of maize growing. The Bordelais vineyards occupy 150,000 hectares

---

* The *département* of Vendée as distinct from the broader region of La Vendée included in the western agricultural region described above.

in the confluence zone of the Dordogne and the Garonne extending 80 kilometres south-east to north-west, and an average of 40 kilometres from south-west to north-east. They produce high quality wine based on large châteaux holdings and on the traditional marketing centre, the Chatrons district of Bordeaux, which formerly exported by sea. These vineyards produce 5 million hectolitres, including some of the greatest French wines, such as Haut-Medoc – particularly red wines, but not forgetting the sweet or semi-sweet wines, such as the Graves and Haut-Sauternes; they represent one of the major bases for the sale of French agricultural products in foreign markets.

Chalosse, Béarn and the Basque country still have an exceptionally dense agricultural population, with one person engaged in farming for every 7 hectares. The land is highly subdivided, more especially at the level of farm operation than actual land ownership. Half of the farms are less than 10 hectares in size and only 250 exceed 50 hectares. A cereal-based *polyculture* with low yields is combined with diversified livestock rearing involving few head per farm except in the case of domestic fowl and pigs, a few fruit trees and a little viticulture. There are yields of 20 quintals per hectare of wheat but double this yield is obtained from maize. Less than 2,000 litres of milk are yielded per cow; working cows give a very poor yield. With a much higher density of population, the *pays* of the Basses-Pyrénées introduce types of farming of the Toulouse area.

The Toulouse region and the *pays* of the middle Garonne are the areas most affected by rural exodus since the middle of the nineteenth century, to such a degree that several attempts have been made since the First World War to renew their agricultural population and farm operators by turning to foreign immigrants. These have included Spaniards, Italians particularly, migrants from densely populated French regions such as Brittany and Vendée, and more recently repatriates from North Africa. A series of vicissitudes have driven out the population in successive generations. The unprofitability of share cropping, which was instituted on the large estates in the nineteenth century when renting replaced the system of paid labour which in turn was derived from serfdom, the heaviness of the *terreforts* and the sterility of the *boulbènes** in dry years, the uncertainty of harvests and the mediocre return for thankless work with inefficient equipment, the repeated attraction of work in public administration (with the complici-

* See Footnote p. 20.

ty of those already in the civil service), and the flight towards stable employment with guaranteed income, have depopulated the countryside in one generation after another without making any noticeable change in the agricultural structures except in the course of the last two decades. In less than a century the rural population has declined by from 30 to 60 per cent. The countryside is nevertheless still overmanned and productivity is particularly low, with 10 hectares per person engaged in agriculture for yields which are among the lowest in France, for example 15 to 20 quintals per hectare for wheat and barley and 20 in the case of maize, 30 hectolitres of milk per hectare for each cow, roughly 1,500 litres per year, except in the case of specialised milk production near the towns. It is true that this is an integral form of *polyculture* with maximum diversity of output. Each share cropping, or each farm, for share cropping is everywhere rapidly declining and even disappearing, has its arable land, its meadows, vines and fruit trees, its stable of draught oxen which are now gradually being replaced by the tractor, its pigsties, turkeys, geese, ducks, hens, its rabbit hutches and sometimes its beehives. As a result there is constant work for an income which remains mediocre. The contribution to national output is low. The *départements* of Hautes-Pyrénées, Ariège, Haute-Garonne, Gers, Lot, Tarn and Tarn-et-Garonne produce 4 per cent of the wheat crop, 2.5 per cent of the barley, 4 per cent of the milk output, from 7 per cent of the arable land of France and 6 per cent of the grassland.

In the centre of this economic gloom the plains of the middle Garonne, and more particularly the confluence zones of the river with its major tributaries, the Tarn and the Lot, seem a prosperous region. Vegetables, orchards, vines and tobacco give good returns there. Peas, tomatoes and table grapes are dispatched and tobacco leaves are treated at Marmande, Moissac and Tonneins. Agen is the centre of plum growing and of plum drying for the preparation of prunes. These fertile lands have attracted investment. Estates have been acquired and replanted by the repatriates from North Africa and act as model farms for fruit tree cultivation.

The central zone of France is divided into two halves from an agricultural standpoint, with very different aptitudes, separated by a diagonal line running north-east–south-west from Périgord to Morvan. To the north-west of this line, on the granite of the Massif Central and on the sedimentary terrains of its foreland, a combination of grazing and cattle rearing with cereals and fodder crops prevails giving average yields. Grassland and a pastoral system tend to predominate and to give satisfactory yields in the beef cattle rearing regions, with fattening on the lowlands, in Nivernais and Morvan. The north-western half of the central zone includes the regions of Limousin, Berry, Boichaut, Bourbonnais, Nivernais and Morvan, comprising the *départements* of Haute-Vienne, Creuse, Allier, Indre, Cher and Nièvre. It produces 7 per cent of the national output of wheat with average yields of 25 quintals per hectare, 5 per cent of the milk production and over 15 per cent of the meat production. The poverty of the soil in the uplands and the persistence of an aristocratic tradition on the plains of Berry, Bourbonnais and Nivernais, increase the proportion of large farms. 20 per cent of the cultivated area is worked by farms of over 100 hectares in the *département* of Indre, 25 per cent in Cher, 18 per cent in Nièvre, 10 per cent in Allier, 4 per cent in Haute-Vienne. In Berry there are 200 farms of over 200 hectares. The rural population density is relatively sparse in the zone, with 24 hectares cultivated for each person engaged in agriculture.

The second portion of central France corresponds with the highest mountains, with the exception of the Limagne lowland, and with the dry *pays* of the Causse and the Mediterranean margins of the Massif Central. It is a zone with high precipitation which ensures a dense cover of grassland and forest, but the harshness of the climate reduces the apparent advantages of the grassland economy. The mountains support 1.5 million head of cattle on 1.8 million hectares of pasture.* The average milk yield is from 2,000 to 2,200 litres per annum. In addition to the cattle there are 1.7 million sheep and 700,000 pigs. A subdivision on either side of a further diagonal, parallel to the preceding one but running from Rodez to Saint-Etienne, distinguishes between a humid pastoral region with a strong emphasis on cattle to the north-west in Cantal, Mont-Dore, the mountains of the Dôme chain, Forez and Haut-Velay, and a drier pastoral region with an emphasis on sheep to the south-east, in Ségalas, Gévaudan, Causses, Vivarais and the Cévennes. The rural population is as sparse as in the north-western half of the central zone, with one person engaged in agriculture for every 25 hectares cultivated, with the exception of the Grande-Limagne lowland and the plain of Velay. However the holdings are much smaller, and although the *départements* of Aveyron, Lozère and Cantal have a total of 1,600 holdings of more than 100 hectares, it is because the land yields poor returns there.

---

* In the *département* of Manche in Lower Normandy, where the problems of wintering do not exist, 406,000 hectares of pasture support 728,000 head of cattle.

Moreover, these 'large' pastoral holdings represent only a fifth of the area that is exploited. By contrast, excluding the Puy-de-Dôme, there are still 80,000 holdings of less than 20 hectares in these bitter mountains, accounting for 38 per cent of the exploited land area. Half of the farms are run by men over fifty-five years old. The replacement of the generations, and especially the generations of farmers, is no longer certain in the majority of the *départements* concerned, except those with large towns, notably Puy-de-Dôme. This *département* is exceptional by virtue of the fertile plain of the Grande-Limagne where high yields of wheat reappear at over 25 quintals per hectare, and because of the town of Clermont-Ferrand. All the other *départements* suffer net loss by migration and between 1954 and 1962 alone lost 2 to 3 per cent of their population.

The Mediterranean Midi occupies a choice position in the inventory of French agriculture, not so much because of any perfect economic balance of its activities but because it obtains high prices for its products and, as far as wine is concerned, guaranteed prices. The essential products are in fact wine, market garden crops and fruit. The region has nearly 600,000 hectares of vines, 43 per cent of the area planted to vines in France and produces 30 million hectolitres of wine or half the national output. Market garden crops and fruit occupy 150,000 hectares, 20 per cent of the area thus utilised in France, but yielding half by value of the marketed produce as a result of the importance of early vegetables and the high yields obtained from irrigated land. Until the Second World War it was usual and fairly accurate to contrast the area west of the Rhône, as being the viticultural Languedoc, with the area to the east of the river, Comtat and Lower Provence, devoted to market gardening and fruit. In fact this idea was already rather far-fetched because for a long time Roussillon had combined market gardens and orchards with viticulture, while the vine held a prominent position east of the Rhône in Vaucluse, the Camargue, the basins of limestone Lower Provence and in the depression of the Argens, not only for the production of table grapes but also for wine. The contrasts have become even less marked in the last fifteen years. Market gardening is gaining ground on the right bank of the Rhône as a result of the constructions and policy of the Bas Rhône-Languedoc regional development company, while east of the Rhône the *département* of Var produces more and more superior quality wines, especially the *rosés de Provence,* much in demand on the national market. New vineyards have been planted on the slopes of

Mont Ventoux and along the Luberon range as part of the policy of upgrading the southern vineyards through improved quality. Bas-Languedoc produces 25 million hectolitres of wine but Lower Provence and Comtat produce as much as 8 million hectolitres. Conversely, the right bank of the Rhône has 75,000 hectares of fruit and market garden produce, half that of the entire region, to which may be added, beyond the Mediterranean zone, 40,000 hectares of fruit trees in the Ardèche.

The viticultural Midi, while maintaining the tradition (brought about by its reconstruction after the phylloxera crisis at the end of the nineteenth century) of monoculture with a major extension of viticulture on to the lowland, has in the last fifteen years been carrying out a change in function which the canal construction undertaken by the Bas Rhône-Languedoc regional development company has perceptibly accelerated. Since the first major crisis of overproduction at the beginning of the century and the violent unrest of 1907, the Languedoc vineyards, which are based on mass production with a huge output of ordinary wine, have struggled against the threat of surplus production, unsaleable on the home market and without outlets abroad, a threat which is aggravated by the many innovations which increase yields;* they have wrested from the central government guaranteed minimum prices and the purchase of the entire output. The economy of the new viticultural zone, reconstituted after the disaster of the vineyards in the *garrigues* and the *costières* zones which were ravaged by phylloxera, mildew and oidium,† has produced a new society which is identified with the entire population of the region. Unusually for France, the town exists here in close association with the countryside. The land is owned by town dwellers in proportions ranging from 40 to 60 per cent and urban businesses live off the income of viticulture. The labour force is guaranteed a minimum amount of work and relatively high wages since the working of the vineyards, pruning, sulphate spraying and treatment against parasites and fungi, tilling and harvesting, are spaced out over the year and require a certain amount of experience. The whole society benefits from the favourable legislation protecting the marketing of wine. It is thus conservative by nature, whatever the opinions held by one or another section on questions separate from the production and sale of

---

* Yields average above 50 hectolitres per hectare and in certain vineyards on the plain can reach 200 and at times even more.
† A parasitic fungus.

wine. Nevertheless the society is aware that an artificial economy is fragile and admits certain types of change in activity. In particular it accepts the substitution of high quality vineyards for those producing in quantity. There has been great progress in this field since the end of the Second World War, whereas until 1940 legislation and local habit sacrificed every attempt to improve quality, preferring the income, guaranteed by law, which was derived from mass production of wine sold according to its alcoholic strength.* Bas-Languedoc nevertheless has its superior quality wines and is also trying to make its new vintages more familiar. The traditional vintages like Frontignan are being improved and its new specialities, the *clairettes*, for example, which are an innovation in a *pays* which has for a long time produced red wines, are being publicised. Similarly, the people of Languedoc have spontaneously created vineyards producing table grapes, as at Clermont-l'Hérault. On the other hand there are more reservations about all the projects of conversion to any economy other than viticulture. In fact only market gardening and fruit growing, and locally intensive stall-fed animal rearing based on massive fodder production, could secure incomes equivalent to those of the protected vineyards, and this is what the construction of the irrigation system installed by the regional development company of Bas-Rhône-Languedoc† is making possible. But today, as at the beginning of the century, without a fundamental reorganisation of the land ownership structure, irrigated market gardening and fruit growing are ill suited to the system of absentee landlords. For his part, the vineyard worker considers that he has more to lose than to gain from the market garden revolution, even though mechanisation extending to sulphate spraying and pest and fungus dusting by helicopter threatens gradually to rob him of work in the vineyards and of his power to put pressure on the town-dwelling land owners. In order to gain acceptance for the irrigation network in the vine growing areas, it has proved necessary, against initial intentions, to permit the use of water for irrigating the vines. The market garden revolution has taken place

* The price level per hectolitre was fixed according to test samples of its alcoholic strength.

† This company, founded on 10 May 1955, has achieved a major instrument for irrigation and regional development by building a main canal, which once completed as far as the Aude, will extend for 240 kilometres, fed from the Rhône by the syphon at Fourques and the pumping station of Pichegy with a capacity of 75 cubic metres per second. The canal dominates an area of 210,000 hectares, of which 160,000 are irrigable, equal to more than the irrigated zones of the lower Durance, Comtat and Roussillon combined which total 100,000 hectares. 443 kilometres of secondary canals and 3,000 kilometres of distribution canals are being completed.

where there was no opposition from viticulture, in the Vaunage, Vistrenque, Petite Camargue and the Costière areas. However, gradually, as though it were treason against the regional tradition or a serious risk, the attempts at market garden and fruit growing are increasing in number. It is too early to talk of a transformation, but the Bas-Languedoc of 1967 was already profoundly different from the vine growing area of the Midi at the beginning of the century and in the interwar period. It is preceded by a pioneer zone beside the Rhône which has launched large scale market gardening and fruit farming. Fluctuations in the market are anticipated and to avoid being at the mercy of the crop contracts of foreign canning firms the producers are financing new plant for canning, fruit preserving and making fruit juice, at Saint-Gilles, Nîmes and Beaucaire. This development is a matter of concern to the growers in the older established market garden regions, set up at the very end of the nineteenth and the beginning of the twentieth centuries in the Comtat Venaissin and the lower Durance valley.

Specialised market gardening, for dispatch to the major centres of consumption in France and abroad, began alongside the irrigation canals diverted from the lower Durance and near a number of railway depots equipped for quick handling by trucks and by complete train loads, as at Carpentras, Cavaillon, Châteaurenard-Barbentane and Avignon. This system has been in use since the beginning of the century. It is based on approximately 15,000 small family farms of less than 10 hectares, almost all owner-operated, which sell their daily output at the evening or early morning markets to distribution groups who dispatch the produce to the zones of consumption. In the last thirty years and especially since the end of the Second World War speculation in market gardening has extended to new regions where newer and cheaper land was to be found, spreading up the Durance as far as Manosque and up the Rhône to Orange, Bollène and even Donzère, with road transport making it easier to break away from the original early vegetable and market garden regions. The improvement schemes and irrigation systems undertaken on the Rhône and on the Durance at Cadarache are opening up new possibilities. The internal market still has some elasticity but the European market is highly competitive, because of both Italy and the Dutch glasshouse forced crops.

Provence is like a patchwork, chequered alternately with uncultivated land, *garrigues* and *maquis*, pinewoods, periodically devastated by fires, the high gaunt mountains and the interior basins with their red or black soils where the ancient cultivation of wheat and barley still persists but which are now being invaded by vines and orchards. To the west the Camargue is divided between the vine upstream and rice downstream, which has taken the place of the former flood pastures of the *manades*.* To the south the coast combines tourism with market gardening and flower cultivation, which proliferate in the vicinity of Grasse and Nice. Between the old massif of Maures and the high limestone plateau of Plans, the plain of the Argens is covered with vines fringed by orchards as in the basins of Lower Provence. The high valleys of the Maritime Alps, in the historic Comté de Nice, are milk producing areas, with 10,000 cattle, but Provence remains overall sheep country, with nearly a million sheep, 12 per cent of the French total.

By virtue of its interior highlands, the Luberon range, the Vaucluse mountains, Mont Ventoux, the Pre Alps of Digne and Grasse, the Alpes-Maritimes chains and the Argentera-Mercantour massif, Provence belongs to the Alpine system. Provence contains its driest mountains, which follow on from the Upper Durance, Ubaye, Queyras and the Gap dome as far as the limits of Dauphiné. These are the sheep rearing Alps, with small scale cereal growing, based on mediocre agricultural resources and undergoing a massive exodus. In total there are 20,000 farmers in the two *départements* of Hautes-Alpes and Basse-Alpes, 30,000 in the entire Southern Alps including those portions within the *départements* of Drôme, Vaucluse and Alpes-Maritimes.

From an agricultural point of view, the Alps begin at the southern limit of cattle rearing combined with fodder crops, orchards and even a few vineyards in the major interior valleys. Small scale subsistence grain growing has gradually faded away and today it is a mere relic. Half a million cattle are raised, producing 8 million hectolitres of milk, and fruit crops are grown in the Combe de Savoie and the Grésivaudan.† The northern Alps, the humid Alps, are characterised by the contrast between the forested mountain, the *alpages* which precede the great summits and play a much less important role in the agricultural economy than formerly, and the agricultural and pastoral valleys, widely opened out by the Quaternary glaciers. Nevertheless

* The estates on which herds of wild bulls and cows are reared. The term is also applied to the herds as a collective noun.

† The Combe de Savoie and Grésivaudan are the names applied successively to the Isère corridor upstream from Grenoble.

there is a striking impression of relative wealth on leaving the mountain for its foreland in Dauphiné and Savoie.

The Northern Alps are enveloped, to the west and north, by a fertile crescent which encompasses the plains and basins of the middle Rhône, the lands of very varying quality in Bas-Dauphiné, and the heterogeneous zone formed by Beaujolais, Lyonnais, Dombes and the southern Jura, dominated by the presence of the large city of Lyon. The vine has first place here, since the vineyards produce the high quality and superior wines of the Côtes du Rhône, Gigondas and Tavel on the borders with Provence and Languedoc, in addition to Beaujolais and the Savoie wines. In total 2 million hectolitres are produced, of which roughly a third is Beaujolais. It is also an orchard area, especially the peach orchards in Bas-Dauphiné, the valleys of Ardèche descending from Mont Pilat, the walnuts of Royans and Savoie, the market gardens and orchards of the Costière de Dombes. Cereals hold quite an important position too, with 2.5 million quintals of wheat, 1 million of maize and half a million quintals of barley being produced. The entire foreland zone rears almost a million cattle and has high grade pig production, chickens, geese and turkeys. Here again there is a traditional economy with relatively high prosperity, and although the demand for manpower of the Lyon region has dug deeply into the agricultural population, the ratio between employed agricultural population and the agricultural land area is 1 to 10 for the whole foreland zone of Savoie and Dauphiné and 1 to 9 in the Beaujolais, the Costière de Dombes and the Lyonnais.

V WOODLAND AND FORESTRY IN FRANCE

Woodland and forests cover 23 per cent of the national land area. A quarter consists of thickets and brushwood, 12 per cent of broadleaved stands, 33 per cent of coniferous forests and a little under 30 per cent is exploited as timber coppices. Forestry yields an average of 30 million cubic metres of timber per annum.

The mountain forests are mixed, combining firs, spruce, scots pine and rigid pine with beech, as in the Vosges, Jura, Alps, Pyrenees and the highest parts of the Massif Central. These account for the major exploitation of timber. The plateaux and hills of the Paris Basin support an extensive forest cover, including the large broad-leaved woodlands of oak, beech and hornbeam in Normandy, Maine and

Touraine, and the woodland, usually exploited as coppices, of the eastern plateaux, the Ardennes, the Lorraine plateaux, wet Champagne and the Pays d'Othe, Lower Burgundy and Nivernais. Pinewoods are still important in Dry Champagne, in spite of the reclamation for cultivation of woodlands planted at the end of the last century, and are also very extensive in the Sologne, where reafforestation has been in progress during the last thirty years, and on the sandy heaths of the West; but they are only dominant in the Landes of Gascony and on the old massifs of Provence where unfortunately they are devastated every year by fires.

The distributions of the land area under woodland and of the output of timber and lumber, show a clear predominance in eastern France, even though some of the finest and most vigorous forests are to be found in the West. The *départements* with a woodland proportion above the national average form a continuous belt along the eastern frontiers, from the Ardennes to the Mediterranean. The mountains of the East, especially the Vosges and the Jura, and secondarily the Northern Alps, supply 20 per cent of the wood felled in France, and the eastern plateaux 15 per cent. However the greatest volume of production in relation to the surface area is achieved in the Landes of Gascony, where the two *départements* of Gironde and Landes yield 17 per cent of the timber felled in France, exclusively pinewood.

The diversity of regional agricultural aptitudes, which accounts for the no less than 350 agricultural regions which have been listed, complicates France's agricultural policy making. Each type of crop and each regional vested interest, calls for particular attention which does not always correspond with the wishes of other regional interests. The diversity of output is partly responsible for the complex commercial organisation and legislation concerning agriculture.

In practice, certain products benefit from guaranteed prices, minimum prices or price ceilings, for example wine, milk and wheat. These prices are established by agreement between the government and the producers' professional organisation for each farm year. They make accounted forecasting for farming operations possible and protect the producers from falling market prices, but on the other hand they preclude all hope of speculation. The output of meat, fruit and vegetables is not regulated by compulsory taxes but certain prices are controlled. The cause of irritation and conflict in this case is the size of the profit margins of wholesalers and carriers who provide for the collection, transport and distribution of produce. In theory the produce which is not subject to price controls offers a speculative sector open to the farmers' initiative, but farmers are afraid of being unable to find a market, and, especially if they have only small farms and limited funds, they very often prefer to obtain advance contracts with wholesalers. This system is extending notably in the new market garden and fruit growing regions of the Midi, particularly in the form of contracts between farmers and conserving factories. However, in the face of the requirements of the purchasers, the farmers are becoming more favourable than in the past to the idea of cooperation for grading and dealing with produce. The example of the Jura, unique until recently, will probably be followed by other regions, notably Bas-Languedoc.

The fact remains that the present system makes the farmer an increasingly important consumer of industrial products, agricultural machinery, tractors and motor vehicles, farm electrical equipment, fertilisers and all kinds of chemical products, and thus a purchaser at market distribution prices. But at the same time the prices at the production stage suffer severe pressure from a complicated distribution mechanism supporting a large number of middlemen. This situation irritates and discourages the farmers, the more so as their yields and their productivity on the whole are still too low to absorb without great difficulty the deficit resulting from the gap between wholesale and retail prices.

CHAPTER FIVE

Recessions, Transformation and Innovations in Industry

The industries which established the greatness of French industry, like all European industry during the nineteenth century, are now declining for many reasons. In the case of the coal industry it is because the initial uses of coal are technically obsolete and their decline is not made up for by forms of solid fuel use, for example in the coal-derived chemicals industry. The traditional textile industries, especially cotton, are in decline because they are no longer 'the cheapest in the world' and are suffering from the competition of countries with low wages as well as from synthetic textiles. The iron and steel industry, especially in Lorraine, is suffering because Thomas process steel based on low grade ore is meeting competition from Martin process steelworks using high grade ore. The shipbuilding industry is experiencing difficulty because productive capacity has grown considerably in relation to limited demand. A variety of light industries are declining either because of changes in demand or because they face competition from new products, and again because their structure is outmoded.

Certain industries ensure their survival and take on a new lease of life by carrying out changes which may or may not be accompanied by geographical shifts. Thus the textile industry is being absorbed by the synthetic chemicals sector, new energy complexes are appearing, the iron and steel industry is gravitating towards the ports which import rich iron ores, the clothing and leather industries have adapted to new demands of fashion and sportswear. But the most spectacular development has been by new industries related to new sectors of demand, like mechanical engineering, constantly changing in character, electrical engineering and electronics, the chemical and chemical by-product industries and especially the group of industries based on petroleum. The number of products offered for consumption and to various service activities increases as a result of increased average living standards and the growth of demand. Industry is becoming more diversified both in terms of the raw materials used and of the end products and, through a variety of methods of packaging and presenting its output, it now has great opportunities to make the market aware of what it has to offer.

I CRITICAL SITUATIONS AND REGIONS

1 The Coal and Textile Industries: The Case of the Nord

The first major contradiction in French industry concerns the exploitation of coal and hence the mining regions. In relative economic terms production is expensive. However it is doubly important since it is a guarantee against the risk of an energy supply based on importing, and a crucial element in achieving a regional social balance. The economic policy followed in relation to coal production is therefore a compromise between the two considerations.

French coal is expensive in relation to international market prices. The French deposits are very unevenly placed in the ranking of costs within the European Economic Community. The Lorraine coal is competitive even in comparison with the Ruhr, that of the Nord-Pas-de-Calais field has a much higher market price and some mines have ceased to be viable. The Centre* deposits are only of value in so far as they provide a geographical coverage which makes them worth using in their immediate vicinity or if their output is converted into electricity directly at the pit-head. Even then it is necessary to distinguish with each deposit between the mines which are still worth exploiting and those which have excessive operating costs.

Coal production is subject to two converging pressures – the competitive prices of foreign coal, including coal imported by sea from the United States, and of petroleum products. This is a general phenomenon in Europe, and even West Germany, although it has more advantageous conditions of extraction in the Ruhr than France has, plans to reduce its production before 1980 to a third of the maximum of 150 million tons achieved in 1957. In 1959, purely on the basis of calculations of profitability, it was envisaged that French output would be reduced to 25 million tons in 1970, of which 15 million would be produced by the Nord-Pas-de-Calais field. The social

* The scattered small coalfields of the Massif Central, the exploitation of which is rapidly being phased out.

problems created by the sudden interruption of the work of tens of thousands of miners made it necessary to slow down the reduction of output and labour retraining. Drastic closures are however already disturbing the coal-mining regions, as in the particularly severe reduction of output in the Saint-Etienne field and the diminished extraction in the Pas-de-Calais. For a number of years now it has been necessary to accelerate the cutting back of the coal sector. In 1959 an output of 48 million tons by 1970 was considered an acceptable limit. In fact output has fallen below this figure since 1967 and in 1970 the national output was only 37 million tons of which 17 million tons were produced by the Nord field.

During an initial period until 1965–66, the rate of reduction in mining employment, at 8,000 per annum, corresponded to natural wastage and retirement. Since 1967 it has been necessary each year to redeploy several thousand miners and this imposes a policy of relocating employment in the mining regions. At first attempts were made to find new employment by developing industries based on coal as a raw material, thus permitting the continued output of the most viable coal deposits by establishing coal-derived chemical industries in association with the nationalised coal board.

Although the output of bituminous coal is tending to decline and to be supplemented by imports, a positive factor for reanimating zones depressed by the decline in output and in coal mining employment is the development of waterfront iron and steel making, as at Dunkerque. Increasingly an effort is being made to attract to the coalfield regions industries which act as growth leaders, principally the vehicle construction industry which is becoming firmly established, especially in the Nord field. The fact remains that such conversions will not work on the one hand without major internal migrations which are opposed by the people concerned through a high degree of inertia and because of individual problems of industrial reclassification, and on the other hand without investment in the infrastructure and investment of development funds. These investments are doubled by subsidies to the coal industries made in order to lower the sale price for the benefit of coal users. The policy on coal, while having a purely national significance, forms part of a general protection of the European coal industry, made necessary by the social effects of the coal crisis and by the wish to retain the unity of regional industrial structures where many industries and service infrastructures are intimately interwoven with mining activity.

As a result, social and political imperatives and a number of economic considerations guarantee a slower rate of the run-down in investment in the mining regions. However the regions where the factors of economic conservation and the possibility of local redeployment are weakest are in far more immediate danger than the others of rapid abandonment. In this context the small fields of the Centre are the most vulnerable. The Blanzy and Saint-Etienne fields benefit from the proximity of Lyon and the Saône axis; this makes their output worthwhile and gives them a better chance, all things being equal, of profiting from industrial reconversion comparable to that undertaken in the Nord region, with the installation of new industries which can consume, on or very close to the deposits, a certain amount of coal and, especially, which can re-employ the redundant miners.

The second ageing structure, on a European scale, is the textile industry, and especially the cotton industries. This is why the Nord region, whose fortune in the nineteenth century depended on coal and cotton, has particular difficulties to overcome. The traditional textile industries, the processing of cotton, wool, linen, and jute, made no progress during the period 1960–65 (and indeed underwent a marked depression, although this was in fact general, at the end of 1964 and in early 1965), while the chemical industry increased its output by nearly 100 per cent and the total industrial output increased by nearly 30 per cent. Late 1964 to early 1965 was a particularly bad period, but the upturn which began during the second quarter of 1965 made it possible to recover the 1963 level of production by mid 1966. Since then a slight growth has been registered. In order to compete in external markets, which is essential, these industries are obliged to reduce their employment levels by investing in machinery, this generally being preceded by mergers of firms. The French textile industry processed 143,000 tons of wool and almost 250,000 tons of cotton in 1970, as against 120,000 and 250,000 before the last war. The production index of the textile industry, based on 100 in 1938, was 115 in 1954 and approximately 110 in 1967, while the chemical industry jumped from 100 to 200 in 1955 and approached an index of 500 in 1966, and while the engineering industries also continuously accelerated their growth, even though they had to follow marked variations in market requirements. As a consequence both economic and social problems have arisen, for example a reduction in working time and the search for cheap labour – women and particularly apprentices. The scale of these problems may be measured by the number of firms and workers involved: 1,600 woollen factories, nearly 1,000 cotton factories and 100 factories processing linen, hemp and jute, involving over 100,000 workers in related and sometimes integrated industries such as dyeing and finishing, not counting the workers in artificial and synthetic textiles. The principal cotton, wool and linen regions and the jute processing areas, where the labour released is not taken up by chemical-based industries, such as the Lille and Rouen areas, Alsace, Forez and Languedoc, are hit by these problems.

TABLE NINE

THE EVOLUTION OF THE FRENCH TEXTILE INDUSTRIES 1960–70
(Output in 1960 equals 100)

	1965	1968	1969	1970	1971
Total	105	115	128	127	136*
Synthetic textiles	192	292	345	387	480
Artificial textiles	109	98	110	110	111
Wool cloth	90	91	97	88	94
Cotton cloth	82	78	81	78	78

* Estimated figures.

2   The Iron and Steel Industry

Following a spectacular rise after the Second World War, stimulated by the needs of reconstruction, the iron and steel industry marked time at the beginning of the 1960s, because of the effect of unexpected competition from foreign steel industries. The operating conditions of French production based on low grade Lorraine ores ceased to be competitive. The planned output had to be readjusted to a lower level than forecast, more closely in balance with the absorptive capacity of the internal market. It was only in 1969–70 that the targets originally fixed for 1965 were reached and surpassed, with an output of 26 million tons in 1970. With this reservation, the iron and steel industry seems to be a strong sector now that a number of technical and financial reorganisation measures have been carried out. Two combines each produced a little over 8 million tons of steel in 1970. Small scale producers are becoming increasingly specialised in the manufacture of high grade steels and alloys by electrometallurgy. The state-encouraged concentrations have made modernisation and thus the survival of Lorraine plants possible. At a purely technological level, it is necessary to regroup the processing into units with a capacity of 6 to 8 million tons. The Usinor complex at Dunkerque is approaching this scale as will the plant under construction at Fos.*

3   Shipyards and Small Scale Dispersed Industries

Over the last ten years shipbuilding has seemed a particularly vulnerable section of French industry. In spite of a by no means slender order book – the gross tonnage launched was almost 500,000 per annum between 1960 and 1965 – the shipyards are not always able to employ fully their labour force of 35,000 workers. The crisis is the more spectacular because the shipyards are very concentrated, at Saint-Nazaire, in the Marseille region at La Seyne, La Ciotat and Port-de-Bouc, Le Trait and Dunkerque, and because, except for Dunkerque and Le Trait near Rouen, shipbuilding consists of isolated industrial groupings, a fact which makes for great difficulties in industrial reconversion. Competition from countries with cheap labour or those, like Sweden, with first class organisation, makes it difficult to regain a share in a tight market. Nevertheless the position improved at the end of the decade with a million gross tons launched in 1970 and orders for specialised vessels including giant tankers. Certain branches of the shipbuilding industry, especially electronics, telecommunications and radar installations in the military dockyards of Brest, Lorient and Toulon, have been easily converted and have supplied excellent technicians and managers for land based industry.

The final group of industries in difficulty is a group as mixed in character as it is geographically dispersed. It gathers together all the traditional industries which have not known how or have not been able to re-adapt to present day market conditions and production costs. These industries, which are usually small firms, are typical of small old towns; they contribute to their sterilisation and hamper development by hanging on to their last chances of survival against competition in the labour market from pioneer industries which offer better financial and material conditions to their work force. They vary from place to place; in one place it is clothing, as in Berry, in others it is leather working, as in Lower Normandy, Upper Maine and

---

* On the Rhône delta thirty-five kilometres west of Marseille.

Touraine or Limousin, spinning at Ganges, or the manufacture of sandals at Mauléon. They correspond to a particular social environment of small factory owners faced by enormous difficulties, threatened by bankruptcy or take over and controlling a poorly paid labour force which has no choice but to put up with an unrewarding situation or leave the area, since the last defence of economically marginal firms is to resist the installation of decentralised pioneer firms. The critical condition of the firms' financial resources prevents all attempts at modernisation and reconversion, and condemns them to work on hopelessly with machinery which is amortised but obsolete, in buildings a century old.

II TRANSFORMATION

1 The Rapid Change in the Energy System

The output of energy, which is the basis of the entire industrial economy, has been in a state of continuous transformation for the last twenty years. In 1938 France consumed 67.7 million tons of coal, of which 47.6 million were produced nationally, 11 million KWh of electricity supplied by hydro-electric stations and 9 million tons of imported petroleum products; an equivalent in coal respectively of 67.7, 18 and 20 million tons.* The balance in 1970 is shown in the table.

TABLE TEN
THE BALANCE OF ENERGY PRODUCTION 1970

	Million tons coal equivalent
Solid fuels	57.5*
Petroleum products	132.3
Natural gas	14.3
Hydro-electricity	20.4
Nuclear energy	2.5

* Including a net import of 15 million tons.

* In terms of coal equivalence in 1938.

The forecasts for 1985 show an increasing role for hydrocarbons and the slow rise in nuclear energy.

TABLE ELEVEN
PROJECTED ENERGY PRODUCTION IN 1985
Million tons of coal equivalent

	Assuming a small production of nuclear power	Assuming a large production of nuclear power
Solid fuels	50	50
Petroleum products	195	168
Natural gas	43	40
Hydro-electricity	27	27
Nuclear power	50	80

In an initial stage immediately after the Second World War, coinciding with a major effort to expand coal output which came to an end after 1955, a parallel attempt to exploit national resources stimulated remarkable achievements in the sphere of hydro-electric installation. The output of the hydro-electric stations increased from 11 to over 55 billion KWh between 1946 and 1970, while the total output of electricity increased by only 400 per cent. The installed capacity of the French sections of the Rhine and Rhône basins, including the barrages on the Grand Canal d'Alsace, the power stations of the Compagnie Nationale du Rhône, the Durance development and the whole of the Alpine power stations, rose from 6 to 7 billion KWh in 1948 to 33 in 1970, that of the Massif Central from 3 to 10 and that of the Pyrenees from 2.5 to 7. During the first part of this period the development of hydro-electric installations took the lead over thermal installations, but during the second part the proportions were reversed. The improved technology of energy extraction in thermal power stations, using less than 400 grams of good coal to produce 1 KWh, the use of petroleum products and natural gas and in certain cases refinery gas, as at Bec d'Ambès near Bordeaux, the forecast of a simple conversion of the machinery of thermal power stations to the transformation of nuclear energy into electricity, and also the increasing cost of hydro-electric installations once the most accessible sites had been developed, resulted in a slowing down in the undertaking of hydro-electric

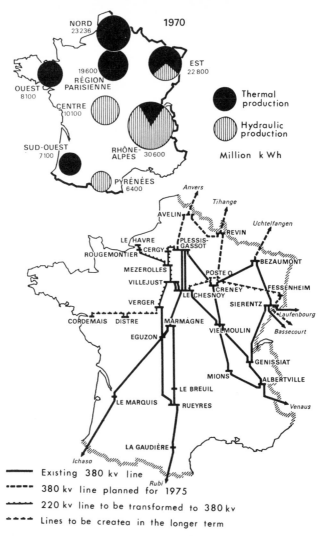

FIG. 10a. Electricity production and distribution. Above: Thermal and hydraulic production in 1970 (after Electricité de France, 1970). Below: The planned 380 kV grid system (after Revue française de l'énergie).

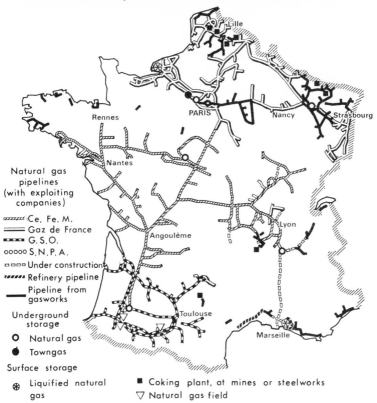

Natural gas
pipelines
(with exploiting
companies)

▱▱▱ Ce. Fe. M.
═══ Gaz de France
▬▬▬ G.S.O.
ooooo S.N.P.A.
▱▱▱ Under construction
▰▰▰ Refinery pipeline
━━ Pipeline from
    gasworks
Underground
storage
O Natural gas
● Towngas
Surface storage

⊛ Liquified natural
   gas

■ Coking plant, at mines or steelworks
▽ Natural gas field

F IG. 10b. The French gas pipeline network (after Gaz de France)

development. In any case, the national consumption of energy increased annually by 4 per cent and the consumption of electricity by
7.5 per cent.

The geographical consequences of this evolution are as important
as the technical consequences. In fact, although it is convenient to distinguish a zone of thermal production corresponding with the coalfield
power stations and the treatment of refinery gas, with plants concentrated in the supply area of the urban agglomerations in the northern
half of the country and a zone of hydro-electric production combining
the great rivers and the mountainous complexes (see Fig. 10), the fundamental geographical fact is the ubiquitous and instantaneous nature

TABLE TWELVE

TOTAL CONSUMPTION OF ENERGY

	1960	1967	1970	1985*
Total consumption (million tons of coal equivalent)	130	183	227	345–385
Consumption of electricity (billion KWh)	72.3	105	137	410–450
Percentage of consumption as electricity	25.9	28	29	44

* Estimate.

of distribution by means of the grid system within which interconnection and feeding to the point of demand is made simultaneously to any point in the nation. The concentration of a considerable proportion of consumption in the Paris region, with almost 20 per cent of the national total, implies a relative concentration of the grid in the direction of Paris, amalgamating the hydro-electric production sectors of the Rhine, Alps and Centre with the thermal sector of the Paris area. However the French electricity grid system, unlike the transport network, is by no means a factor promoting geographical concentration of industry. It is much more supple, and proximity to certain major centres of power generation can also work as a location factor in that distances transmitted are balanced by progressively increased losses of power. The Centre-Sud-Est region seems exceptionally well placed in this respect. It is interesting to note that the foremost geographical consideration in the initial preparation process of harnessing nuclear energy calls for the location of nuclear power stations in regions already well supplied with conventional electricity and having at their disposal at the present time a surplus output which could be used locally. As a result, some of the first nuclear plants capable of delivering energy to the grid system are to be found in the major hydro-electric production zone of the Alps and Rhône,* which has an installed capacity of 30 billion KWh, and in Alsace.†

To some extent the increased use of petroleum products tends to have the same result. The importing of petroleum and the exploitation

* The nuclear stations of Marcoule, Pierrelatte and Cadarache.

† The nuclear station of Fessenheim being located close to the Rhine power schemes.

of gas only establish small amounts of industry and in specific locations at the importing ports and the extraction fields. By nature this form of energy is mobile and is expected to be mobile. The refinery capacity now exceeds 120 million tons and in 1970 was 116.5 millions. The 'natural laws' of industrial location in the nineteenth century, laid down by the economic requirements of heavy transport at a time when coal was the sole source of power, are now a dead letter. If the old industrial regions, founded on coal or on coal transportation systems, still continue to exert a power of attraction, they express this power through the cumulative effect of the investments from which they have benefited, the presence of large populations and of a service infrastructure system.*

2 The Chemical Industry – Source of Substitute Products

The present time in all industrial countries is marked by the dizzy rise of the chemical industry. At the moment it represents almost 10 per cent of the total industrial output, and makes available substitute products at low sale prices to the majority of the traditional industries, thus facilitating their reconversion. Moreover, its expansion rate on average is double that of the whole of industrial production, at 9 per cent per annum from 1960 to 1969, although slowing down in 1970–71.

TABLE THIRTEEN
THE GROWTH OF THE CHEMICAL INDUSTRY 1965–71
Production 1962 by value = 100

	1965	1968	1969	1970	1971
Total	136	177	211	230	244
Mineral based	133	158	167	176	191
Organic	149	219	291	330	351
Parachemicals	121	146	164	168	177

* The need to take into account the risks of imports being interrupted means there has to be a twofold effort to increase the capacity for stockpiling energy sources; for instance three-month stocks of petroleum products and the stockpiling of fissionable materials, and also the search for diverse sources of supply, at home and in different political and geographical areas abroad, especially in the case of petroleum and natural gas.

The chemical industry is both a creator of new products (in this respect it should be placed in the third section of this summary of French industry) and a factor in the transformation of a large number of traditional industries for which it provides a means of renewal. This is particularly the case of the textiles industries. While it does not escape from the general crisis of the textile industries, the manufacture of artificial and synthetic textile seems to be a palliative to the crisis, by lowering the sale price of finished goods and compensating, through its technology, for the harm done by competition from countries with low wage rates in the processing of traditional textiles. Since 1938 French output of artificial textiles has almost doubled, from 80,000 to over 130,000 tons. The output of synthetic fibres, which was practically non-existent just before the Second World War, now exceeds 150,000 tons, whereas the use of cotton has remained stationary.

The phenomenon of substitution is also of considerable importance in the silk and schappe* industry, where the degree of replacement is almost total. But new textiles are entering into all fields and conquering them all. The creation of new specific industrial zones applies only at the stage of producing the raw materials. The case of the Lyon region is as complex as it is revealing about the intervention of different influences. The Lyon chemicals industry was drawn to research into new fibres since it existed side by side with textile industries in a precarious condition and sought new solutions to their problems. By creating the principal French production centre Lyon encouraged the location of industries using the new fibres. One therefore finds both reconversions, as in the Albarine valley, and new creations, like the Rilsan firm at Valence. More commonly artificial and synthetic textiles are totally or partially substituted for the traditional raw materials in the already existing textile industries, bringing them the revival that they need without always managing to save them from all their difficulties. This is notably the case of the silk spinning area of the Cévennes foreland, now converted to manufacturing from nylon. The generally depressed state of the textiles industry is not very favourable for the creation of new regions or new centres working directly and solely with artificial and synthetic threads and fibres.

A parallel evolution can be seen in the traditional wood, metal, pottery and glass industries, now conquered by plastics. In fact the

---

* A dull silk fabric made from silk waste.

chemical industry offers a growing range of substitutes for wood, bone, horn, textile furnishings like carpets, tinplate, zinc, pottery, ceramics, glass, cardboard, paper and leather. It has stimulated conversions, some of them spectacular. A prime example is the town of Oyonnax,* where plastics have been substituted for celluloid, horn and wood, accompanied by a considerable widening of the range of products offered to the market; these are displayed in a permanent exhibition centre and range from household goods to toys and bizarre jewelry, as well as the traditional manufacture of combs and spectacle frames. It is at the stage of the finished product that the real evolution of production can be measured, and not at the level of each branch of traditional manufacturing, the decline of certain products being compensated by many types of innovation which occur at different stages in the production process. Depending on the technical considerations governing the introduction of chemical replacements, the former structures, forms and locations of production may be retained, as in the case of Oyonnax, or else there may be competition and change in the distribution of production, for example in the substitution of plastic floor coverings supplied by industries in Lyon or Paris for wooden parquet or for carpets formerly manufactured in the west, Picardy or Berry.

The changes are far from complete. Although the production of plastics in France multiplied ten-fold in the ten years from 1952 to 1962, the rate of usage remains well below that of foreign countries like West Germany or the United States. In West Germany the annual consumption *per capita* is 20 kg, in the United States 16 kg and in France only 10 kg, and it is likely that the growth of this industry will continue in France in the course of the next decade. Output in 1970 was 420,000 tons of chlorinated polyvinyl as compared with 240,000 in 1965, 130,000 tons of polyethylene and polypropylene as compared with 45,000, and 170,000 tons of polystyrene and comparable products compared with 82,000 in 1965. These are light, easily transported products. Although the manufacture of the intermediate products or organic synthesis is technically and geographically tied to the petrochemical and coal derived chemical industries, the products themselves can be used anywhere. The location of the manufacture of the finished products depends on the initiative of the firms which incorporate the derivatives into their production cycle and on the localisation of the demand, especially in the case of the output consumed by the

* In the Southern Jura.

manufacture of complex end products, as in the electrical industries, vehicle building, aeronautics industries, rolling stock and the manufacture of furniture and building materials. Nevertheless, the future of the French chemical industry depends on its concentration* which alone can ensure a competitive position in Europe. This concentration is taking place at a rapid rate at the present time.

3   Changes Provoked by Diversification of Demand

Some types of product disappear through lack of customers and reduction of demand. The evolution of technology, fashion and the internal pattern of household spending suppress or reduce certain uses. Some manufactured goods are condemned to extinction or seem to be – for example, the manufacture of sails and ropes for boats and harnesses for horses, linked to obsolete methods of transport; barrelmaking has been ruined by wine making in cement vats and transport in tanks; some articles of clothing are less in use than before, such as leather gloves and men's hats. Firms disappear or struggle to open up a new market within the traditional scope of their manufacturing activity. From one year to another the demand for water sports equipment increases and winter sports have revived the manufacture of articles in fine leather like boots and gloves. The increased attention given to hygiene has made it possible for textile industries to become specialised in medical dressings, as at Voiron. The changes brought about by the age structure of the national population have opened up new outlets which some firms have been able to exploit, for example the manufacture of children's shoes. In a more specifically technical field, the Savoie nail works have given birth to an industry of international standing, the screw cutting of the Bonneville and Cluses area.

Public attention is often more drawn to the decline of obsolete traditional industries than to their replacement. In an economy characterised by the growth and constant diversification of demand, the number of firms that are adapted or newly created must exceed the number that are abandoned, taking into account the general trend towards the concentration of firms. The problem is one of management, and geographically it is a local problem. Once a town feels the

* This implies a geographical concentration into chemical industry complexes and a structural concentration between companies, as in the case of Perrefitte-Auby for the manufacture of chemical fertilisers.

effects of the unremitting decline of obsolete or stagnant industries, like Saint-Claude, or the leather working towns of the Massif Central, Saint-Junien or Millau, and transfers its activities to a fresh footing or, like Annecy, receives new firms, the economic and social climate is totally changed.

The best example of an industrial sector transformed as a result of changes in demand is undoubtedly the food processing industry. Eating habits change as a function of the age structure of the population and households' way of life. Consumers increasingly dislike cooking preparation and want ready made foods which are both nourishing and simple. The demand for vast amounts of foodstuffs in the densely populated zones calls for special processing, unknown in the past when there was direct and immediate consumption of natural products. Techniques of refrigeration and the increasing use of deep-freezing, drying and concentrating, replace or supplement the traditional manufacture of conserves, biscuits or confectionery. The last decade has even witnessed widespread penetration of the market for prepared foodstuffs for domestic pets. The retail price can be appreciably reduced by the modernisation of production methods which have often remained more artisan than industrial. Also, although a continuing increase in demand by 2 to 3 per cent per annum is envisaged, it seems unlikely that the labour force employed in the whole of the agricultural and food processing industries, which is already considerable at over half a million persons, will need to follow the evolution of consumption and in consequence to adapt its machinery, which accelerates the process of concentration induced by the need for investment. It is worth noting that this sector is one of those in which the penetration of foreign technology and capital is most apparent and where the most spectacular mergers have taken place. Among the major groups recently formed or enlarged notable examples are Générale Alimentaire, Olida-Capy, Gervais-Danone, Genvrain, Perrier-Sapiem, and Moët- and Chandon-Hennessy-Dior. However, business turnover is still less than in other major industrial groups. Less than ten have annual turnovers above a billion francs. No doubt this makes it easier for the smallest firms to be regrouped by subsidiaries of large foreign companies, especially American ones.

There can be no transformation, and as a result no rescuing of the traditional industries which are now outmoded by the progress of technology, unless there are on the one hand new industries to supply the material elements for change to take place, and on the other more and increasingly diversified consumption, requiring the production of larger quantities of new or modernised products. The industries undergoing transformation are thus tributaries of new industries. The safeguarding of inherited industries by modernisation depends on progress towards future forms of production and consumption on a national scale.

III   CREATIONS AND CONSTANT RENEWALS

Between the group of industries in process of transformation and the group of completely new industries comes the solid mass of engineering industries which include both mature industries like vehicle construction, which are however constantly changing, and industries like electronics, born in the last fifteen years. Language changes less noticeably than technology; for example Concorde and an aircraft built at the outbreak of the Second World War, already completely different from the first Bleriot or Farman models, have scarcely anything in common other than the name. It is in this respect that the engineering industries may be termed new industries, or at any rate industries in a state of constant renewal, and the same applies to the basic chemical industry. These are the two sectors where the greatest investments are being made at the present time.

1   The Engineering Industries

In the last ten years the gross product of the engineering industries has grown by nearly 10 per cent per annum. This overall growth rate covers some very different states of development. One should distinguish between a sector in constant renewal, tested by several decades of operation and progressing by a process of unceasing change, and a new sector, less than twenty years old proceeding with successive new creations which involve massive investment.

The traditional sector concerns the manufacture of industrial plant and the construction of transport material. It is perpetually changing in character. The demand factor counts most for heavy equipment for public works and civil engineering, building, lifting gear, pumps, boilers and machinery for the food processing industry. It is an industry which is becoming more and more complex in the sphere of equipping factories with transfer machines,* which are tending to replace the classic specialised machine tools in the process of automation. In the course of the last twenty years France has distinguished itself by the quality of its rolling stock, especially electric locomotives. It holds a very competitive position in this field, but the internal market is reaching saturation point. The vehicle industry is experiencing pressure on the internal market from foreign competition from the Common Market members, especially West Germany, Italy and Britain, as well as from countries outside the community like the United States. On the other hand, France exports to her Common Market partners as well as overseas. The growth rate matches that of the engineering industry as a whole, almost 10 per cent per annum. 1971 was a particularly favourable year, with a 10 per cent increase in output, a 6 per cent increase in exports and a turnover increase of 18 per cent, reaching 31.4 billion francs. Over half of the 2.7 million vehicles built were exported, 1.5 million units, while the national market absorbed only 300,000 foreign vehicles.

Production is shared by four groups; the nationalised Renault company with 44 per cent, Citroën-Berliet with 20.5 per cent, Peugeot with 21 per cent, and the American firm Simca, in which the Chrysler corporation has had a majority shareholding since 1963, with 14.5 per cent. Commercial agreements for exporting have been established between Renault and Peugeot on the one hand, and between Citroën and Fiat on the other. The largest company building heavy vehicles is Berliet, with an output of 15,000 lorries per annum, which also forms part of the Citroën group. The head offices and parent factories of three of the four large groups, including the two most important, are in the Paris region, and at the present time occupy 57 per cent of the labour force in the vehicle industry. Peugeot at Montbeliard, Berliet at Venissieux within the Lyon agglomeration, and Saviem at Blainville near Caen, Annonay and Limoges, employ less than a quarter of the labour force. However the decentralisation of factories by the great Paris companies has transferred roughly a fifth of the employment to the provinces, especially to the West, and the Nord region is now receiving new car factories too, at Lens, Douai, Valenciennes and Charleville. On the other hand, the large number of component firms,

---

* Single machines capable of executing a variety of processes in succession, selecting multiple tools by a system of programming, as opposed to the working of material on a range of separate machines individually.

working for the vehicle companies as suppliers and sub-contractors, are almost all located in the Paris region.

Along with the manufacture of rolling stock, the aircraft industry is one of those which permits France to face up to international competition with the best prospects. It is also one of the fields where innovation is a constant necessity and determines exactly the degree of success in competition. To a greater extent than the automobile industry or the manufacture of industrial plant, the aircraft and ballistic rocket construction industries are a synthesis of the most technically advanced sectors, and call in large measure on innovating industries and on industrial research laboratories. At least 150,000 people are employed in the aerospace industries, which occupy an intermediate position between the group of industries inherited from previous decades and the group which is currently being created. They need permanent contact with other engineering industries, laboratories, research and testing centres which are concentrated in the major industrial and urban agglomerations, and at the same time large areas for industrial plant and testing grounds. As a result there are new types of location, close to large provincial centres, which are being supplied with adequate scientific and technical facilities, with annexes situated on the land which is least valuable from an agricultural point of view. The chief examples are Toulouse and Bordeaux, with reserves of land in the Landes, and, as far as the development and stockpiling of rockets is concerned, the plateaux of Vaucluse and Banon. Technically, the aerospace industries are associated with the electrical and electronics industries, which are indispensable supporting activities.

The electrical construction industries also belong partly to the traditional engineering sector, in the case of power station machinery, electric motors for factories, locomotives and vessels, electrical equipment for building and town services, telecommunications and the manufacture of electrical domestic equipment. However they are also prominent in present day sectors, in the electronics branch which is being subjected to strong pressure from American investment by I.B.M., Bull General Electric and Control-Data. The increase in demand in the last ten years has been considerable, to the extent of saturating the initial market and making necessary a renewal of the products on offer by technological change. The electronics industry benefits from a double market, the market for consumer goods, like television sets, and the market created by supplying collective users

● Aircraft construction   ◇ Manufacture of aerospace equipment
M Engine manufacture   E Research and testing centre

Fɪɢ. 11. The aircraft and aerospace industries in France

and the State, including the national military market. The demand for computers and calculators in public administration, banks and the head offices of major firms and for micro-electronic components stimulates the work of the laboratories and research centres of one of the most forward-looking industries which has become indispensable to the development of other manufacturing industries and activities of all kinds. Its expansion depends on exceptionally large medium and long term investment. If the investment were to be lacking or parsimonious the market would rapidly be invaded by the competition of wealthier or more enterprising nations. It is an industry with a difficult role to play. France protects its home market and at the same time its chances of exporting, but it has to contend with very powerful foreign industries, like I.B.M., already located on its territory. In this context the role of government orders and subsidies is absolutely essential.

The importance of the electrical construction industries in the national economy is indicated by the business turnover − over 30 billion francs compared with 31 billions by the vehicle industry − and by the labour force of over 400,000 of whom 100,000 are managerial and qualified technical staff.

To a greater extent than in the period between the two world wars, the engineering industry, and especially the advanced technology industries, aerospace construction, electrical and electronics construction, are based on high technology, combining a large number of production processes all of which require constant research and permanent checking and testing. The proportion of highly qualified workers and skilled technologists is very large. These industries constitute a distinctive technical and social category which can only function in certain types of location, in direct and rapid contact with client industries or the public services which order from them, and in contact with technical centres which train skilled workers, carry out applied research and have different facilities. These are industries which belong to highly developed regions, major urban agglomerations, university towns and centres of scientific research. However, their components move about as individual units, the production of which can be relatively dispersed to find land free for development and available labour supplies, so long as there is a high density and an efficient transport and communications network. The whole industry is based on a highly complex centre, like Paris, the Lyon-Grenoble-Geneva area, Dijon and Strasbourg, but the factories can spread over a wider perimeter, provided that it is well served and has a high density of active population, as in the Lower Seine valley, the Saône plain, the foreland of the Northern Alps and the Lyon region. Nevertheless, in spite of the powerful attraction of the scientific and technical centre of Grenoble and in spite of the systematic decentralisation schemes, over three-quarters of the high technology electrical industries remain in the Paris region and its extensions into Normandy.

2   A Post War Industry, the Aluminium Industry

Until the Second World War, the French aluminium industry reached only a modest level, with 29,000 tons produced in 1929 and 45,000 in

TABLE FOURTEEN
BUSINESS TURNOVER IN SELECTED INDUSTRIAL
BRANCHES 1971*
Billion francs

Iron and steel	19
Engineering	55
Electrical construction	30
Vehicle construction	31.4
Chemical industries	46
Textiles	28.5
Building and public works	77.2

* For the number of persons employed see Table Six, p. 54.

1938. It was not until the decade 1955–65 that it assumed the proportions of a major industry exporting a third of its output, producing 130,000 tons in 1955, 360,000 in 1968 and 381,000 tons in 1970.* It appears that a ceiling has now been reached, in the sense that French exports in the future will meet strong competition from foreign industries under construction in Greece, Africa and the United States. The internal market capacity is of the same order as the output already guaranteed, that is 1 million tons of alumina and 380,000 tons of aluminium. The rapid expansion of the French aluminium industry is linked to the possibility of exploiting on a large scale the indigenous resources of bauxite, amounting to 3 million tons in 1970, and to the use of electricity supplied at prices, which although not comparable with those of the most favoured nations, Canada and the Scandinavian countries, guarantee competitive prices, not only on the domestic market, but for export to many countries. Electricity can be supplied at preferential prices in relation to the general tariff, since it is consumed in the areas of high generation and away from the areas of heavy local demand. The aluminium industry, exceptionally, remains an industry of the Midi, using the hydro-electricity of the Alps and Pyrenees and the power stations burning Provence lignite and at Salindres the coal from the Gard field. The presence of the main bauxite deposits in the same part of the country guarantees a real geographical unity to this industry which has hardly been modified by the construction of a factory at Noguères using current generated from the Lacq natural gas, which has stretched the distribution a little further westwards.

* To which must be added nearly 90,000 tons at the second stage of fusion.

However, once launched into international competition, the French aluminium industry can no longer be satisfied with internal production conditions and it is extending subsidiaries into countries where bauxite and electric current are cheaper – West Africa, Cameroon and Guinea.

3   The Chemical Industry; Progress and Delay

The role of the chemical industry in the reconversion of traditional industries in difficulty has already been described (pp. 101–4). This role is possible only if the basic chemical industry supplies products which are suitable for many different treatments and applications. It has, in fact, a double function; to supply products which are directly usable, like fertilisers, detergents, natural and synthetic rubber, pharmaceutical products, photographic and cine-photographic film and perfumes, and also to offer semi-finished products which serve as raw materials for the plastics and synthetic textile industries already mentioned.

The two series of products are governed by the expansion of the basic chemical industry. There are several distinct production cycles:

1   The manufacture of fertilisers, which involves nitrogen (ammoniac), sulphuric acid (treatment of phosphates) and potassium.
2   The production of sulphur and its derivatives.
3   The chlorine industries and their derivatives, vinyl chloride, chlorinated organic solvents.
4   Synthetic organic chemicals controlled by the pharmaceuticals industry, plastics and synthetic rubber industries, the manufacture of dyes and detergents, insecticides and fungicides.

The first three groups derive from raw materials either supplied in France, for example the sulphur separated from the Lacq natural gas and extracted from pyrites, rock salt and marine salt and potassium, or imported, as in the case of phosphates. The fourth category derives from coal and, especially, petroleum. It is this category which has developed most rapidly in the last fifteen years, under the name of petrochemicals, and it continues to grow at a fast pace.

However the general impression is that the French chemical industry took off too late. Certain essential products are clearly insufficient, and the French plants are not of the size needed to supply cheaply some products as important as ammonia, vinyl chloride, olefin and styrene. The French chemical industry is thus called on to make a major effort of investment accompanied by the regrouping of firms. It must also double the finance for research in five years. The position of an advanced technology industry is not without its obligations.

The French chemical industry made a real leap forward between 1960 and 1970 by carrying out amalgamations and major investments. The value of its output increased by 150 per cent in ten years, but the difficulties of the European situation throughout this branch, as well as some increases in internal production costs, seriously slowed down its growth in 1971. From an annual average growth rate of 10 per cent in gross production in the period 1960–70, the rate fell to 6.5 per cent, and net production fell even more steeply. All the same this very real crisis is not necessarily to be interpreted as a long term malaise.

From the point of view of location, there are two distinct levels. The first is that of basic industries involving heavy materials, linked to the existence of national or imported raw materials, as in the case of coal-based chemicals on the Nord/Pas-de-Calais coalfield at Mazingarbe and on the Lorraine coalfield at Carling, or petrochemicals dependent on refineries at the importing ports, Marseille-Berre, Bordeaux-Bec d'Ambès, the Lower Seine valley and Dunkerque, or the extraction of natural gas at Lacq, the treatment of petroleum transferred by pipelines, as at Strasbourg, chemical industries of the soda works in Lorraine and the manufacture of superphosphates in the ports importing raw phosphates. The Lyon chemical industries, initially created by the proximity of pyrites at Sain-Bel, are in a rather exceptional situation and have the greatest need for the opening up of the canal route to reduce their transport costs. The completion of the Pierre-Bénite* scheme is important in this respect, concluding the first stage of the Rhône improvement by the Compagnie Nationale du Rhône.

The second level is that of the industries using semi-finished products supplied by the basic chemicals industry, and it includes light chemicals and parachemicals. They consume expensive products in small amounts and can be more independent geographically. This involves the pharmaceutical industry, perfume manufacture and

---

* An integrated scheme to the south of Lyon involving improved navigation with new docks, a hydroelectric station and an extensive industrial estate.

photographic products. This level also corresponds to a greater structural dispersal of firms. Nevertheless, the manufacture of medicines or perfumes is mainly the province of large companies which combine and control the two levels of production in the same geographical area. This applies to the Lyon based group of companies, such as Progil and Rhône-Poulenc. On the other hand, the very large sales markets like the Paris region, attract a proliferation of laboratories specialising in pharmaceutical production, the manufacture of cosmetics and perfumes. Some changes imposed on the detergent industries by restrictions concerning water purification (they are now required to manufacture products which break down biologically without polluting the rivers into which used water is discharged) will result in structural modification through the disappearance of small firms incapable of conversion, and concentration benefiting the firms which are able first to meet market demand while conforming to the new laws. The chemical firms rank among the largest French companies, with Ugine-Kuhlmann-Produits Azotés, amalgamated in 1967, Péchiney-Saint-Gobain and above all Rhône-Poulenc reaching turnovers of from 2 to 5 billion francs each, but their scale is still smaller than that of the great German and even Italian companies, not to mention the British groups, and the pressure exerted by the petroleum based companies on the chemicals industry is becoming ever more severe.

4   The Nuclear Industry

The nuclear industry is obviously the most typical of the new generation of industries. Because of the size of its gross national product France is stretched to the limit of its powers for the independent development of the nuclear industry as a result of the enormous investment required for research, the manufacture of pre-products and the construction of plants, not to mention the question of viable operation. For this reason the programme of research and equipment was integrated into an European organisation, Euratom. However, the wish to keep exclusive national control of the military aspects of atomic equipment led to the establishment of strictly national enterprises in the framework of the Atomic Energy and National Defence Commission. The strategic character of the operation prevents the publication of precise information concerning the scale of investment and the stage of advance of production processes. The centres of research, experimental studies and production of semi-finished materials, enriched uranium and plutonium, are scattered throughout France. Several of the largest installations, however, are grouped in the South East, at Pierrelatte, Marcoule and Cadarache, although the first plants were located in the Paris region which still has important research laboratories at Fontenay-aux-Roses, Chatillon and Saclay. Toulouse and Bordeaux have received large investment especially for research laboratories, experimental testing and the applications to ballistic missiles. Electricité de France built its first nuclear power station in the Loire valley, near Chinon. The overlapping of research with an economic significance, involving 'productive' investment on a comparatively long term basis, and the achievement of strategic objectives, like plutonium bombs, means that it is difficult to distinguish in terms of both structure and location between what is civil and concerns the economy, and what is military.

There can be no doubt that by the complexity of its technological processes the nuclear industry acts as a driving force for a very large number of industries. However the question still remains whether this pressure has productive results, providing a fund of information for a later phase of technical and economic development, or whether it simply means a large consumption of the national income for expenditure with no economic effect other than stimulating the growth of suppliers and sub-contractors. In the latter case the development seems artificial, because it is based on purely adventitious orders which in the end are only justified by the need to maintain a self-created economic set up.

The decision taken by Electricité de France to invest huge sums in a new programme based on enriched uranium and natural water gives an economic motive to at least some of the operations. Apart from the experimental plants of Chinon I, II and III, Saint-Laurent-des-Eaux I and II and Bugey, France has undertaken with Belgian collaboration the construction of a nuclear power station at Chooz in the Ardennes, and in addition to the combined plants of the Atomic Energy Commission and Electricité de France at Brennilis in the Monts d'Arrée and at Marcoule-Phenix, the construction of a series of high capacity stations, the first being at Fessenheim. The forecasts for 1975 indicate the launching of a programme in the order of 8,000 Mw of installed capacity.

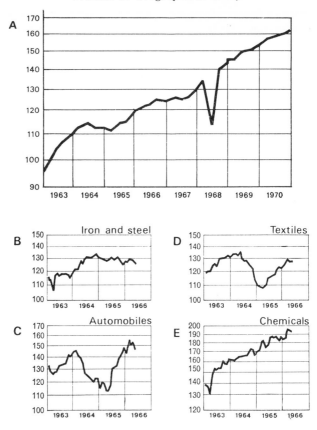

FIG. 12. Industrial output. (A) Quarterly index of industrial output, excluding building (base 100 in 1962). (B, C, D, E) Indices of specified industries (base 100 in 1959)

5   Adjustment to the Scale of the World Market

Until the Second World War and up until the beginning of the decade 1955–65, France still had an industrial structure of small and medium sized firms, with much smaller dimensions than American or West German companies. Even the largest French firms seemed small scale in comparison with the international giants. The creation of the Common Market placed French companies in competition with foreign firms, and especially with German firms. The smaller size resulted in a smaller

FIG. 13. French foreign trade, customs data in billions of francs, corrected for seasonal variations. (Source: Rapport sur les Comptes de la Nation de l'année 1970, I.N.S.E.E., 11, June 1971)

capacity for investment and thus a reduced potential in the quicker pace of technical progress. The pressure of American banking and industrial corporations seems overwhelming if it can only be met by scattered, under-equipped firms in precarious financial circumstances. It is expressed in concrete terms by the purchase of firms in difficulty and by increased capital participation which guarantees control of the firm by the foreign group. The size of French companies is no longer on the scale demanded by European and world competition.

The largest firms were the first to understand the danger and to carry out the most spectacular mergers or marketing combines. In the vehicle industry Renault and Peugeot are one example, in the chemicals industry Kuhlmann and Ugine, in non-ferrous metallurgy Péchiney and Tréfimétaux, in the iron and steel sector Usinor, de Wendel and Sidelor, and in special steels Creusot-Loire. The Commissariat Général au Plan* encourages research cartels and the creation of joint study teams in the absence of total regrouping. Without intervening directly in the structural reform of industry, the government warns against the dangers of dispersing the industrial effort and itself takes in hand a large part of the technical and scientific research, either by creating specialised services, like the Industrial Development Committee,

* The supreme French planning body, responsible for drafting the national economic plans and supervising their implementation.

responsible to the Commissariat Général au Plan, or by equipping the nationalised sector, which as a result acts as a public service alongside the private firms. University and institute laboratories and government research centres also contribute to applied research. Grenoble is the clearest example of collaboration between university and industry.

The fear of foreign competition on the home market and even of foreign industries settling in France, and the need to compete on equal terms with the European partners with no customs protection since 1968 speed up the process of association and amalgamation in all branches of industry. During the completion of the Fifth Plan,* the structure of French industry changed fundamentally. Small and medium-sized firms will only have a chance of success in very specialised sectors, or will only have an appearance of independence, being sub-contractors of large firms or organised groups.

* The Fifth Plan extended from 1965–70.

CHAPTER SIX

The Establishment of a New Consumer Economy

While still far from reaching the American standard of living* and way of life, France has entered the economy and society of consumption and recreation. The average margin of disposable income is nevertheless small in comparison with the situation in the richest countries. As a result consumption and leisure activities involve an element of selection which depends on a whole range of conditioned demands; fashion, as expressed by advertising through the press, radio and television, can direct these demands, according to the combined strength of industry and the retail outlets concerned, towards selected sectors of consumption or purchase of services. Experience shows that the increased means of households during the last twenty years have been directed towards the purchase of manufactured goods, new types of services and tourism. The centre of gravity in business, especially in the retail trade, has moved from the sector of foodstuffs and everyday mundane goods towards new sectors involving the sale and after-sales service, with or without sales guarantee, of cars, domestic electrical equipment, radios, televisions and record players for example. In spite of the criticisms which have been levelled at the type of housing provided for the increasingly concentrated populations of the urban regions, the investment and the service expenditure tied to housing have considerably increased compared with the residential patterns of the 1920s and 1930s. In a very short space of time commerce has experienced changing demands, which are also regulated by the marked difference in the age structure of the French population compared with the period between the two world wars. In this sphere too, there appears to be a poor structural adaptation to the new market

---

* The per capita gross national product is in the order of 60 per cent that of the United States.

119

conditions. The general trend is towards concentration in the distribution system, but the circuits are still complex and their complexity weighs heavily on retail prices.

1   Changes in the Distributive Trades

Trading employs approximately two million persons in France in a little over a million firms, which means that one in ten French workers is employed in trading. These figures show the fragmentation of the distribution system. The internal migration of population, on the one hand by rural exodus and on the other by the growth of urban agglomerations, has appreciably modified the distribution of customers and even more of purchasing power, especially during the last twenty years. While the population is deserting the villages with their tiny businesses, chainstores and supermarkets are catering for the *grands ensembles** built to house the new urban dwellers. Business structures are evolving towards a concentration of distributive trading, but the geographical pattern of the different kinds of structure reveals the transition from one commercial structure to another. The former population groupings, in villages, small towns and the old districts of large towns, still have miniature shops which feel the effect both of population migration and of competition from modern businesses. The new districts, now the major centres for everyday shopping, have department stores with a much lower ratio of employees to business turnover. Modern retailing, with supply lines running from wholesale depots, simplifies the circuit between suppliers and customers. It makes it possible to put pressure on prices and to dazzle the customer with a constantly changing variety of goods.

It requires a complex organisation, especially in the case of perishable goods, to meet the demands of a market made up of huge nuclei of localised consumption and redistribution. In this situation the organisation depends on professional groups of collectors, or collectors-assemblers-dispatchers, and agents, operating in the markets of the large towns and supplying the specialised groups of retail-wholesalers and retailers; fish merchants, carcass butchers, fruit and vegetable retailers. To help dispatch and delivery, the public

---

* The term applied to major apartment complexes housing many thousands of inhabitants.

authorities, government, *départements* and towns, have organised central markets and depot markets, guaranteeing the concentration of wholesaling activities and the fixing of prices for perishable goods. Before 1970 twenty-seven large markets in urban agglomerations formed the basic network from which regional redistribution of the assembled and packaged produce operated. The vegetable and fruit market of Rungis and the new meat market of La Villette are situated as part of this network in Paris. A parallel network of twenty-three large abbattoir-markets for meat is being organised, covering all the major producing regions and situated in the principal centres of consumption.

The degree of concentration in the sale of consumer goods varies and depends on whether items sold occasionally, known as irregular items, or everyday sales are involved. There is less concentration in the case of irregular items, at least at retail level, where the shops are still specialised and are even tending to become more and more specialised. On the other hand, in the case of items of everyday use the degree of concentration is accelerating, with huge shops supplying a wide range of goods and replacing a relatively large number of categories of retail shops. The concentrated shops, such as the big department stores, Uniprix, Monoprix, supermarkets and all the chainstores and cooperatives, accounted for 16 per cent of the business turnover of the retail trade in 1962 and over 25 per cent in 1971. Some small shopkeepers have combined into associations, simplifying their purchasing arrangements to avoid being suffocated by the large shops. At the beginning of 1972 France had 144 *grandes surfaces** as against 115 a year before. The concentration of retailing is accompanied by new geographical trends; for example the location of American-style hypermarkets with parking areas on the edge of agglomerations, as at Parly II and La Belle-Epine in Paris.

Behind these figures and these decentralised developments, a fundamental change is taking place in French retailing. Its visible effects are attenuated by the increasing diversification of demand. In the place of shops selling everyday goods, which are disappearing as a result of concentration, shops selling specialised goods and service businesses are being set up; for instance shops selling fashions, fancy goods, gimmicks and gadgets, sport and holiday articles, household equipment, radio and television sets, records or children's goods, driving schools, estate agents, hairdressers, launderettes and

* Shops in the largest category according to floor space.

physiotherapists. A comparison of a 1938 town trade gazette with an edition for 1970 or 1971 indicates the changes which have taken place both in the economy of the distribution market and in the landscape of the shopping streets. To an increasing degree general shopping is being concentrated in the markets and chainstores, with the exception of a few specialised chains notably for milk and dairy produce distribution, and is being replaced by a new type of business seeking out and suggesting needs unthought of thirty years ago.

The importance of major purchases has also increased considerably, but with a change of items, involving, for example, a decline in the purchase of jewelry, clocks, porcelain and gold plate. At the outbreak of the First World War, occasional household expenditure simply involved buying furniture and certain purchases coinciding with the major events of life and especially the setting up of a home. It was at the time of these expenditures that the supply of credit first appeared. Gradually the number of purchases representing a heavy financial outlay has expanded and has involved an increasingly wide stratum of society, acquiring motorcycles and cars, then electrical domestic equipment, and more recently radio, transistor and television sets. An expansion of the credit system has followed this growth of the market for irregular and expensive acquisitions, and has in large measure conditioned its growth. However, people are looking for credit for increasingly expensive and varied purchases. Two new markets have appeared on a mass-market scale during the last twenty years; the housing market and the market for leisure activities.

2   The Housing Market

The sudden expansion of the housing market is a consequence partly of urbanisation and population growth and partly of the sterilisation of speculative building by the low rent policy pursued since the end of the First World War. The housing crisis has continued to get worse since 1920 and has stimulated private initiative in building individual houses or buildings in co-ownership. The largest building boom was recorded after the Second World War and in spite of a twenty year effort, including the restoration of housing destroyed during the war, it is estimated that 200,000 new housing units per annum must be built over the next twenty years to satisfy the new demand and to renew the housing stock. The investment potential of public organisations concerned with building to meet social needs is limited, in spite of measures taken under the auspices of the Habitations à Loyer Modéré departments,* and the financing of building works by the Caisse des Depots et Consignations.† The private rented apartment building is becoming less common. There is thus an increasing need for investment by the householder, either directly or through housing cooperatives or building societies supported by long term credit arrangements with government support or guarantee. At the same time a liquidation of speculative buildings is taking place as these are sold off as apartments. An enormous property market has been formed, which absorbs a large proportion of private income. The development of this market does not escape the usual effects of demand. On the contrary, prices are under exceptional pressure, both in the case of building land and completed housing. The rapid accumulation of population in the major urban agglomerations increases these pressures, and property speculation has reached impressive proportions in the last forty years, especially in recent years. As an indication, one square metre of building land ten kilometres from central Paris was sold in 1946 for the value of less than half an hour's work by a qualified worker; to acquire this twenty-five years later required the equivalent of twenty-five hours' work. Even more exaggerated is the disparity between the price of agricultural land which has been converted into building land and subject to several transactions over a few years, and its present day sale price. Dealings in land, buildings and construction projects have led to the proliferation of estate agencies, developers and specialised credit firms. Paris is an ideal place to make a survey and study of this phenomenon, but the large provincial towns and even centres which seem less involved in these transactions have been affected by the spread of this style of business.

Far from absorbing all available savings, the property market for first homes is duplicated by a housing market for secondary homes; this is related to the now general existence of retirement pension schemes and to the development of seasonal and weekend leisure activities, and it is located with respect to the suitability of the different regions as bases for these recreations. The market includes the sale of land and buildings, especially in the great tourist and seasonal holiday

* Low rent apartment blocks intended for renting by lower income groups. The almost uniform blocks, built by industrialised techniques, most commonly referred to by the initials H.L.M. are typical of the skylines of most French cities.

† A public investment scheme financing housing construction.

regions, like the Côte d'Azur and the Nice area with its many residential estates and housing investment companies, the Basque and Landes coast, the coasts of Brittany and Normandy and the high mountain valleys. It also includes the acquisition of rural houses and in some cases entire villages in the most depopulated areas like the Southern Alps, which are then renovated often at great expense. In relation to the market for principal homes, the market for second homes acts as a counterbalancing force by encouraging some decentralisation of expenditure on building, furnishing and various services and by correcting the general tendency to withdraw investment from rural areas. It is true that it is a highly selective development, as the map of secondary homes shows.

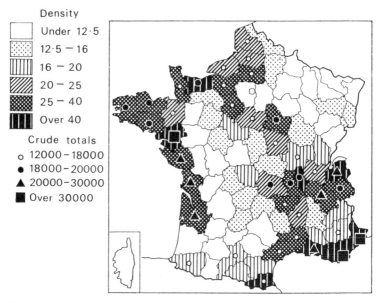

FIG. 14. Density of secondary residences by *départements*. (Number of residences per 10 square kilometres, 1968 census)

3   The Market in Leisure Activity

Since 1936 the amount of free time available to the French has markedly increased with the shortening of the working week to forty hours and the introduction of holidays with pay. In all jobs, in one way or another, more leisure time has been released, although this is partly absorbed by increased travelling time, especially in the form of commuting to work.* The organisation of daily life in material terms has also been affected by the desire for free time through the simplification of household chores and the smaller amount of time spent on meals. This is a general evolution in all industrial countries which has reached France during the last thirty years and particularly since 1950. As a consequence, a complete market has opened up to use the time saved from employment. The pressure of leisure even gradually reduces the amount of time given to rest, and paradoxically it tends to prolong working hours again because of the inevitable expenditure that it creates. In many households the wife has gone back to work and the husband takes on overtime and part-time jobs to make the payments on the car, television or holidays.

The leisure market can be divided into several sectors as regards both the type of activity and where it is based; leisure spent at home, in residential areas, recreation involving weekly or periodic movements, holiday leisure involving long distance travel including travel abroad.

Home based leisure is characterised by the mechanisation which is taking the place of reading and traditional manual activities. Until the Second World War, free time in the home, according to the degree of occupational qualification and the level of training of the people concerned, was spent in cultural or practical activities like reading, music, painting, tapestry making, embroidery, doing odd jobs or gardening. The market for books was conditioned by the educational level of a region or a town. It developed around the quality and the tastes of a clientele which might be concerned with knowledge, entertainment and collecting and at the same time interested in art books, book collecting and bookbinding. It was a high class market, dealing essentially with the cultured – or anxious to seem so – bourgeoisie or aristocracy. Having a collection of books, going to book shops, subscribing to magazines, encyclopedias or literary collections were an index of social standing. Gradually the growth of free time and the democratisation of leisure activities have caused this market to decline, replacing it with other pastimes which are more immediately accessible to the greatest number of people and which are at the same time to some degree imposed on those who were culturally privileged

* See P. George, *Sociologie et Géographie,* Presses Universitaires de France, 1966, p. 167.

in the previous period. Industrial techniques have provided a range of pastimes which is shaped by the new free time and purchasing power of the vast majority and is at least partly orientated towards easy solutions, like record players and record collections, radio and television. The sudden rejuvenation of the population following the increase in the birth rate after 1945 has widened the gulf between the home pastimes of the inter-war generation and that of the 1960s. Housing conditions and the crowding together of all members of a family make it more difficult to have individual pastimes like reading or playing a musical instrument. There has been a remarkable attempt to democratise reading by the mass publication of high quality books and classics as low cost paperbacks, an attempt hindered by the proliferation of the popular press which attracts advertising revenue; however, except as regards school and university texts the book market is far from keeping up with the increase in the potential number of readers. The number of titles published annually is scarcely greater than thirty years ago and the outlay on book purchases, including school texts,* accounts for less than a thousandth part of French household spending.†

The slack has been taken up by the market in gramophone records, where the demands of a brainwashed youth, eager for rhythm and sensation, count for more than the preference of music enthusiasts. The number of shops and listening kiosks, as well as the number of juke boxes in cafés, is astounding, and they have reached even the smallest towns. An echo effect links the record market with radio and television and thus a radio controlled programming of family entertainment. First radio, by means of mains sets and then portable transistors, reached almost all homes in rural areas as well as in the towns. The market for television sets grew more slowly because of the technical difficulties in transmitting programmes to all areas. The network now covers virtually all the country and the sale of sets has become correspondingly widespread. In spite of the high price of television sets, the number of users has grown rapidly because of hire purchase. The sale of sets, and the mechanical operations connected with installation, erecting aerials and carrying out repairs, have appeared even in villages, often combined for technical reasons with the retailing of

* In France parents are generally responsible for buying the books used by their children in school.

† P. Angoulvent, *L'Edition Française au Pied du Mur,* Presses Universitaires de France, 1960.

domestic electrical equipment. Television, which devours family recreation and rest time, often takes the place of the clock which used to tick away the time in more intimate days. This is not the place to analyse the social and psychological effects of a transformation of which all the consequences have not yet been recorded.* The present observations simply concern the growth of a market and the economic behaviour of French society in the 1960s, especially in relation to the distribution of its share of purchasing power between the different types of goods and services offered.

Home based pastimes to a large extent conflict with outdoor recreation, at least as far as everyday leisure activities are concerned. It has been suggested that they have led to less frequenting of drinking places, although many public establishments try to keep their clientele by installing television and various kinds of slot machines. Cinema going is experiencing a crisis similar to book selling, and has been worse hit than the theatre, which still attracts a cultured audience. However, the rejuvenation of the population, and especially the relative youthfulness of the industrial and urban regions, has called into being other types of recreation to release the need for physical activity through games and sports. Here the idea of a market is inextricably linked with public investment and the use of urban land. Usually the practice of a sport calls for improved open spaces and covered halls which local authorities must provide. Development is slowed down by the price of land and the cost of installation and this is not unconnected with the use of energy, unreleased through games and sports, in various kinds of violence which threaten public order. The increase in leisure, particularly for young people, is a major problem in town planning schemes and the allocation of public funds. There is no doubt too that present day types of housing, apartment block complexes for example, handicap the development of traditional everyday leisure activities like gardening and handyman jobs for a large proportion of the urban population, especially in the working class, and pose another problem for the planners and the use of land in major urban agglomerations.

The narrow confines of everyday life and the monotony of a daily routine within which people try unsuccessfully to find their own private niche stimulates another search, a periodic search triggered by a more or less conscious need for contact with the natural environment. This is expressed in a simple way by a longing for the sun and

* P. George, *Sociologie et Géographie.*

the need for an activity which takes people out of built up areas – like camping, fishing and hunting, or more simply a trip including a meal away from home in a country inn. This search results in the periodic mobility of an increasingly large proportion of the urban population, reaching its height in summer, at Easter and the All Saints Day holiday. The mass ownership of cars means that this periodic mobility becomes a rhythmic flow every weekend and at each public holiday, with long weekends* causing the largest number of departures; major road improvements are needed to facilitate the flow of the traffic and to reduce the risk of accidents. Each major agglomeration is surrounded by a zone for weekly recreation, with favourite routes depending on the opportunities that they offer for recreation. This zone is equipped with reception businesses, cafés, restaurants and camp sites. Secondary homes proliferate in both the forms mentioned earlier – new housing and renovations of disused rural dwellings. Building, renovation and repairs support a number of commercial activities which essentially live on urban income transferred in the form of expenditure on leisure.

The most spectacular phenomenon of the leisure society is certainly tourism – the enjoyment of annual or quarterly leisure activities during the holiday periods. The problem was formerly confined to school holidays and was solved according to social category by holidays spent at the seaside, in the mountains or the countryside by children accompanied by their mother, often staying with their grandparents, or by sending children to socially sponsored hostels like the *colonies de vacances.*† The extension of holidays with pay, their prolongation and often their division into two seasonal periods, summer and winter, has fundamentally altered the situation. The general social phenomenon has become adult tourism. The pressure of the young age groups makes it even more of a large scale upheaval. A very important holiday market has been created, which combines daily board and lodging, travel there and back, excursions, entertainments, the purchase of adequate equipment, the services inherent in some types of leisure activities and the installation of facilities

* The French term 'pont' translated here as long weekend has no exact English equivalent. It refers to the practice of granting an extra holiday when a public holiday falls midweek in order to take advantage of the following or preceding weekend and thus converting a single holiday into a more substantial break.

† Hostels sponsored by religious, social or professional groups, providing low cost holidays with an emphasis on outdoor recreation under the supervision of monitors, bringing healthy holidays within the range of the children from low income families.

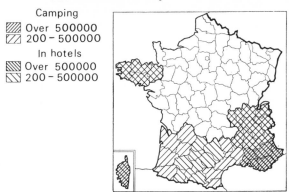

FIG. 15a. Number of holidays in France spent in hotels, camping or in caravans, in 1964, by planning regions

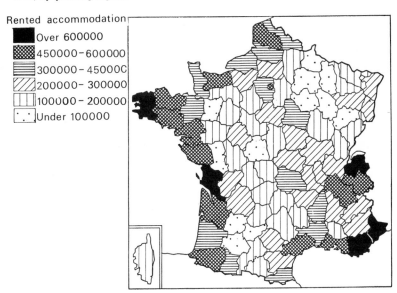

FIG. 15b. Location of holidays in rented accommodation by *département*, in 1964

necessary for them, for example ski lifts. This market is geographically concentrated in a small number of regions favoured by their natural environment and drawn to the attention of the masses through well organised publicity in all the media capable of stimulating the public; the press, radio, television and the world of fashion. It is so important and lucrative that it benefits from the intervention of the major banking companies which finance leisure and holiday organisations and developments with as much attention as they devote to industrial enterprises. In fact, tourism has come to occupy an important place in the budget of most families. In many ways it has replaced the habit of saving which seemed a characteristic feature of the preceding generation. A vast amount of money is spent every year in the course of summer holidays and winter sports. The market is highly mobile and it crosses national frontiers with ease. More and more French people not only visit foreign tourist areas, especially for several years now the Costa Brava in Spain, but invest abroad in land purchase and the building of holiday villas. The economic problem is one of balance: will the revenue from foreign tourists in France compensate for or exceed the flight of French capital to foreign tourist areas or to the profit of foreign tourist agencies? How can the balance sheet be kept in the black: by retaining more French tourists in France and attracting more foreigners to France? This is the problem which faces the development of tourism in a country which fortunately has natural qualities to help it keep and attract the people involved, and which also faces the organisation of a profession which is all the more tempted by quick profits since the season of activity is short. At the present time the balance is negative because of the increasing numbers of French tourists going abroad and the loss of interest in holiday visits to France on the part of foreigners. The probable deficit in the immediate future has been estimated at over a billion francs. As a result a major investment in hotel and tourist facilities is planned. Between 1965 and 1970 over 30,000 new rooms, of which 25,000 were in the holidaymaking areas and 5,000 in Paris and the regional capitals, were added to the existing total of 350,000 hotel rooms, including 610,000 beds in classified hotels. At the same time older buildings have been modernised, involving 60,000 rooms. In the realm of popular tourism, the target is to create 400,000 places on camp sites and 41,500 in country inns, holiday villages and country lodgings. Technical facilities like marinas, swimming pools and ski lifts in the mountain resorts are being multiplied, and training for the profession is being improved. The improvement of the Bas-Languedoc and Roussillon coast and the facilities built around Grenoble for the 1968 Winter Olympic Games, are two essential elements in the list of recent achievements and developments under construction. The general concentration process of businesses naturally extends to the tourist industry. Increasingly the hotel trade is being integrated into chains managed by companies with shareholders. The S.O.F.I.T.E.L.* company is a grouping of banks, insurance companies, transport companies and travel agents, which invests in the creation of hotel chains. A semi-public group, Inter-Hotel, in which public lending bodies participate, is involved in new hotel construction and contributes to the modernisation of old hotels. Foreign chains are appearing in France in their turn.

Camping has become the basis of a very large market in which individual initiative overlaps with the organised camps and 'villages under canvas' in the shape of holiday clubs. Fifty factories, employing 5,000 workers, are concerned with the manufacture of camping equipment. Their business turnover is increasing by 15 per cent annually, greatly exceeding the average rate of expansion of French industries.†

The State is involved in the entire operation, not only because of its participation in certain investment projects, but also through the need to maintain transport services and access to the tourist zones, the improvement of rail services and of the road network for French and foreign traffic and the creation of air lines and specialised airports. It also keeps a watch over the improvement of the market, an indispensable condition if French customers are to be kept and foreign visitors attracted, by the inspection of prices and management methods.

In a geographical sense the phenomenon of tourism is strictly localised, involving a small number of regions whose economy and ecology are completely transformed by this new activity and new type of use; the coastal regions, the snow covered mountains, spas and archaeological zones and centres like the Loire valley and Mont Saint-Michel. Tourism in the large cities, and principally Paris, is less noticeable in the middle of the other activities of large agglomerations. The seasonal displacement of the consumer market, especially the market for perishable produce, is a direct consequence, and often poses very difficult problems for professional organisations and transport systems.

* La Société Financière de Gestion et d'Investissement Immobilier et Hotelier.
† Ginier, *Géographie Touristique de la France*, S.E.D.E.S., 1965.

PART THREE

New Regional Structures

The government and public opinion can no longer fail to notice the lack of balance in the nation brought about by the excessive concentration in the Paris region of the power of decision and much of the country's productive capacity. The self-evident effects of excessive growth and of the general overloading of the capital make everyone aware of the many growing disadvantages of a rapidly increasing population; this cannot be absorbed by the infrastructure created by previous generations which it would be very costly, if not impossible, to adapt to the needs of an agglomeration with an expected population of between 12 and 15 million within twenty years.

The reawakening of the major provincial centres, the reorganisation of the nation into large regional units and a revival of the provinces which the Constituent Assembly wished to destroy to the advantage of Paris as capital of all the *départements,* seemed more necessary than ever with the entry of France into the European Economic Community which showed up starkly the underpopulation of the country's land area outside the Paris region and a few secondary centres of concentration corresponding with the oldest industrial areas, like the Nord region and the greater Lyon area. It is not for the geographer to draw up programmes for reorganising the national space that has been in large measure sterilised by the excessive centralisation on Paris, or to recommend particular investments in preferential development. However, he must describe the present state of affairs and analyse development plans and policies in so far as they shape action in the short term and already act as a differential stimulus, until it is time to draw up a restatement. Part Three deals in turn with the country's present situation as revealed by geographical analysis, the outlook for regional development resulting from the options chosen in the investment policy defined by the development and modernisation plans, especially the Fifth Plan, and finally the problem which is the most important and the most difficult to resolve in a satisfactory manner, the place in France of the Paris agglomeration and the problem of regulating its growth.

Development planning is the concern of various public bodies, working at a national or regional level. The 1964 decrees established in each of the so-called planning regions, or administrative units for regional action (see p. 37 above), alongside a regional prefect, a Commission for Regional Economic Development (C.O.D.E.R.), which brought together representatives of the elected *département* administration, representatives of economic associations and trade unions, and others chosen for their special expertise. At a central level, development planning is integrated into the framework of interministerial coordination by the Délégation à l'Aménagement du Territoire et à l'Action Régionale (D.A.T.A.R.). Certain projects with precisely defined objectives may be delegated to research and development teams, as in the case of the improvement of coastal tourism in Bas-Languedoc, or to mixed economy companies, like the Compagnie Nationale d'Aménagement du Bas-Rhône-Languedoc. At the level of the major urban complexes, nominated as metropolitan areas, structure plans have been called for from Organismes d'Etude d'Aménagement des Aires Metropolitaines (O.R.E.A.M.), and from town planning agencies for urban communities.

CHAPTER SEVEN

Problems and Trends

More than a century of industrial development based on the exploitation and movement of coal and iron and on a transport network which followed natural lines of direction and suitable inherited axes (the canals and railways followed the lines of the royal highways) and confirmed the supremacy of Paris, ended in a division of France into two specialised and economically unequal major units: a northern and eastern unit, roughly bounded in the south west by a line drawn from the Seine estuary to Valence, where three-quarters of the national industrial capacity and activity is grouped; and a southern and western zone where industrial activity is very restricted as regards location and small in scale, while the agricultural activities which are dominant here do not compensate with high yields and productivity, except in a few privileged sectors like the vine growing and market gardening areas.

The demand for labour in industry and the activities stimulated by industry, commerce, transport, services and administration at all levels, had the effect of transferring population and also fertility, since it constantly caused the rejuvenation of populations in the industrial regions and the ageing of those in the regions from which labour was recruited. The regions of exodus reacted differently to this repeated depletion of population which took place over a century. The Midi, western and south western France have not all been equally afflicted. The West resisted longest, and until the Second World War the uneven distribution of demographic fertility showed a distinct crescent with high fertility running from the Vendée to the Jura via the Nord, from a central area and the Midi which were depopulated and aged (Fig. 6). Over roughly the last fifteen years, there has been a loss of momentum in Brittany and the Vendée in the West, and the spatial distortion in demographic terms has moved closer to the distribution of industry. The ageing process has been exaggerated by the settling in the country or in small and medium sized provincial towns of retired people and workmen or employees from various kinds of firms who set up businesses on an artisan scale in their late middle age, as a semi-retirement after twenty or twenty-five years of paid work in the industrial regions and especially in the Paris region.

The spatial disparity is also a disparity of capital, income, occupational training and the creation of highly qualified workers. The absence of large industrial plants, except in the seaports, and often the fact that government intervention takes the place of private capital, at Toulouse for example, have discouraged the investment of local or regional profits made from agriculture and commerce. Savings, like the young population, have taken flight to the northern and north-eastern half of the country and above all to Paris, to such a degree that the money to finance basic facilities can no longer be raised locally and to keep up with the pace of contemporary life, these regions must resort to outside aid in the form of public subsidies and investment. The distribution by *départements* of business turnover shows particularly clearly the spatial distortion of France in economic affairs.

Thirty-three *départements* situated to the north east of the Le Havre-Valence line account for 77 per cent of the business turnover of commercial and industrial firms, with 52 per cent of the population and approximately one-third of the land area. It is a fact that the Paris region accounts for almost half of the nation's business turnover, the remaining 25 per cent being shared between the Nord regions and the east, together with the Lyon region in its wider setting. Fifty-eight *départements* covering two-thirds of the national land area contribute only 23 per cent of the business turnover. If one excludes the *départements* with ports, Loire-Atlantique, Gironde, Bouches-du-Rhône, Haute-Garonne and Alpes-Maritimes, which benefit both from a concentration of regional commercial activity and from an inflow of income from tourism and the settlement of retired persons, there remains 17 per cent of the national business turnover for fifty-three *départements* occupying over half of the national land area (Fig. 16b). The data on taxed income shows the same disparity as business turnover, with only a slight attenuation. Payments into savings banks, which, however, do not only express the build-up of industrial and commercial income and the distribution of wages, show the same contrast, with half of the deposits being made in the thirty-three

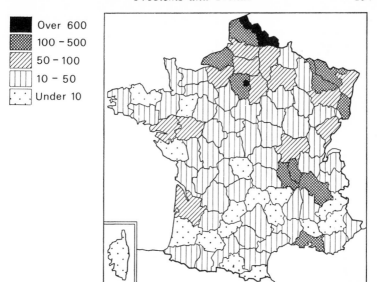

FIG. 16a. Industrial firms with over 200 employees by *départements*

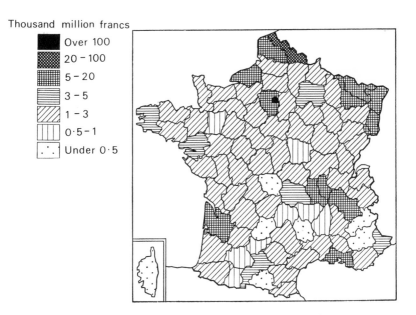

FIG. 16b. Business turnover of industrial and commercial firms by *départements*

départements already mentioned, in the North and East, and a sixth in the Paris region.

The first consequence of this spatial disparity is the existence of two different types of spontaneous areal organisation. The group of industrialised areas in the widest sense of the term, including industrialised zones and service centres of all kinds concerned with industrial processes and activities, is present in the form of ranked and organised units which, in spite of some imperfections, seem to be regions integrated by regional metropolises, in turn linked by high density flows to the capital. These can be considered economic regions with a network of interconnections in an urban hierarchy. The importance of the business transactions which take place here and the financial volume of transactions, exchange and distribution flows mean that there is a high level and a complex variety of different service activities and of commercial and financial business, which give the regional metropolises a high standing and because of their tertiary sector facilities put them on a footing with the great cities of industrial Europe. It would be an exaggeration to think that when a region's life is animated by an intensification of its activities and the flow of people, goods and money this means that the whole of its economic, social, cultural and scientific life is concentrated at a purely regional level. It was pointed out before and it should be emphasised that regional life was integrated into national life and as a consequence depends on the power of decision at the highest level, that is at the level of the capital city. Moreover the promotion of regional development is deliberately following this direction at the present time; within a spatial framework defined according to specific forms of activities, a package of incentives and encouragements is being applied according to national priorities and European and international market prospects, controlled by government intervention by means both of tax regulations and of direct or indirect subsidy. It is thus applied in the context of the overall management of the national economy. These few preliminary remarks make it possible to define a first category of region in France, which is far from being uniform.

The West, Centre and South of France belong to a completely different kind of geographical space. One feature which makes this type different from the preceding one is the weakness of internal flows and of all kinds of contacts. A second characteristic is the general by-passing of the scope and prerogatives of the towns, which are under-equipped in relation to the regional functions that they could be called upon to fulfill, by flows and channels of communication directly connected to Paris. In other words, the degree of regional polarisation is minimal. Regional unification resides less in the power of control being exerted by a regional metropolis and an urban network, than in a more or less pronounced uniformity which, according to the place, can spring from positive characteristics or from a common degree of inertia. This is projected onto the general map of contrasted uses of the national land area, and in this respect the regions are here more geographical and to a large degree natural, rather than economic. At this level of analysis, one may well ask whether these are not homogeneous and continuous regions, constructed literally on an articulated framework in which the joints are the towns as functional centres and points at which traffic converges and is dispersed.

The economic significance of the large towns, even when they take on the status of regional metropolis, is very different from that in the major centres of industrialisation in the north-eastern third of France, and especially the Paris region, as the following table shows.

TABLE FIFTEEN
THE POWER OF CONTROL OF PARIS AND THE REGIONAL
METROPOLISES
(after Le Fillatre)

	Number of workers in firms outside the agglomeration whose head office is in the agglomeration	Number of workers in firms situated in the agglomeration whose head office is elsewhere	Dependence on Paris. Number of workers in firms with head offices in Paris
Paris	1,329,900	52,027	—
Lille, Roubaix	23,000	49,000	40,000
Nancy-Strasbourg	17,000	33,000	25,000
Lyon, Grenoble, Saint-Etienne	73,000	81,000	68,000
Rouen, Le Havre	10,000	61,000	54,000
Nantes-Saint-Nazaire	10,000	42,000	37,000
Bordeaux	7,000	31,000	28,000
Toulouse	5,000	23,000	21,000
Marseille	15,000	28,000	23,000

Any hypothesis, and even any exercise concerning regional organisation, presupposes an analysis of the regional reality, which means that two elements must be considered: the qualitative study of the towns considered as regional capitals, and then the search for the limits of the urban spheres of influence. In other words, any attempt to draw up a regional inventory begins with an attempt to classify the urban hierarchy. As a first step, a classification based on the population size of each agglomeration and on the rates of increase can be revealing.

Outside the Paris agglomeration and the regions with mining conurbations, seventeen urban agglomerations in France exceed 200,000 inhabitants. A first group stands out, that of towns with populations of between 500,000 and 1 million inhabitants. At the lower end of the scale Bordeaux scarcely passes the half million mark, at the upper end Lyon verges on 1 million, and the larger agglomeration of Lyon-Saint-Etienne-Givors exceeds 1.5 million. Between the two extremes, the Lille-Roubaix-Tourcoing agglomeration and that of Marseille have both approximately 900,000 inhabitants. This size level of course implies a range of activities suited to a very large city but does not on its own qualify each agglomeration to the title of regional metropolis. One must be even more careful about the next size category, the agglomerations of from 200,000 to 500,000 inhabitants, in descending order Toulouse (439,000), Nantes (393,000), Nice (392,000), Rouen (328,000), Strasbourg (302,000), Toulon (288,000), Clermont-Ferrand (204,000) and Tours (201,000).

Professors Hautreux and Rochefort* have attempted to refine and correct this quantitative assessment, by introducing the idea of service functions. Agglomerations with a regional function might be considered to be those which as well as their own population, have a clientele of several million inhabitants, and which are characterised by the existence of highly specialised services related to the needs of large numbers of population and to the unfolding of a region's life. In fact, if certain goods or services are not available in an easily accessible centre, and especially if the persons concerned are unable to find all the goods and services they require grouped in the same place, the search is automatically transferred to a better equipped centre, and in fact to the capital, which has the advantage of making available simultaneously a wide range of provision. A system of standardised classification has been based on this set of observations, taking into account population size, the service provision for the economy and individuals, and criteria relating to external influence, such as the intensity of telephone flows and short distance train services. This system

* By applying the principle of the method suggested by A. Piatier.

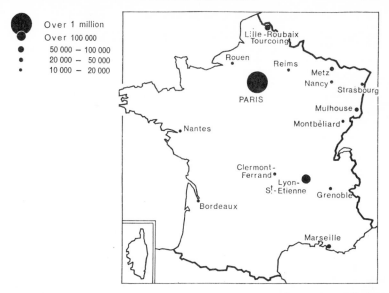

FIG. 17. The power of control of major French towns according to the number of employees dependent on head offices located in them

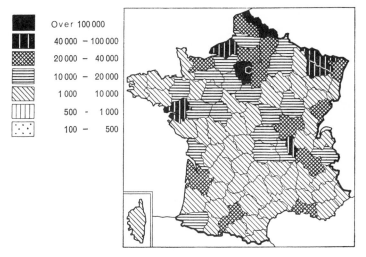

FIG. 18. Number of employees in each *département* in firms whose head office is located in the Paris agglomeration (after Le Fillatre)

FIG. 19. The number of employees in each *département* in firms controlled by head offices in the agglomerations of:

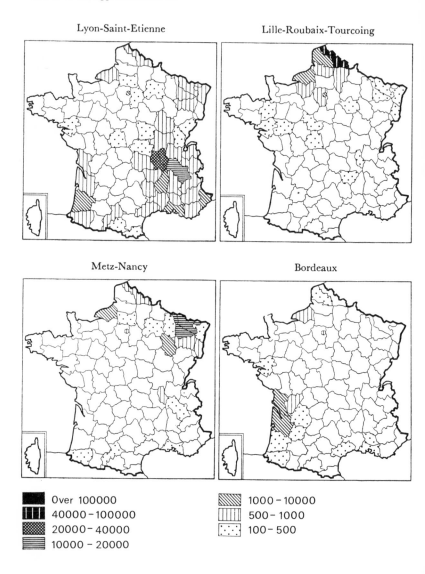

Lyon-Saint-Etienne   Lille-Roubaix-Tourcoing

Metz-Nancy   Bordeaux

■ Over 100000	⬛ 1000 – 10000
▥ 40000 – 100000	▥ 500 – 1000
▦ 20000 – 40000	⬚ 100 – 500
▤ 10000 – 20000	

reveals the primacy of eight well equipped urban centres, both in terms of public services and of private activities, which exercise a definite external influence as indicated by the frequency of telephone calls and the intensity of daily and periodic population movements: Lyon, Marseille, Bordeaux, Lille, Toulouse, Strasbourg, Nantes and Nancy, followed quite closely by Grenoble, Rennes, Nice, Clermont-Ferrand, Rouen, Dijon and Montpellier. These towns are characterised by having services and businesses which, with a few exceptions, are able to meet the entire needs of a population and consequently make it unnecessary to turn to the capital city. They have universities and scientific facilities, the highest level of hospital provision, offices and agencies for research, study and all kinds of expertise, branches for the sale, installation and repair of specialised equipment, a range of specialised wholesale depots, banking offices which can act on their own initiative, responsible administrations capable of resolving complicated problems in the shortest time and an international level and capacity of accommodation so that they can attract foreign representatives and visitors and stage commercial exhibitions, conventions and study conferences. They are rightly able to exploit an historical site and heritage to some degree enhanced by recent planned urban development.

The eight cities mentioned above may deservedly be described as regional metropolises with an infrastructure favouring the exercise of this function, while Grenoble, especially since the investment made for the Winter Olympic Games, Rennes, Nice, Clermont-Ferrand, Dijon and Montpellier have the role of supporting urban centres. Rouen has been forced to develop within the framework of satellites in the Paris region. There remains the far from easy task of defining the limits of the sphere of influence. Economists and geographers have tried by various methods to map the regional areas defined according to the criterion of urban influence.* The most reliable methods are those based on reference to the use of urban services and to the distribution range of products and merchandise from urban depots. In practice the regional influence of a town is expressed more by the intensity and frequency of services and contacts, than by the mere existence of these features. However, it is difficult to quantify the intensity of flows and the frequency of recourse to urban centres, and the results are of varying accuracy, according to the character of the flow or the system of contact under consideration. Nevertheless, the increasing number

---

* In particular the map drawn under the direction of Professor G. Chabot.

of measurement techniques make it possible to distinguish between areas covered by frequent and high intensity contacts which may be considered representative of generalised and constant spheres of influence and areas of more specialised contacts, and also to detect, beyond certain distance thresholds, the falling off of the flows most representative of regional influence. It is thus possible to discern approximate limits and a hierarchical ordering into sets of spheres of influence. All attempts of this kind reveal how imprecise the synthetic outlines* are, how frequently spheres of influence overlap and how everywhere there is conflict between control from the regional metropolises or regional centres and control exerted by Paris. In particular, the functions of towns of the second level, like Grenoble, Clermont-Ferrand or Montpellier, are complemented not by the nearest regional metropolis but directly by Paris.

The idea of a region thus appears to be partly relative, in that one cannot rely on objective criteria to define boundaries which are both rigorous and stable. From a geographical point of view, the awkward thing is that if one relies on objective criteria in defining limits and considers that the spatial convergence of several important criteria indicates a true urban hinterland, the regions which are clearly defined are not contiguous, but form organised areas which, in terms of a map, seem to 'float' within an ill-defined space, unsuitable for regional purposes, and which in fact falls directly under the control of Paris. Conversely, one may just as easily observe that real regions are few in number and have a peripheral distribution around a large area covering roughly half the national land area, directly dominated by Paris, in spite of the sketching in of polarised zones around the regional centres of 100,000 to 300,000 inhabitants situated within a 100 to 200 kilometre radius of Paris.

* i.e. hinterlands delimited by multiple criteria which reveal inconsistent boundaries.

CHAPTER EIGHT

Polarised Regions and Inorganic Areas

France has two regions which are completely polarised, although in very different ways, the Nord region and the Lyon region. Both are old established industrial regions, where commerce and artisan activities preceded the machine age. The traditions of regional organisation, originally provincial organisation, are very old, but the forms, like the outlines of the regional control of the power centres, spring from more recent considerations and initiatives which have existed for a century. Both are located in the industrial and economically dominant north-eastern half of France and both have tried to extend their control, but with different degrees of success. The influence of Lille meets obstacles, competition or zones of inertia on all sides; the Belgian frontier, competition from Paris and the indifference of industrial Lorraine towards an axis linking Dunkerque with Thionville; for this reason a high capacity canal was never built during the period when the canal was the supreme link between heavy industrial regions. The Nord region is blockaded on its coalfield, threatened with annexation by the great Paris region, only two hours from Lille by express train, and facing difficult problems of reconversion. The Lorraine industrial region, far from forming a complementary and solid unit with the Nord region is instead trying to direct its development towards the Rhine axis by the canalisation of the Moselle, without in any way lessening the authority and personality of Alsace, which benefits from the stimulus inherent in all north-south European routeways between the North Sea and the Mediterranean.

The Lyon region seems to be having more success than the Nord in extending its control. The economic independence of the Saint-Etienne region has not been able to survive the crisis in coal mining. The Saint-Etienne depression has been absorbed into the Lyon system, and Lyon is designated as the capital of the 'Rhône-Alpes' region,* or of a 'Central South East', including ten *départements* and approximately five million inhabitants. Situated on the European North Sea-Mediterranean axis, Lyon competes for influence over the middle and lower Rhône with Marseille, which has also recently assumed the function of a regional metropolis.

I THE NORD REGION

4 million inhabitants, 8 per cent of the national total on 3 per cent of the area of France; nearly 10 per cent of the gross national product; highly intensive agriculture combining the highest yields with highly productive labour and investment; above all, an industrial complex combining all the industries which figure in the nation's range of activities, based on the tradition of the Flemish cloth manufacturer and on the use of coal; over three million urban dwellers of whom nearly one million live in the regional metropolis of Lille-Roubaix-Tourcoing; these, briefly, are the main descriptive elements of this regional unit. At first sight everything seems to be in its favour, but the Nord region also has many weaknesses and these weaknesses often explain the flight of population and capital to Paris. The region, however, keeps its distinctive character and solid power, particularly as it tries to cope with the difficulties caused by the ageing of its heritage and the need to face up to the European era.

1 The Regional Structures

Like all regions created by the nineteenth century industrial revolution, the Nord is in large measure the creation of business families. After the eighteenth century local capital made up the Anzin Company which was the first shareholding company founded in France. The discovery of coal at Oignies in 1847, coinciding with the first railway building, was the point of departure for speculation in mining, iron and steel and railways, based on coal. These developments coincided with those at Lille which converted textile manufacture from an artisan activity to an industry. The coalfield was the domain of a

* One of the twenty-two planning regions; see Fig. 4.

highly enterprising aristocracy which acquired major interests in the Nord railway companies. The textiles industry founded the fortunes of great bourgeois families in Lille, which were joined at the end of the nineteenth century by several major firms of the new chemical industry which originally served the textile industry, like Kuhlmann-Agache. The complex was originally backed by the Lille banks. These business families, Thiriez, Motle, Prouvost, Le Blan, Scrive, Desurmont, Lorthios, Flipo, Masurel, Tiberghien, Descamps, Delesalle, Wallaert, Droulers, Delattre, Pollet, Requillart, Dansette, Leuront, Coisne-Lambert and Toulemonde in the textiles sector, Joire, Scalbert, and Verley-Decroix in banking, and Beghin in sugar refining, were the creators of an economic region after 1866. The Credit du Nord bank, which launched the iron and steel industry on the coalfield at Valenciennes, was involved in the early stages of the chemical industries. Lille had a stock exchange from 1861. At the outbreak of the 1914 war, the financial and economic unity of the Nord was confirmed by the action of banks and administrative councils based on Lille. Lille capitalism financed many operations outside France, especially in wool and cotton producing countries. It founded technical colleges at all levels to guarantee the training of its qualified workers, before the government intervention which set up the university, by stages, between 1854 and 1897.

After the First World War, the autonomy of the Nord was gradually reduced by increasing difficulties. After the reconstructions following the war which made it possible to modernise plant and infrastructure, the crisis of the 1930s created severe financial problems for the textile industries and hastened the increasingly large input of capital from outside the region, especially from Paris. The nationalisation of the railways, and, after the Second World War, of the coal mines, reduced the controlling power of the regional metropolis and the coalfield towns, although a regional administrative structure still continued in the nationalised sector. As a result, the centralisation based on Lille was frustrated, and the coalfield now tends to escape Lille's control more than in the past. The textile crisis has encouraged groupings to a greater extent than formerly. The crisis has inspired inter-regional combines in the textile sector, for example Thiriez of Loos* and Droulers-Vernier of Lille with Dollfus-Mieg of Mulhouse, and in the metallurgy sector between Fives-Lille and the shipyards of Penhoët et

* In the south-western sector of the Lille conurbation.

de l'Atlantique,* the S.A.C.M. and Alsthom companies. These mergers indicate a technical breakthrough beyond the region's boundaries. The Lille region requires more and more materials from other regions and from various European countries, in the shape of synthetic and artifical thread and fibres, petroleum products and foodstuffs.

The head offices of its firms have been transferred to Paris, as in the case of Kuhlmann, Fives-Lille-Cail, Usinor and Vallourec. The regional banks resist this trend, headed by the Crédit du Nord, followed by the old family banks of the Nord, like Scalbert, Dupont, Joire, Pajol and Martin, the Société de Banque du Nord and the Banque Régionale du Nord, but a large proportion of the financial transactions affecting the region escape them: the major credit operations are controlled by phone from Paris, while less traditional speculations extend beyond the region and the purely industrial context.

2   The Output

The regional activity of the Nord can be defined in terms of three essential features: agriculture, the coalfield and the Lille region. There are some important extensions which complete the economic contribution of these three: the industries of the Sambre valley and in Ardenne of the Meuse Valley, the industrial port of Dunkerque and the fishing port of Boulogne which is also surrounded by different industrial activities.

The two *départements* of Nord and Pas-de-Calais occupy a little more than 2 per cent of the national land area and produce 5 per cent of the milk, 6 per cent of the barley, 8 per cent of the wheat, 10 per cent of the potatoes and nearly 20 per cent of the sugar-beet harvested in France. The yields are among the highest recorded by French agriculture, over 30 quintals per hectare for cereals, over 200 quintals for potatoes, over 400 for sugar-beet and over 3,000 litres of milk per cow per annum. These results are mainly obtained from farms with an average size of 25 to 35 hectares. The smallholdings are increasingly being absorbed by average sized farms, which ensure that family labour and machinery are more profitable. The large farms, which have difficulty finding labour, are tending to be subdivided. The Nord

* France's major shipbuilding company, based on Saint-Nazaire.

region is thus a region of intensive cultivation practised on family farms of on average 30 hectares. Incomes are high and the farming is directly linked with agricultural industries, the most typical being the sugar industry, symbolised by the Beghin company which still has some of its head offices in the heart of the sugarbeet growing countryside, at Thumeries.*

The coal basin is 110 kilometres in length and has the shape of an elongated crescent; it has very nearly a million inhabitants living in a group of towns, most of which are immature and give an impression of being unfinished. Above all it is an industrial region with mining and industrial *cités.*† 16 million tons of coal were produced in 1971, mined by 60,000 coal face workers. The record levels were 32 million tons in 1939 with 101,000 miners and 28.5 million tons in 1946 with 132,000 miners. However, some of the mines, especially in the western part of the field, in the Pas-de-Calais section where the coal seams plunge below 1,000 metres, are no longer viable in the competitive situation of the Coal and Steel Community and the European Economic Community, and for over ten years it has been necessary to follow a policy of mine closure, relocation of machinery and manpower to the best mines and a reduction in the number of miners. Coal acquires an added value locally, by being processed into a higher form and into a more transferable type of energy in the coalfield's electricity power stations, by its use in the chemicals industry and the manufacture of 5 million tons of coke per annum, 200,000 tons of coal tar and 2 billion cubic metres of coke oven gas; this guarantees a certain degree of industrial stability to the coalfield at a deliberately reduced level of production. The coalfield's iron and steel industry, getting its iron ore from Lorraine and the Normandy-Anjou fields, and scrap produced within the region, produces 4 million tons of steel, from plant at Denain, Valenciennes and Anzin. It supplies the heavy engineering industry, producing for the mines, transport and heavy industries located on the coalfield, and the Lille engineering industry.

The specific role of the Lille region is as a major textile centre, turning out 90 per cent of the nation's combed wool and combed woollen yarn, nearly 20 per cent of the carded wool, 33 per cent of the woollen cloth, 90 per cent of the carpets, 33 per cent of the cotton thread, 26 per cent of the cotton cloth, 90 per cent of the linen thread, over 50

---

* South of Lille, between Lille and the coalfield.

† Immense housing estates, built and usually owned by the industrial firms for their work force.

per cent of the linen cloth and three quarters of the jute thread and cloth. The urban region of Lille, Roubaix-Tourcoing and Armentières is the largest textile industry area in western Europe, with a capacity for processing 90,000 tons of combed wool, 5,000 tons of carded wool, 25,000 tons of woollen cloth, 100,000 tons of cotton thread, 60,000 tons of cotton cloth and 30,000 tons of linen thread. However, these industries are passing through a crisis. In ten years the textile industries have made 40,000 people redundant. There were many factory closures between 1952 and 1957, with over twenty cotton spinning mills in Lille and Roubaix-Tourcoing and at least as many weaving mills being closed. On the other hand, metallurgy and the engineering industries, after serious difficulties, have shown some signs of progress. The food processing industries, firmly established in the Lille urban region, are consolidating their position, while certain branches until now of secondary importance, like the paper and printing industries, are making progress. Nevertheless, the industries of the regional metropolis as a whole are in a critical situation and this contributes to a slower growth of the power of decision and the provision of service facilities in the Lille agglomeration.

On either side of the huge industrial complex formed by the coalfield and the Lille urban region which are closely linked by daily journey-to-work movements, there are two important technical and industrial units, namely the heavy industries of the Sambre valley to the east, and the port industrial complex of Dunkerque to the west. The Sambre basin appears as an extension of the Valenciennes iron and steel zone. While the coalfield extends into Belgium to the east of Valenciennes in the direction of Mons, the Sambre valley forms an iron and steel corridor outside the coalfield, aligned along the Paris-Brussels rail route. Aulnoye, Louvroil and Haumont produce 20 per cent of the pig iron and 22 per cent of the steel in the Nord region, nearly half of the rolled finished steel. The manufacture of tubes, and especially tubes for petroleum and gas pipelines, is one of the local specialisations, while Maubeuge deals predominantly with iron sheets and bars. The factories of the Sambre valley employ a total of 40,000 people.

The other extension to the central industrial region of Nord is the Dunkerque group of industries. The port, formerly considered as a service port for the Nord region, has been transformed into an industrial port by the construction of a petroleum refining industry with a throughput capacity of over 5 million tons, and above all by the con-

struction of the highly automated USINOR steelworks, capable of
producing 4 million tons of high grade steel per annum and in the
course of enlargement. The coastal zone as far as the Boulonnais, is
scattered with factories which become denser around the great fishing
port, including iron and steel industries, as at Isbergues, and
employing approximately 15,000 people in manufacturing.

3   Problems and Plans

In spite of appearances, the Nord region does not at present qualify as
a balanced industrial region. In the nineteenth century it was
dominated technically by coal, and financially by the textile
bourgeoisie of Lille and Roubaix. As a result, there were a certain
number of gaps in the general development which are now very apparent. At a time when the coal industry is contracting and the textile
industry is seeking a new level of profitability by amalgamating companies, increasing productivity and cutting down on labour, it is
regrettable that the motivating industries in the forefront of growth are
not all present and adequately represented in the region. High growth
rate industries are exceptional; the electro-technical and electronics industries as yet employ only several thousand workers and qualified
staff in the Lille agglomeration, although the founding of large firms
and amalgamations suggests a new direction, exemplified by the setting up of the Institut Supérieure d'Electronique du Nord and by the
taking over of old textile mills by Alsatian telecommunications companies. Similarly, modern chemical and chemical derivative industries
are poorly represented. Consequently, the gross product has increased
more slowly than the gross national product. The coalfield and the
Lille urban industrial region give the impression of being working class
regions with a relatively low standard of living threatened by partial
unemployment. An indication of this malaise is the inertia of the
building industry.

Social life faithfully reflects economic life. Although considerable
efforts have been made to improve housing conditions, notably during
the reconstruction periods after the two world wars, the towns of the
Nord, especially the 'pseudo-towns' which is what the majority of the
mining and industrial *cités* are, and even large portions of the Lille
agglomeration, provide only mediocre standards of comfort for a population which in other respects too has little experience of modern

living standards. Infant mortality and tuberculosis here reach the highest levels in France. The level of school attendance beyond fifteen is well below the average for France. Although its facilities have been remarkably improved over the last fifteen years, Lille University ranks only sixth in France in an Academy* which comes immediately after Paris in terms of the number of children of school age. The activity of private higher education institutions is not enough to explain this difference. The Catholic university accounts for less than 20 per cent of the Lille student population.† Given the visible characteristics of its economic and social life, the Nord region seems to be an old region, living on the glorious past of its coal and its great mill owners.

As a consequence, the service and distribution activities are not what one would expect to find in such a densely populated and urbanised region. The sale of goods other than foodstuffs has not grown at a comparable rate for this sector in the nation as a whole in the last decade. Shops selling luxury and special articles are less frequent in Lille than in Lyon or Bordeaux, and the entire service provision of all kinds seems slender.

The problem of regional development is therefore on the agenda, but it is difficult to solve because the most important problem is attracting investment and new industries. To stimulate them the government has looked towards operations with multiplier effects. In the first instance new industries must be developed in the coalfield coordinated with the decline in mining which is occurring from the west towards the east of the basin. The dismantling of the mines has accelerated since 1965 and is accompanied by a policy of installing new industries and re-employing the labour force. Initially it involved chemical and chemical based industries especially plastics. Increasingly the car industry is being relied on to exercise a multiplier effect by attracting component industries. Renault and Peugeot operate at Douvrin-La Bassée with 6,700 employees, Simca at Bouchain, between Valenciennes and Cambrai, with 6,000 employees, Chausson at Maubeuge with 600

---

* The administrative subdivision of the French education system, initiated by Napoleon 1, consisting of groupings of *départements* coinciding with university spheres of influence. The Academy of Lille includes the *départements* of Nord and Pas-de-Calais.

† On the other hand the private technical colleges, in the main religious foundations, absorb a larger proportion of the Nord's youth, as for example the Catholic Engineering College, the Institut Supérieur d'Electronique, the Institute of Business Management, the Hautes Etudes Industrielles, the Agricultural College, the School of Journalism, the Roubaix Technical College and the Ecole Nationale Supérieure des Arts et Industries Textiles at Roubaix.

workers, and Renault at Douai with 12,000 employees planned by 1975. Douai has also benefited from the transfer of 3,500 jobs from the Government Printing Office. An enormous effort has been made to improve the infrastructure of transport and business direction to attract new firms. The major canal axis from Valenciennes and the Scheldt to Dunkerque has been increased to 3,000 ton gauge and it is destined to become an axis of location for new industries. The planned development of the terminal zone of the Channel tunnel near Calais is also capable of attracting new firms. All the functions of control and regional communication in the Lille-Roubaix-Tourcoing agglomeration are being reinforced.

4 Lille

In terms of size and intensity of functions, the Lille agglomeration dominates the urban structure of the Nord region. With a population of 881,000 it accounts for rather less than 1 million inhabitants out of the region's 3 million urban dwellers, but the largest agglomerations of the coalfield do not reach 200,000 inhabitants and only their principal nuclei, generally with 30,000 to 50,000 inhabitants, may be considered as real towns, like Douai, Valenciennes, Lens, Bethune and Liévin. The largest towns outside the huge industrial concentrations, Calais, Boulogne and Arras, have under 80,000 inhabitants. The urban function at its highest level seems concentrated, therefore, in Lille, or more exactly in the agglomeration of Lille-Roubaix-Tourcoing, which includes the three towns and forty suburban communes.

The two essential characteristics of the Lille agglomeration, in comparison with the other French regional metropolises, are its peripheral location in relation to its tributary region, and its heterogeneous urban organisation, with its three heads, even though most of the essential functions are centred on Lille. Blocked along the Belgian frontier, with a suburban population of 110,000 in Belgium, the Lille agglomeration cannot achieve total economic control over the Nord region. Many of the region's towns escape its influence and have the bulk of their contacts with Paris. The various indices for measuring urban polarisation, like daily population movements, telephone flows and the transit of goods, define the limits of concentration on Lille. The Lille agglomeration has less power of control than Lyon. Its regional position in relation to the beams of attraction radiated from Paris is partly responsible. In addition, the unity of this large urban organism of a million inhabitants, including the Belgian section, is better expressed as a conurbation than as an agglomeration in the strict sense of the word. The centre of Lille does not seem to be in proportion to the size of the conurbation. It is cramped and in direct contact with old and run-down working class area industrial zones and railway yards, badly linked to the main access roads and the different sections of the urban region. The town of Lille itself seems heterogeneous and without logical order, subject to the pressure of industrial growth rather than following a harmonious plan, and there are still dilapidated enclaves that no one thinks of saving from demolition by a conversion to tourist use.* Open spaces survived until very recently along the major boulevard linking Lille with Roubaix and Tourcoing. Roubaix's activities have for a long time been different from Lille's, and have tried to keep their distance from the economic and financial control of Lille. Plans currently being prepared or applied aim to accelerate the process of unifying the agglomeration by the opening of new urban routeways, a redistribution of administrative and university services, new infrastructure facilities adapted to the city's industrial and commercial functions, the creation of a new urban complex, Lille-Est, with a capacity of 300,000 inhabitants and the opening up of possibilities for the growth of service industries and housing to the south, in the direction of the coalfield and along the Paris motorway. Nevertheless, at present this vast urbanised mass of 30,000 hectares still gives the impression of an intermingling of working class housing, with the industrial areas, railway yards and canal basins characteristic of great industrial regions rather than of a major regional metropolis completely polarised by a nucleus acting as a command post. However, one can find a few quiet retreats with villas shaded by century-old trees, symbols of success on the part of a bourgeoisie which could choose, away from its magnificent but now rather unfashionable town houses, pleasant sites in a landscape which is not by nature very attractive and which is now spoiled by industry.

The possible opening of the Channel tunnel during the 1970s is considered to be a growth factor for the regional economy and especially for the Lille metropolis by exploiting the crossroads function between the north-south Paris-Lille-Brussels-Amsterdam route and the

* Unlike the old centres of cities like Strasbourg or Rouen which have lent themselves to this kind of conversion.

transverse London-Liège-Dusseldorf-Ruhr and Metz-Sarrebruck-Frankfurt axes.

II REGIONAL PROBLEMS IN THE EAST

The regional evolution of Lorraine appears to have two simple alternatives, either a provincial unity built on a regional unit based on Nancy or an industrial combine of iron and coal in the context of the French nation, in other words a union between Lorraine and the Nord region. In fact, a complicated history full of contradictions and internal rifts, means that this choice has been postponed. Provincial unity, which was imperfectly developed before the Revolution of 1789, could not withstand the repeated breaking of the administrative boundaries and national frontiers. There is a Lorraine preserved around Nancy, but it is not the whole of Lorraine, and the more industrialised section of Lorraine is outside the traditional sphere of influence of the Ducal capital,* while Metz and Thionville do not have sufficient power to become metropolises of the industrial regions of northern Lorraine. In spite of projects which on several occasions seemed likely to be carried out, the absence of a high capacity north-east canal providing low cost transport has discouraged attempts to organise an inter-regional Nord-Lorraine complex. Lorraine has looked in other directions across the frontier for energy supplies and coke. The canalised Moselle has made communications with the Saar and the Ruhr easier than in the past. In the context of a regional reconstruction stemming from European economic integration, Lorraine is becoming aware of its position on one of the branches of the North Sea-Mediterranean axis via the Meuse and Moselle valleys and to the south towards the Saône. It is therefore tending to become a separate region, with strong north-south lines, cutting across the lines of centralisation on Paris. The functions of direction and control tend to be located along these strong north-south lines, and especially on the axis of the Meurthe and Moselle. The historical capital, Nancy, which is also the cultural capital and an important economic centre, is far away from the industrial areas which sprang up with the exploitation of iron ore and coal, but it is located at the intersection of major north-south routes with the east-west route from Paris to Strasbourg. Metz, an ancient

* Nancy was the capital of the Duchy of Lorraine.

bishopric and garrison town, aspires to the role of controlling centre for heavy industry and commercial centre for a group of working class *cités* and small towns with altogether 500,000 inhabitants in scattered rectangular grids of small working class houses, in newly built housing blocks, and in small traditional urban centres which now seem anachronistic.

Unevenly endowed by nature, alternating between predominantly clayey damp plains with heavy soils punctuated by meres, exposed stony escarpments crowned with woods, on which valued wines can be produced, and limestone plateaux with little fertile soil, Lorraine has witnessed the continuous decline of its agriculture over the last fifty years, if not in terms of absolute value, at least in relation to the progress of the agricultural revolution in the rest of France. Nowadays the peasantry is sparse, elderly and rather badly equipped, only obtaining crop yields equal to or below the French average in all farming activities. Agriculture has failed to attract investment and industry has robbed it of its labour force.*

Industry had its moment of greatness when the production of Thomas steel brought into use the *minette*† ores of the Nancy, Briey and Longwy basins, especially between the two world wars, within the context of a recovered province,‡ and when the Lorraine coalfield, overcoming the disdain previously felt for it because of its limited ability to produce coke, became the main hope for boosting coal production after the Second World War. However, these moments of glory have always been limited technically and in kind. Lorraine has the distinction of possessing four industrial regions with a minimum of contact between them; the textile and wood-working valleys of the western flanks of the Vosges, the salt deposits, the iron ore field and steelworking valleys of the Côte de Moselle, and the mining region of the Lorraine coalfield.

The vast forests which cover the long and abundantly watered slope of the Vosges Massif on the granite and the permo-triassic cover of red sandstone which envelopes it, have been exploited since early times from the long valley corridors, with lacustrine or grassy bottomlands strung with villages occupied by smallholders combining crops with cattle rearing and woodcutting. The swift flowing waters of

---

* R. Haby, *Les Houillères Lorraines et leur Région*, Paris, S.A.B.R.I., 1965 C. Prêcheur, *La Lorraine Sidérurgique*, Paris, S.A.B.R.I. 1959.

† The name applied to the rather lean phosphoric ores.

‡ With the return of territory occupied by Germany after the Franco-Prussian War.

the upper Moselle, Moselotte, Vologne, Fave, Plaine and the Sarre supplied energy which attracted first sawmills and paper works, then wool spinning and weaving mills. Cotton working spread into the southern Vosges from Alsace after the Treaty of Frankfurt. But there have been severe crises during the twentieth century and whereas industry in the Alsatian valleys sought a solution through a regional reorganisation of production based on Mulhouse, the process of concentration in the Lorraine valleys originated in Paris via the Boussac textiles group. The modernisation process is accompanied everywhere by factory closures and a reduction in employment. Although it is more stable, the wood-working industry which increasingly works for the furniture stores of the Paris region, cannot absorb the excess labour released by the textiles crisis. Moreover, the industrial and urban region of Nancy is nearly a hundred kilometres away from this micro-regional setting which the Vosges towns of Saint-Dié and Epinal, with 25,000 and 50,000 inhabitants respectively, control only at a rudimentary level of service provision and distributive trade.

Salt is found in the Trias of the Lorraine plain and has given its name to the Saulnois area, a confluence region upstream from Nancy where the rivers flowing from the northern Vosges, the Mortagne, Meurthe and Vezouse, unite. It is the domain of the Solvay Company, an international concern with Belgian origins, and of the Saint-Gobain Company, with origins in the Nord region. The salt extraction and soda works have created industrial landscapes, a few concentrations of factories and working populations like Varangéville and Dombasle, built along on the canals which make possible the bulk transport of salt, limestone and coal, but this cannot yet be termed an industrial region. The controlling centres are outside the area, while towns like Lunéville, Château-Salins and Sarrebourg are on the whole not concerned with this branch of industry.

The same inability to create a true regional structure is found on the coalfield. Certainly the massive exploitation of coal, with 15 million tons per annum just before the last war and 13 million tons in 1970, is of recent date, and the late exploitation of this regional resource goes some way towards explaining the impression of improvisation which is created by this fragmented industrial landscape. Coal mines and integrated industries, like the huge chemical complexes and power stations at Carling and Grossbliederstroff, alternate with vast agricultural and forested lands, and small pre-industrial towns, surprised but scarcely changed by the recent appearance of large scale industry on their doorsteps, like Forbach and Saint-Avold. It is a curious *pays*, where the proliferation of housing mainly built by the coalmining industry has not produced towns.

The situation is no different on the iron ore field. Certainly Nancy has benefited from being near the basin in the neck of the Moselle meander around Neuves-Maisons and Pont-Saint-Vincent, but heavy industry has settled elsewhere, at Pompey-Frouard and even at Pont-à-Mousson outside the Nancy ore basin. Moreover, the centre of gravity of the Lorraine ore basin is sixty kilometres to the north of Nancy, between Metz, Thionville and Longwy. Industry has produced its own installations and its own settlement pattern, in the narrow winding valleys of the Côte de Moselle, in the form of chains of long amalgams of factories and workers' housing, as in the Orne and Chiers valleys. Attempts at settlement separate from industry, like Saint-Nicholas-la-Forêt, are exceptional. Industry has brought little to the towns left over from the pre-industrial epoch, except where iron mining and the steel industry coincided with the former urban settlement which, as at Longwy, was rapidly submerged. In turn these towns have contributed little to industrial growth. Industry very rapidly assumed a different dimension from the towns. It was national and even international. At the same time it was limited to a specific sector and to almost exclusive concentration on iron and steel; it seemed to be unconnected with the urban network and played no stimulating role in relation to the development of urban activities. The towns grew only slowly, in spite of their double function as market and garrison towns. Metz, which by its location seems well placed to be the controlling centre of the industrial region, was a town of only 80,000 inhabitants in 1940 in a *département* of 700,000 inhabitants. Today Metz has a population of 170,000 out of a *département* total of nearly a million, and has a serious rival in Thionville, with 136,000 inhabitants. Great importance has been attached to the decision to route the new eastern motorway through Metz, but it might be argued that the speeding up of communications presents as many dangers as advantages. As in the Nord region, and in spite of the greater distance, the attraction of Paris is strong. The full express trains and the way they are used are already evidence of this. Moreover, Nancy also has an increasing role to play. The geographical anomaly of the region has led to the idea of a linear urban complex based on Nancy-Metz-Thionville; the major facilities and functions would be shared out, but Nancy, with 260,000 inhabitants in its agglomeration, seems suited to be the dominant authority. The university and cultural facilities, the distributive trades which are diversified on the scale of a regional metropolis, the variety of employment which is so uncommon in Lorraine and the importance of the location on the rail and road routes to Strasbourg place Nancy clearly at the head of the urban complex, although this does not exclude the growth of Metz and Thionville by virtue of specialised functions.

The structure plan for the Lorraine metropolis, drawn up by the O.R.E.A.M* and approved in 1970, takes into account the various difficulties which the region is undergoing. It envisages the creation of two major industrial zones each capable of supplying 15,000 jobs, one between Metz and Thionville, the other to the north east of Toul, and the unification of the Moselle economic complex by intensifying the north-south communications system, a process already begun by the introduction of a rapid passenger train system called the 'Metrolor'. The plan foresees that two extended agglomerations will be formed: Metz steel district-Thionville, with 600,000 inhabitants in 1968 and 780,000 forecast for 1985, and Nancy-Toul-Lunéville, with 460,000 inhabitants in 1968 and 620,000 forecast for 1985, and the partial reconversion of the coalfield, which involves 250,000 people. Nancy will be expected to receive in particular advanced technology industries, supported by the existing higher level services in the university, advanced technical colleges, laboratories and research centres.

Nevertheless Lorraine will not achieve a sound regional balance unless the iron and steel industry, even if it is strengthened and modernised despite its particular problems, is complemented more than at present by other industries offering a variety of employment opportunities. The presence of food processing industries, biscuit factories, confectionery, breweries and flour milling, and the glass and porcelain industries, the only ones situated outside the Vosges and its foreland, the coalfield and the orefield, are not at present enough to employ all the labour supply, and the female workforce especially.

Alsace has a separate place among the regions of France. It is the most completely structured, and yet this cohesion and the way all its components form a homogeneous and distinctive whole are not due to the effects of the industrial revolution, even though the region did experience them; it stands out today as being one of the regions most representative of Europe as a whole. Alsace is above all an historical region, fashioned by long periods of isolation and constraint into a

* The metropolitan area planning authority.

political and cultural unit which is now seeking an economic reality. A land of peasants and small town bourgeoisie, there are still 500,000 rural dwellers out of a total of just over 1.3 million inhabitants. Alsace has only 8,309 square kilometres, of which 3,500 square kilometres are usable agricultural land. The land has been extensively subdivided and has the most extraordinary strip field pattern to be found in France. It is one of the zones of heavy peasant overpopulation, a land of exodus for generations, but one which has nevertheless maintained high fertility levels. Industry absorbs part of the excess population and labour force in the workshops and factories of small towns like Wissembourg, Hagenau, Saverne, Molsheim, Selstat, Saint-Marie-aux-Mines, Ribeauville, Munster and Thann, in worker-peasant* employment systems or employment of peasant wives and daughters. Industry here appears in forms which are unique in character in France and which may just possibly be compared with certain methods of employment found in the Lyon region before the 1930s. The crises are severe, however, and the valleys of the southern Vosges, which were equipped with cotton spinning and weaving mills by Mulhouse, suffer chronic under-employment accompanying the amalgamation and rationalisation of firms.

The former economic and social organisation, which was highly decentralised in the life of large villages and small towns, is now contracting and being reorganised around the large towns, which in turn are becoming centres for reanimating the little towns on the basis of changed functions and modernisation.

At first sight the region appears to have a double character. Firstly, Upper Alsace has the cotton industry, potash mines, the small-scale farming of the Sundgau, and Mulhouse as the centre, with 199,000 inhabitants. The area does not escape the influence of the neighbouring Swiss city of Basle, whose agglomeration reaches into Alsatian territory in Saint-Louis and Huningue. Secondly, Lower Alsace is a loessic region, with grain farming, hop gardens and the Rhine port of Strasbourg with 334,000 inhabitants. At the junction between the two regions, Colmar with 65,000 inhabitants, capital of the vineyard area, has its distinctive character and its own sphere of influence, at least in specific fields and notably in the Alsatian wine business. In fact, this division of Alsace, real though it is, only underlies a unity centred on Strasbourg and with the Rhine as its axis.

The small twelfth century town which at that time had 5,000 in-

* i.e. part-time farm work combined with an industrial job.

habitants but already had an active bourgeoisie of artisans and merchants, has asserted itself through varied and often dramatic events as a great Rhine city. As such it has become an industrial town; moreover, this is as much by investments from outside the region and even outside France* as by the initiative of the Strasbourg bourgeoisie. It is also in its capacity as a Rhine town that it acquires a European function. The Strasbourg agglomeration now features as a port, industrial town and regional metropolis, with a greater degree of power than might be automatically expected from the control of a region of some 8,000 square kilometres and less than a million and a half inhabitants. Strasbourg owes this power to its Rhineland and European scope, which stretches beyond the regional boundaries and gives it an international function in culture, science and politics. It has major regional banks and national banking companies, warehouses and commercial companies with influence radiating over the whole of the Rhineland and the neighbouring French regions of Lorraine and Franche-Comté, and also one of the great French provincial universities with all its accompanying scientific facilities. Direction and service activities employ 50,000 people. Strasbourg is also a major industrial city in which 40,000 urban dwellers work with 20,000 commuters from the environs and the neighbouring small towns. The industries are partly linked to the presence of products handled by the port and partly founded by companies seeking easy transport by canal, rail and the node of main roads and easy recruitment of labour. Partly, too, industry is a heritage of the former urban artisan activities. The main industries represented are the food industries, with huge mills, breweries, jam making and confectionery, wood industries, cellulose, paper, leather working, and above all engineering and metalworking industries, forges, motor and machine construction and the manufacture of electrical machinery.

The Strasbourg agglomeration is fundamentally different from most of France's cities and agglomerations, in the first place because of its very large expanse of 14,500 hectares. Only the old town, an historic tourist centre which also still has some of the classic functions of a central business district, is tightly clustered around the cathedral in a network of canals. In 1870 Strasbourg covered only 202 hectares with a population of 70,000 inhabitants. A new town was built in a very open geometric style during the German period, with a much lower density of 300 to 500 persons per hectare, falling to 200 in the middle

* During the period of the separation from France.

class residential districts. The city expanded progressively between the two wars in the direction of the Rhine and away from the railway station. This extension is now being completed by the building up of the Esplanade military land. The suburbs form a bunch of separate nodes of urbanisation, separated by a loose pattern of woods, market gardens and agricultural zones. The suburb of Schiltigheim has 25,000 inhabitants, and with Bischeim, 37,000. Neudorf and la Meinau have a little over 50,000 inhabitants and there are a dozen other urbanised communes, occupied initially by detached houses but where *cités* of appartment blocks of the *grand ensemble* type are springing up. Strasbourg is an expanding agglomeration in the process of complete transformation.

Leaving aside the character of Alsace itself, if one tries to define the place of this small but exceptionally active region in France and in western Europe, one finds that its location along the major transverse axis of the continent is the principal cause of its importance and the essential factor which makes it distinctive. Unfortunately the canal is still a cul-de-sac. It serves Basle, which the construction of the Grand Canal d'Alsace has made accessible to 2,000 ton barges, but the links with the Rhône are nominal, and the Saône itself, with its capacity limited to 300 ton units, cannot at present serve as a link between the two rivers. The main function of the Rhine here is the production of energy. Four billion kWh are delivered annually to the grid system by the five power stations of Kembs, Ottmarsheim, Fessenheim, Vogelgrün and Markolsheim, arranged in a chain and soon to be reinforced by a sixth power station at Rhinau. The passage of the major pipeline,* carrying crude petroleum from the Mediterranean to the refineries of Strasbourg and the Palatinate, defines the function of Alsace as an energy crossroads, and of Strasbourg in particular. The industrial vocation of Alsace and of its metropolis, Strasbourg, seems likely to express itself during the next decades in the context of the development of European contacts along the Rhine axis. The existence in the area of a stable and extremely large and fertile rural population is related to this achievement.

III   THE LYON REGION, THE RHONE-ALPES REGION

The third really coherent major French region is the Lyon region. It is defined not in relation to natural crude resources, but as a result of

* The South European pipeline.

organisational and productive action by the Lyon bourgeoisie, encouraged by the natural tendencies of a great crossroads of routeways. The region's boundaries have varied in the course of the last 150 years.

Before the development of large scale industry, Lyon was a town of cloth merchants, directing the production of thread and weaving and known as *fabricants*. The making of silk in Lyon, like the old printing trades, was initially an essentially urban function. The social crises of the first half of the nineteenth century brought about an integration of the Lyon economy with the whole of the poor regions surrounding the town and supplying both pools of cheap labour and the driving power of the numerous rivers; the Albarine in the southern Jura, Azergues and Brévenne in the Lyonnais uplands, and the Bourbre in Bas-Dauphiné for example. In the period up until the First World War a Lyon region in the strict sense was established, assimilating new techniques; it maintained and widened its industrial and commercial position by a succession of changes. Electrical energy was substituted for water power, artificial textiles were combined with silk and the chemical industries developed from the original firms processing pyrites from the Lyonnais uplands at Sain Bel* and from the manufacture of dyes. The Lyon region remained no more than an aggregate of *pays,* in the sense of physical and historical geography; the Lyonnais uplands, the Massif du Pilat, Southern Beaujolais, the Dombe and its flanks, the Mont-d'Or Massif, the base of the Saône plain, the southern Jura, Bas-Dauphiné and the basins of the middle Rhône as far as the entry to the Valence plain, extending into three *départements* and covering a little under 10,000 square kilometres.

Two other units, at different distances from Lyon, assumed a distinctive character, the Saint-Etienne coalfield region, fifty kilometres from Lyon and with a different physical, economic and social setting, and the major region of the northern Alps. The latter is at least one and a half times as large as the Lyon region, but it is centred on several nuclei and valley axes equipped with electrical energy which supply a complex of new industries derived from the technological applications of electricity, like electrometallurgy and the electro-chemicals industry, stimulating totally new kinds of research of which Grenoble has become both the centre and the symbol.

According to the traditional images of regional life, the three towns of Lyon, Saint-Etienne and Grenoble were seen until the Second

* In the Brévenne valley, north-west of Lyon.

World War as having specifically different, though rival, positions in relation to technology and the exercise of control. The realities of the post-war period and the European horizon have posed direct problems. In the Saint-Etienne region these are the crisis in the coalfield and in the traditional textile industries. There is a paradox, often hidden, in the expansion of Grenoble, where the cost of growth has been the loss of the last forms of local and regional economic and financial independence, while Savoie is fortunate in being able to combine reconverting its traditional industries with acquiring decentralised firms and the expansion of mass tourism.

The dispersal of initiative and the contraction of activities to medium sized centres are factors which lead to sterilisation. Given the counterweight of Paris on a national level, neither the Lyon agglomeration with a million inhabitants, nor the Saint-Etienne region with 600,000 and the Grenoble urban region of 300,000, nor even the vast mountain region of the Northern Alps with a million inhabitants, can be considered equivalent to a Frankfurt or Milan region. The basis for real economic power exists, but this power can only come from a regrouping into a region of over 40,000 square kilometres and with 4.5 million inhabitants (the planning region of 'Rhône-Alpes'), or even from a region which also absorbs part of the Saône et Loire *département,* giving 45,000 square kilometres and approximately 5 million inhabitants. This would cover 8 per cent of the nation's land area, 10 per cent of the population, 10 per cent of the employment and 15 per cent of employment in the provinces, 7.5 per cent of the business turnover achieved by French companies and 15 per cent of those directed from the provinces. It would account for 16 per cent of the nation's electricity consumption and 25 per cent of that consumed in the provinces, with a little under 15 per cent of the urban population of the French provinces.

1　The Exploitation of Energy

The Rhône-Alpes or South East Central region has in turn mobilised its solid mineral fuel resources, its hydro-electricity potential and exploited the easy links with the importing bases of petroleum products on the Mediterranean coast. It also benefits from being served by natural gas from south-west France.

Coal was supplied by three fields; the Blanzy basin incorporating

Blanzy, Montceau-les-Mines-Montchanin, the Loire basin and the Dauphiné basin of La Mure. All these fields are difficult to exploit, and the reserves and mining conditions do not justify large investments and systematic modernisation. Output has gradually declined; at Blanzy from a maximum of 2.7 million tons in 1958–59 to an annual level in the order of 2 million tons at the beginning of 1970, at Saint-Etienne from 3.5 million tons on average throughout the first half of this century to 1.5 million tons, with only one mine still producing and complete closure imminent. Coal extraction is suspended at La Mure. A proportion of the remaining output is burned locally in coalfield power stations with a total capacity of 325,000 KW. Two major power stations each of 250,000 KW capacity built by the nationalised electricity industry, one beside the Saône at Chalon-sur-Saône using coal from Blanzy, and the other at Givors on the Rhône absorbing the output of the Saint-Etienne field, bring the total electrical energy at present supplied from thermal power stations to over 5 billion KWh. Natural gas and petroleum refinery gas contribute over 1.5 billion thermal units. The refinery of Feyzin* treats crude petroleum arriving by pipeline from the Mediterranean which transports approximately 4 million tons per annum, but the region still receives refined products from the Etang de Berre refineries, mainly by canal, both for use in power stations and in the Lyon chemical industries.

The region's chief distinctive feature in relation to energy is its important hydro-electricity supplies of over 25 billion KWh. Half is supplied by mountain power stations in the Alps and the other half by the stations belonging to the Compagnie Nationale du Rhône at Génissiat upstream from Lyon, Bourg-lès-Valence, Beauchastel, Baix-Logis-Neuf, Châteauneuf-du-Rhône and Bollène downstream, and recently at Pierre-Bénite on the edge of the Lyon agglomeration. The production capacity of the middle Rhône power stations, including the thermal plants, exceeds 30 billion KWh, or over 20 per cent of the national energy production. This allows both the development of industries consuming large amounts of electricity, like electro-metallurgy, electro-chemicals, and the manufacture of aluminium, and the exporting of current to other French regions, especially to the Paris region. The energy supply position will be increased, before 1975, by a nuclear plant modelled on those of Touraine† at Saint-

---

* On the southern fringe of Lyon.
† Chinon and Saint-Laurent-des-Eaux in the middle Loire valley.

Vulbas in the *département* of Ain with an installed capacity of 400,000 KW and a production capacity of 3 billion KWh per annum.

It is too early yet to see the Rhône-Alpes region as a bloc. It is not even certain that such a bloc will materialise in the short term. Although an economic union is being established between Lyon and the Saint-Etienne region, after generations of independence and mistrust, the Grenoble firms are magnetised by the major direction and development centres in the electrical and electro-technical industries, Beifort and Paris; up until now, Grenoble has apparently preferred to accept as inevitable the initiatives and attractions of Paris rather than try to protect its autonomy within the context of a true Greater Lyon city region. In an analysis of the present situation one must therefore examine the elements in a potential Greater Lyon Region, corresponding with the Rhône-Alpes planning region, enlarged by part of the Saône-et-Loire *département* which is administratively attached to the planning region of Bourgogne.

2 The Lyon Agglomeration and its Environment

The Lyon agglomeration contains over a million inhabitants, provides work and attracts daily population movement over a radius of thirty to forty kilometres, representing a population mass in the order of a million and a half people. This restricted* Lyon region is one of the most individual and lively in France. Historically, and even now socially, it has been dominated by a class of businessmen which refused to abdicate in the face of the centralisation on Paris. Obviously, there is no longer any question of independence on the part of Lyon's capital resources, and the Lyon stock exchange cuts a sorry figure, but the financial and administrative autonomy of her firms is still a reality. The counter offensives of Lyon based firms on the national market are by no means negligible. Their catalysing effect at the level of the Lyon metropolitan region is the best rejoinder to the process of concentration. This is why one must go beyond the traditional image of the Lyon economy. It is no longer by virtue of the silk and textile industries that Lyon maintains and can extend its regional sovereignty. It is through the chemical industry which instigates changes in the traditional industries such as the replacement of traditional textiles by artificial and synthetic textiles, the electrical

* As opposed to the wider city region for which Lyon acts as metropole.

construction industries amounting to nearly 10 per cent of the French output in this branch, and the engineering industries, like the Berliet lorry company, the manufacture of civil engineering machinery and industrial plant. Nevertheless, the textile industry was at the origin of the foundation of the Lyon bourgeoisie, which now leads the region's business and is negotiating for the creation of a major region on a European scale. Some significant names evoke this creative power, which has greatly expanded beyond the context of the former textile industry; Gillet, Péchiney, Berliet, Usines du Rhône, Crédit Lyonnais and Société Lyonnaise des Dépôts.*

In the sphere of commerce, Lyon has become the collecting, processing and distribution centre for an area which has rapidly extended beyond the limits of the immediate Lyon zone. This zone is itself expanding by the proliferation of factories. To the north along the Saône it stretches beyond Villefranche and even Belleville. To the south, the chemical industry has gradually colonised the plains and basins of the Middle Rhône as far as Valence, which was one of the most rapidly expanding towns in France between 1962 and 1968, with a 21 per cent growth rate from 75,000 to 92,000 inhabitants. There is no longer any break with the Saint-Etienne region which abuts on to the Rhône at Givors opposite the metallurgical factories of Chasse. In Bas-Dauphiné the no-man's-land between the Lyon agglomeration and the Grenoble region is more marked between Bourgoin and Voiron.

The main present day activities, by numbers employed in descending order, are the metallurgical industry, with over 40 per cent of the industrial work force, the textile industry with 16 per cent, the building industry with 15 per cent and the chemical industry with 13 per cent. In terms of business turnover, the chemical industry moves into second place, close behind metallurgy and a long way ahead of textiles. It is the most diversified, modern and technologically based industry, and as a result the executive class tends to be one of engineers and laboratory directors, replacing the former bourgeoisie of merchants, financiers and travellers. In this respect Lyon is moving closer to Grenoble (but is orientated towards chemicals whereas Grenoble is centred more on electro-technical and electronic activities), even though it was metallurgy which took the leading position in the old silk merchant city of Lyon. In terms of industry, Lyon is a centre with a complete range from which few branches are missing. The scale is in

---

* Prominent companies at a national level in chemicals, engineering and banking.

the order of 300,000 industrial workers. The tertiary sector, excluding the tertiary workers in industry such as industrial laboratory and research staff, amounts to roughly the same size as the industrial work force. It includes workers in trade, public and private services, administration and the professions.

3   The Saint-Etienne Region

The Saint-Etienne region corresponds with the topographic and structural depression between the Loire and the Rhône, from Firminy to Givors, between the Lyonnais uplands and the Mont Pilat range, and occupied in part by the 'black country' of the coalfield. It has an area of 3,758 square kilometres, and approximately 600,000 inhabitants of whom four fifths are urban dwellers. The main centres of the conurbation are Saint-Etienne, with 331,000 inhabitants, Firminy to the west with 30,000 inhabitants and Saint-Chamond to the east with 73,000 in its agglomeration. Two thirds of the working population are employed in industry. Almost all this industry is in a critical state. Over three quarters of the industrial labour force work in three branches; metallurgy, mining and textiles. The mines employ 10 per cent of the industrial labour force, textiles 10 per cent and metallurgy a little over 51 per cent. The present difficulties do not merely affect the coal mines and textiles, as in the Nord region. Metal working is represented here by traditional manufactures which, through lack of conversion, are seeing a decline of their markets. The predominant manufactures are light armaments, cycles and hand tools. The industrial structure is old and difficult to adapt to new types of production. The number of artisans working as sub-contractors for large firms remains high in Saint-Etienne itself and in Firminy, Chambon-Feugerolle and Saint-Bonnet-le-Château. Wages are low, female employment is scarce and family incomes are small.

The first problem is the re-employment of the miners. The power station and coke works of Chambon-Feugerolle are condemned to disappear. Lacq natural gas has already replaced coal in the major firms. The arms, cycles, hand tool, silk ribbon and straw hat industries see their clientele getting smaller daily. The region's future lies in a general reconversion requiring more use of synthetic products in light industry and renewing the range of engineering goods. Such a reconversion assumes a restructuring of finance and management systems. Amalgamations have taken place, as in the case of the merger of the forges and steelworks of La Marine and of Firminy, the steelworks of Saint-Etienne and the Jacob Holtzer company, to form the Compagnie des Ateliers et Forges de la Loire, which immediately created research laboratories and offices for improving new special steels for the ballistic and nuclear industries. In the space of a few years, Saint-Etienne has become one of the principal French research centres in the field of steel manufacture and metallurgy. At the same time, hunting guns and light arms factories have changed over to toy making, which is tending to become one of the region's industrial specialities, especially in Firminy. Only the venerable Manufacture d'Armes de Saint-Etienne remains loyal to its tradition. The textile industry and the artisans practising their trades at home all around the conurbation are also changing very little.

The Saint-Etienne region suffers from having been one of the first French mining and metallurgical districts, and also from having had semi-rural high-class artisan activity from a very early date. It has grown old within the narrow confines of the old mountain furrow with its smoke and soot. It lacks water. Far from attracting modern industries and their highly qualified employees, it repels them. An enormous cleaning up job is essential. This has been resolutely undertaken in Firminy, which prides itself on being a pilot centre for urban renewal in industrial environments. Regrouping of communes have made possible town planning in Saint-Chamond and Saint-Etienne. New neighbourhoods have sprung up on the slopes of Mont Pilat. The difficult and slow traffic conditions, channelled along narrow streets, have been improved by the opening of the motorway between the Loire and Rhône which provides an easy link with the Lyon agglomeration.

A labour force used to all kinds of industrial work and accustomed traditionally to frequent conversions, infrastructures which are being modernised and fertile contacts with a mountain hinterland which also supplies reserves of skilled artisan workers, make it easier for the Saint-Etienne region, as it undergoes renewal, to be integrated into the major Lyon complex without capitulating and to make a contribution in quantity and quality which places it at a high level in the hierarchy of French and European urban-industrial complexes. The entire urban region of Saint-Etienne and Lyon exceeds 1.5 million inhabitants at the heart of a framework of *pays* which has over two million inhabitants dominated by the economic activity of the two cities.

4 The Northern Alps

In contrast to the old *pays* of Saint-Etienne, the Northern Alps, which have more recently reached the stage of modern industry through electricity, give the impression of being an industrial pioneer front and a zone of fast expanding tourism. Everything here seems to progress without obstacles, although a more careful examination reveals contradictions and difficulties in adapting to an extremely rapid, and in some respects, authoritarian evolution. The principal centre and the most prominent town is Grenoble, but Savoie also contributes to this major alpine development, far to the east of the Lyon and Saint-Etienne heartland.

5 The Grenoble Region

A lively town, technically and economically controlling the development, especially the industrial development, of the major northern alpine corridors since the First World War, Grenoble has become since the Second World War the target for decentralised firms. Its rapid expansion and the success of its firms seem to give the lie to the inevitability of the processes of centralisation. A provincial capital of 60,000 inhabitants at the beginning of the century, Grenoble only topped 100,000 inhabitants just before the Second World War. In 1962, the agglomeration approached 250,000 inhabitants and now exceeds 330,000.

The building developments carried out in the town and the sports zone of the Grenoble Olympics on the occasion of the 1968 Winter Games, have made it one of the leading areas for winter sports and have accelerated the physical planning of the old industrial, commercial and cultural metropolis of the Northern Alps. Grenoble is in fact the epitome of the Northern Alps. Even when it does not act as the controlling centre, everything that exists in the Northern Alps and everything affecting their economic, social and cultural life, is reflected in Grenoble.

The initial development was triggered by hydro-electricity plant. Until the beginning of the century, the capital of Dauphiné was the chief mountain market because of its excellent situation at the gateway to the Alps and at the crossroads of the major glacial valleys of the Northern Alps intersecting the sub-alpine furrow. Its only industries were glove and straw hat manufacture. The far-sightedness of a small group of businessmen, aware of the prospects of a new specialised industry by the opening of the hydro-electric plants, placed Grenoble in the first rank of French industrial towns. The names of Joya, Bouchayer, Viallet, Brenier, Neyret, Beylier, and later of Merlin and Gérin are associated with this phase of industrial development. The metal-using industries, producing high pressure tubing, turbines and electrical plant, expanded as the mountains got electricity and were industrialised. This expansion encouraged other branches of activity as they became aware of what the comprehensive exploitation of the mountain had to offer to them. Glove making was transformed; the previously artisan based textile activity became industrialised and processed artificial silk. The food processing industry, created on a modest scale during the First World War, spread in the shape of the biscuit factories of Brun, the Cémoi chocolate company and the pasta products of the Lustucru company.

In 1931 there were 25,000 workers in Grenoble. Today Grenoble's industries employ nearly 60,000. The metallurgical and precision electrical engineering industries followed, and sometimes lead, the evolution of the market, acquiring an international clientele and reputation symbolised by the Neyrpic company. Grenoble is now one of the centres of the French electronics industry, based on the Saint-Egrève plant. The demand from dam construction sites and factories in the mountains, and also from the building industry in the continually expanding town, stimulated the creation of factories manufacturing civil engineering plant. The Progil factory at Pont-de-Claix, combined with the Ugine company and the German firm of Bayer, is one of the largest chemicals firms in France. The textiles industries have also attained an international rank with the Valisère firm. Glove making, by the Perrin company, has subsidiaries in the Anglo-Saxon countries. Through the sphere of influence of its industries in France* and abroad, Grenoble gives the impression of a provincial city which, by its vitality, has its own dependent network of centres outside the Paris network and even that of the neighbouring major regional metropole of Lyon.

To a large degree, Grenoble owes its total success to the association between the university and industry, which has since been emulated elsewhere. For the last fifty years, Grenoble university has taken as

---

* The Valisère company for example has factories in the Berry and Vivarais regions.

the theme of its research, from the department of alpine geography to the applied schools of the science faculty, the development of the mountains and all technology related to electricity. In this specialisation it has found the means of expansion and has contributed in very large measure to the concentration in Grenoble of applied industrial research. In this context the university has played a decisive role in the location of industrial laboratories, research offices and headquarters. It is imitated in that it encourages industrial research within the framework of firms themselves, as for example the Société Grenobloise d'Etudes et d'Applications Hydrauliques, which is a department of the Neyrpic company and has done work for the whole world and registered over a thousand patents, or the Grenoble Centre of Nuclear Studies, which combines university research with research for private firms. Other examples are the Centre of Cryogenic Studies belonging to the Air Liquide Company, the Magnetic Study and Research Company, an affiliate of the Ugine and Allevard metallurgical companies, and the Péchiney chemicals company laboratories. The importance of research and higher education in all its aspects is symbolised in the creation of a university campus at Saint-Martin-d'Hères in the Isère Valley upstream from Grenoble.

The ambiguity of this success, from the point of view of regional economic organisation cannot, however, be concealed. The more Grenoble expands its industrial base, the more the disparity between the provincial scale of operation and the national scale acts in favour of centralisation. The firm of Bouchayer-Viallet has had to amalgamate with the Forges et Ateliers du Creusot, in order to increase its capacity and acquire increasingly expensive production and research techniques, and as a consequence it has had to accept the transfer of some of its normal activity to Chalon-sur-Saône. Apparently because of its strength and its international scope, Merlin-Gérin is losing its autonomy. Neyrpic is integrated with the Alsthom company.* The local market for civil engineering plant is dominated by the American Caterpillar Corporation, the chemical industry is controlled by the German Bayer Company and the Brun Company's activity is no longer directed from Grenoble.

In these circumstances, it might seem tempting to rediscover a new activity, based specifically on Grenoble, in tourism. Grenoble can already claim a high rank in this field. It is one of the principal dis-

---

* One of the giants of the French electrical engineering industry with its main factory in Belfort and branches elsewhere.

tribution centres for winter and summer tourism, and it played an important part in hotel construction and the organisation of tourist transport in the Northern Alps. Grenoble capitalises on its site and on its situation close to famous mountain resorts and the main excursion itineraries to attract many meetings and conferences of all kinds; there has been a major effort to provide hotel accommodation, as well as the constant activity of the Hotel Management College based on the Hôtel Lesdiguières. The preparations for the Winter Olympic Games of 1968 stimulated a major programme of innovation in the town and large sports complexes, which have given a new boost to the town but which demand heavy sacrifices which must be made good by a new increase in the value of the gross local output. Unfortunately there is again the same ambiguity as with industrial development. The installation of important winter sports centres, the construction of cable cars and ski lifts and the organisation of tourist itineraries starting from Paris, Lyon or on behalf of foreign agencies are more and more tending to by-pass the local tourist organisation centres which now merely have to provide accommodation information and distribute the clientele from elsewhere.* The bulk of the returns accrue to banking, business and industrial investment companies involved in recreation and tourism, the majority of which are located outside the region. The fact remains that the growing flow of tourists and sports enthusiasts at Chamrousse, l'Alpe d'Huez and l'Alpe du Grand-Serre, and at a lower level, Villard de Lans, Saint-Nizier and Sappey, bring a certain amount of income to Grenoble and its region. This is reflected in the commercial, financial and administrative activities of the town. 5,000 people are employed in administration and public services, 2,000 in banks and finance occupations, 10,000 in trading, especially in the retail trade which handles a very wide range of goods from articles necessary for everyday use for the majority of the town's population to the luxury articles bought by certain categories of tourists. Two local banks still operate in Grenoble, Nicolet Lafanechère and the Banque de l'Isère, but it is particularly in the realms of politics and culture that Grenoble retains most successfully its position as a regional capital, with thirty-two editions of the *Dauphiné Libéré*† and two major publishing houses, Arthaud and Didier-Richard, which rank highly in the national market.

* One might almost say there is a sub-contracting of the tourist industry to Grenoble.

† The regional newspaper, with a circulation of over 500,000 copies a day.

With a continually increasing young population, coming not only from the Alps but from all over France, the town is changing rapidly. Old Grenoble is now only a historic town which no longer has city centre functions. Trade and business are concentrated on the edge of the old town around the Place Grenette and on the main boulevards. The middle and working class town of the early twentieth century and inter-war years has been overwhelmed by recent expansion. The railway, which formed an intolerable barrier between the nineteenth century town and the new districts beside the River Drac, has been raised on a viaduct and the old railway station is to be transferred. New suburbs are spreading urbanisation into the Grésivaudan, the Drac plain, around the disused airport of Echirolles. Industry extends as far as Pont-de-Claix in the south, Saint-Martin-d'Hères in the east and upstream to Saint-Egrève. An urban complex of a million inhabitants is already being envisaged partly based on satellite towns centred on Voiron and Mormoiron. Grenoble is gambling on the future. In the course of its history it has never lost.

6 *The Savoie Mountain Front*

The northern portion of the Alps escapes the control of Grenoble and is situated at a distance from Lyon's enterprises. However, it is more open to influences coming on the one hand directly from Paris, and on the other from Geneva.

Industry, tourism and lively commercial activity based on productive and diversified agriculture in the Alpine foreland, reproduce in a scattered form the conditions which are found in a concentrated form in Grenoble. Industry appears both in the form of traditional activities converted to a highly skilled production with an international clientele, as in the manufacture of screws and bolt fittings in the Arve valley at Cluses and Bonneville, and the classic activities using electrical energy in the Chedde complex, the Arly valley and Ugine, and in the form of decentralised activity, which has found suitable roots in local firms and a pleasant environment in which to set up new factories. Examples of this latter category are the ball bearing works of a Renault subsidiary, the Gillette company and the Société Alsacienne de Mécanique et d'Electronique at Annecy. The tourist industry is also diversified, with the spa development at Aix-les-Bains, summer tourism on Lake Annecy and the French shore of Lake Geneva and in the intermediate mountain zone of the Pre Alps, especially the Chablais ranges, winter sports at Saint-Gervais, Megève, and, at the head of the hierarchy of tourist centres, Chamonix. The nearness of Mont Blanc means that Chamonix has a large number of visitors at all seasons, and it now benefits from the tunnel under the Mont Blanc range as much as from the exceptional facilities for reaching the mountain heights. The real affiliations between the major valleys and Alpine foreland of Savoie and the Rhône-Alpes metropole are unclear. Paris and Switzerland seem as close in spirit and distance as Lyon, but nevertheless the Savoie Alps fall within the zone which the people of Lyon visit and in which they invest.

7 The Rhine–Rhône Axis

The Rhône is a link between *pays* which are still strongly autonomous and attached to their provincial tradition, more as a valley routeway, even though it is still imperfect, than by inland navigation, which is insignificant above Lyon and very disparate in the Saône-Middle Rhône sector, in spite of the improvements carried out by the Compagnie Nationale du Rhône. Obviously it is an important European location; the crossroads of routes from Italy via the Great Saint-Bernard and Mont-Cenis passes, from Switzerland via the Savoie foreland and the *cluses* of the Southern Jura, and from Auvergne across the Lyonnais uplands or via the Saint-Etienne depression, with the Rhine-Middle and Lower Rhône axis. The Rhône valley is gradually assuming the technical and economic importance for which it is naturally suited. The expansion of Lyon's industries as far as Valence, which in a short space of time has become an agglomeration of over 80,000 inhabitants, and the improvements carried out by the Compagnie Nationale du Rhône, which have encouraged various types of growth in the middle course of the valley, for example the creation of the Marcoule atomic plant and the Pierrelatte nuclear centre, and are stimulating the expansion of Montelimar, Orange and of Avignon, the latter now exceeding 100,000 inhabitants, are giving a new significance to this major natural axis. It has become an important communications belt in the course of the last two decades, with the navigable Rhône and loop canals,* the electrified railway now capable of taking heavy high speed train loads, with the motorway south from

* By-passing the power schemes.

Lyon and the Marseille-Lyon-Strasbourg oil pipeline. The facilities of the Saône plain are still backward, in spite of the large investment made at Chalon, especially to speed up the reconversion of the Chalon-Montceau-les-Mines-Blanzy industrial zone, but development has been set in motion and is certainly irreversible; this is the great opportunity for Lyon to fulfil its vocation as a centre of regional polarisation on a large scale.

8 Lyon, Regional Metropolis and Major City

For Lyon to become the uncontested metropolis of one of the most active French regional groupings, or at least uncontested except on the fringes of its sphere of influence, it must play the role of a very large city on a European scale and it is endeavouring to do so. This large city of a million inhabitants has, stage by stage, spread over the contrasted zones of its original site: the hills overlooking the confluence of the Rhône and Saône on the right bank of the Saône at Saint-Just and Fourvière, the interfluvial plain of the confluence, Brotteaux and Bellecour, extended to the south by the development of Perrache, and upstream from Brotteaux on the Croix-Rousse plateau, still between the two rivers. Once the stigma of being in a foreign land belonging to the ancient imperial bank had been effaced, Lyon extended on to the lowlands of the left bank of the Rhône. Industries occupied the river banks on both sides downstream from the confluence, in Gerland, Saint-Fons and Feyzin on the left bank and Pierre-Bénite, Caluire-et-Cuire on the right bank, and also the Bas-Dauphiné plain at Venissieux, with its Berliet lorry factory, and Decines. Now the city is mounting an assault on the hills, and *grands ensembles* are being built in Montessuy-Caluire above Croix-Rousse between the Rhône and Saône and at la Duchère on the right bank of the Saône above Vaise. Suburbs of detached housing are infiltrating the little valleys of Mont-d'Or and the Costière de Dombes, nibbling away at orchards and market gardens. The city is also expanding on the lowland towards Bas-Dauphiné beyond Villeurbanne, La Guillotière and Montplaisir to Bron-Parilly. Commercial activity is itself leaving Bellecour and Les Brotteaux to form clusters on the edge of the agglomeration in peripheral commercial centres to serve the suburban clientele and to intercept customers from outside. In spite of this the city centre is still dense, crowded proudly along the quaysides, with bridges which are constantly enlarged and modernised; the problem has not been solved of renovating old Lyon, which still dominates the Saône from the top of its *ficelles** and under which the road tunnels of Fourvières and Croix-Rousse pass.

Nevertheless, an attempt is now being made to ease congestion in the central business district, the district of the Place Bellecour and the Place des Terreaux, by building a new office centre in an urban renewal zone on the left bank of the Rhône at la Part-Dieu. The metropolitan structure plan also envisages two new towns to encourage industrial and residential decentralisation, at l'Isle d'Abbeau, in Bas-Dauphiné to the west of Bourgoin, and at Meximieux, above the confluence of the Ain and Rhône. Between these new towns and the existing agglomeration a new international airport will be built to replace Bron airport.

IV   THE MEDITERRANEAN REGION

A Mediterranean region undeniably exists in France, but it is a natural, historical and cultural region. Paradoxically it is the region of France which has the most character and yet it is not really an economic region and does not have a structured network or hierarchy of urban poles defining an organised or organic region. The paradox is heightened by the fact that it possesses an agglomeration which has the dimensions of a regional metropolis without actually being one – the Marseille agglomeration which is formed around its function as a national commercial port with colonial contacts.

Physical geography, the use of the land and the natural environment, has revealed two different units, which are also two different historical units; Bas-Languedoc to the west of the Rhône and Provence, Comtat-Venaissin and the Comté de Nice to the east. Since the reconstruction of the vineyard area after the phylloxera crisis a little less than a century ago, Bas-Languedoc has become a wine producing area. Its towns are above all wine markets, while retaining other functions from their past, such as artisan and trading activities in Nîmes, and legal and administrative functions in Montpellier. Provence and the former Comté de Nice have developed the tourist

---

* The familiar name given by the people of Lyon to the funiculars which climb the slopes of Fourvières and Croix-Rousse.

function. The interior here has been increasingly depopulated and all economic activity is concentrated along the coastal margin, with the exception of a rural economy in the interior basins based on viticulture and fruit trees, and in the Grasse area on flower cultivation. Population is clustered along the coast in a string of small and large towns which are overcrowded in the summer season by the flood of tourists to the seaside.

A special place is held by the terminus of the Rhône corridor at the coast. The coastal façade, the delta coast of the Camargue, until recently acted as a dead end. France's most extensive commune, Arles, is practically empty outside its capital, the town of Arles. The botanical and zoological reservations, the salt marshes of Salins-les-Giraud, the watery pasture ranges of the bulls, the rice fields and vineyards to the north of the Etang de Vaccarès, are almost empty from the point of view of settlement. It will probably not always remain like this if the tourist development of the huge beaches of Saintes-Maries-de-la-Mer and the construction of the steel complex on the Gulf of Fos, already operating as a tanker terminal for vessels of over 100,000 tons, are completed. For the present, however, the outlet of the Rhône corridor is outside the delta, beyond the hills bordering the stony wilderness of the Crau to the south and east, via the Etang de Berre, which is the largest centre in France for petroleum handling and the site of the Berre-Lavéra-La Mède refinery complex, and on the other side of the Estaque range, via the port of Marseille. In spite of frequently expressed intentions, and engineering works like the cutting of the Rove tunnel between the port of Marseille and the Etang de Berre at the beginning of the 1930s, which have come to nothing, France's largest port still has no waterway link to the Rhône, which until the middle of this century could not be used by large barges, and was only navigated by picturesque paddle boats. Marseille's traffic, as a colonial port handling relatively light and high value freight, and the existence in the town of industries processing the bulk imports into more refined products, made having a waterway for bulk transit less urgent; these factors also explain why pressure in favour of canalising the Rhône and opening a real waterway between the Mediterranean and the river has come less from Marseille than from Lyon, and was in fact for a long time of no avail. The problem has been raised again during recent years, and partly avoided by the construction of oil pipelines. The profitability of a systematic and complete improvement of the Rhône waterway is still a subject of debate. Nevertheless the lower and middle sections of the corridor are becoming increasingly busy. The improvement of road and rail traffic, the growth stimulus exerted by the launching of the Compagnie Nationale du Rhône's development schemes, and in due course by the creation of electricity power stations, the nuclear industrial centres at Marcoule and Pierrelatte in the Rhône valley and at Cadarache in the Durance valley, have profoundly changed the appearance and activities of regions which until the Second World War seemed dedicated to growing specialised crops in small market gardens and irrigated orchards, sheltered by windbreaks of cypress trees. This zone extends from the south of the Pierrelatte lowland as far as the approaches to Arles, the foot of Mont Ventoux, the Monts de Vaucluse and Luberon, around Carpentras, Cavaillon and Avignon in the Comtat region, and in the Durance valley from Pertuis to Châteaurenard and Barbentane. Industry, which was rare and sometimes in a marginal state at Bollène, Sorgues, Avignon and Arles now occupies more and more space and the towns are growing. Orange, which had only 13,000 inhabitants in 1936 has over 20,000 today. Avignon, which before the war was a town of 60,000 inhabitants is now the centre of an agglomeration of 140,000. In thirty years Arles has grown from 29,000 to 45,000 inhabitants. There is no doubt at all that at present the Rhône axis, in spite of the hesitation regarding its modernisation, has a strong attraction for activities and population growth. Everywhere the mountains and the traditional rural areas, with their alternation of interior basin, *garrigue* covered limestone plateaux and mountain folds with steep rocky slopes, are emptying in favour of the Rhône corridor and the coast.

Marseille's position seems to make it well suited for organising and animating a vast amphitheatre of French regions opening up on to the Mediterranean, but up until now the regional structure has remained very fragmented, and, as always where there is a disintegration, the power of command is transferred essentially to Paris. West of the Rhône, urban functions are shared between the towns lining the old Roman road, the Via Domitia, which skirts the *garrigue* slopes from Beaucaire and Nîmes to the Lauraguais threshold,* leading on the one hand to Toulouse and on the other to Catalonia. By their population size and functions, Nîmes with 125,000 inhabitants and Montpellier with 170,000 dominate the other elements in this chain of towns. Beaucaire has less than 15,000 inhabitants, Béziers 80,000, Narbonne

* Usually known as the 'Gate of Carcassonne' in English.

40,000 and Perpignan 107,000. Each is trying to establish itself as a leading regional centre by attracting new industries, by pursuing building programmes involving new town construction, like La Paillade at Montpellier, and by integrating itself into the internal air network by opening regular services. Montpellier enjoys a privileged position resulting from its past rank as a provincial capital, capital of the *Generalité* of eastern Languedoc and from its judiciary functions and its university, especially the medical faculty, which give an intellectual and administrative gloss to its trading activities and its control of the mass-consumption vineyards. Its artisan and small scale industries, less active than those of Nîmes, have now been succeeded by recent industrial development, stemming from the policy dispersing to the provinces factories not necessarily tied technically or economically to the old industrial regions or the Paris region. Montpellier shares with Nice the honour of housing the laboratories and offices of the I.B.M. Corporation, and it is also striving to create fish, fruit and vegetable preserving industries to serve the region. The prospect of an agglomeration of 300,000 inhabitants by 1980 is not exaggerated. It is not certain, however, that this will procure for Montpellier the status of a regional metropolis, since it will always encounter the competition of Béziers and Nîmes, each sixty kilometres away on either side of Montpellier, and particularly as the region under its control has only a million and a half inhabitants of whom 300,000 are in Perpignan's local sphere of influence and partly escape the control of Languedoc.

The development of the coast might increase Montpellier's scope. The port of Sète has been in a critical condition for a long time. The combination of fishing activities with shell fishing in the Etang de Thau, the transit of wines and products for treating vines, together now with petroleum products for the Frontignan refinery, are not enough to shake it out of its drowsiness. The town of 36,000 inhabitants, which had 37,000 in 1936, is changing little and still has its rather sad charm, but it does not attract investment. The plan to develop tourism on the Languedoc coast from Aigues-Mortes to La Nouvelle, and to organise a tourist complex between the Cévennes and the Seranne and the sea could stimulate the labour market by expanding public and private construction works and, at a later stage, the region's commerce and all the service activities linked with tourism. Montpellier is better placed than Nîmes to profit from this, but it is too early to judge the economic significance of the enterprise

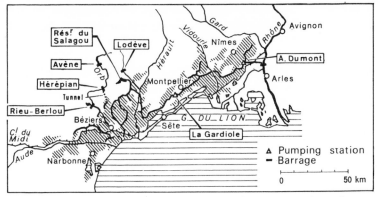

FIG. 20a. Development of irrigation in the Bas-Rhône and Languedoc region

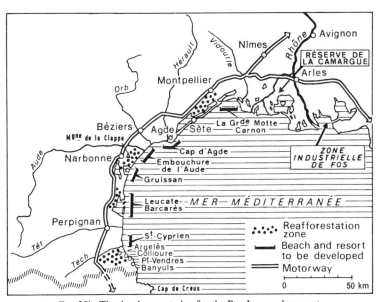

FIG. 20b. The development plan for the Bas-Languedoc coast

and Montpellier's involvement in its operation. The town clings to its prestige as an ancient provincial capital, steering clear of adventurous paths and it is as wary of the plans to extend tourism as it is of the projects for an agricultural revolution by applying irrigation in the area served by the Bas Rhône-Languedoc canal.

In fact it is in the Nîmes area that the Compagnie du Bas Rhône–Languedoc has brought about the most noticeable changes in the rural landscapes, in the economic and social structures and in local incomes. The arrival of water from the Rhône, diverted at Fourques opposite Arles, raised by the Pichegu pumping station to the level of the Costières, has introduced the conditions and methods for intensive market garden farming to land previously dry and used only for non-descript cultivation of vines and in part abandoned to grazing. The Mediterranean Midi's capacity for producing early and main season market garden produce, fruit and table grapes is now considerably increased. The area which can be irrigated by the canal in the whole of the perimeter concerned will cover a much larger area than that at present irrigated and devoted to market gardening in the Comtat-Venaissin, the Lower Durance and Roussillon, a total of approximately 150,000 to 160,000 hectares. However, the desired conversion of a proportion of the mass viticultural zone is only progressing slowly, and the land owners prefer to produce high quality wines in place of ordinary wine rather than risk replacing vines by market gardening. Bas-Languedoc, and the Nîmes and Montpellier areas in particular, are faced with a marketing problem. The Nîmes area, which is more directly involved in the extension of market gardening, is coping with the difficulties of a satisfactory organisation of packing and conserving market garden and fruit produce, and is trying to achieve a new balanced economy by the competition between contract cultivation for the conserving industries, like the Libby company, and the cooperative organisation of marketing and manufacture of preserves. It provides an example of modern market gardening on large scale units very different from the market gardening which was organised during the first third of this century along the irrigation canals and around the railheads in the Comtat and the Lower Durance.

East of the Rhône, Old Provence and the Comtat have their historic towns, like Avignon, the papal town, and Aix-en-Provence, an old Roman town, seat of the Provence parliament and the provincial government, with an expanding university and a population of 90,000 inhabitants. Toulon was the naval base of the royal fleet and Nice, the largest of all, has a population of 392,000 inhabitants. Around each of these towns contacts have been established on the scale of a small region corresponding to an urban size in the order of 100,000 to 300,000 inhabitants. The structure of Provence is not very suited to a concentration of the functions of direction and control. Out of a total of three million inhabitants today, nearly a million live in the Marseille agglomeration, and a million and a half in the coastal fringe outside the Marseille agglomeration reaching over more than 250 kilometres from the Rhône to the Italian frontier. The physical geography and the scattered economic activities, here above all tourist activities, are not suitable for a concentration of urban functions, with the possible exception of Nice. In fact Nice enjoys a privileged position as Professor Blanchard has shown.* It was the historical capital of an autonomous regional unit, the meeting point of valleys flowing down from the interior, the Loup, Var and Paillon. It has a first-class site on a coast rich in concentrations of luxury residences and tourism. It is a port with links with neighbouring Italy and Corsica. A large modern town is being grafted onto the core of the old town centred on the port and the hotels fronting the sea along the Promenade des Anglais, by winding through the tormented relief behind the old town. Nice is now assuming the role of a regional cultural centre with a university. The demographic situation in Nice is still ambiguous. The large number of retired people gives it the highest age structure and mortality rate in France, while new advanced industries, like I.B.M., and the university stimulate a rejuvenation of the qualified workers and the population in general. However, Nice can only claim to control the valleys descending to its riviera and the privileged coastal area from Antibes to Ventimiglia, in conjunction with the function of relaying the influence of a superior power centre, which is Paris rather than Marseille, although Marseille and Aix-en-Provence, in terms of its university, have for a long time claimed the right of tutelage.

Coastal tourism generates a gross business turnover of several billion francs, animating a hundred large and small resorts from the Nice coast to the *calanques* on the eastern side of Marseille. Movement along the coast is difficult, however; the main routes pass through the interior. 250 kilometres of hostile countryside, crystalline massifs devastated by forest fires, plateaux and chains of limestone separate the Nice and Cannes region from the Rhône furrow and Marseille. The railway and the main road, which in part is paralleled by the Esterel motorway, break a way through the mountains to the corridor of red soils planted with vines formed by the Argens valley, between the Massif des Maures and the high Plans plateaux, and then swing around the ranges of Basse-Provence. The attraction of

* R. Blanchard, *Le Comté de Nice,* Arthème Fayard, 1961.

Marseille cannot easily be transmitted across so many obstacles. Contact with Paris is often relatively easier.

Nevertheless Marseille is still trying to overcome the difficulties which prevent it really being a regional metropolis. Marseille both benefits and suffers from its past as the largest French port during the first part of this century. On the profit side are its very important port installations, its experience in commercial affairs and a system of world wide contacts covering particularly the Mediterranean. On the debit side is the lack of balance in port activity, urban development and the demographic situation. The town grew with more vigour than order, and so needs much renewal. The port is under-used and the active population has difficulty in finding work as a consequence of the decline in the traditional port activities and the old industries related to the port. The port traffic of Marseille proper* has declined by nearly 20 per cent in comparison with the period before the depression years of the 1930s. It maintains with difficulty the 1938 level of between 5 and 6 million tons. Mechanisation means that fewer and fewer dockers are employed and the occupation is suffering chronic unemployment. However, the traffic of the Marseille-Berre complex has tripled since 1931, approaching 30 million tons, accounted for above all by petroleum and minerals. Fifteen million tons are discharged and 6 million tons of refined products and derivatives leave the complex. By virtue of its outlets outside France and within the nation, the port of Marseille remains as in the past a national rather than a regional port, but with a changed type of traffic. Its hinterland is the Lyon region and eastern France within the nation to a much greater degree than Basse-Provence, Bas-Languedoc or the Bas-Rhône region.

The industries have passed through difficult periods, often finding themselves in a marginal economic position and have suffered from the dispersed structure of the firms.

The conversion of industries, and the amalgamations which affected particularly the sugar and vegetable oil industries, have been accompanied by serious reductions in employees. In 1962 100,000 people were registered as industrial workers, including those out of work, or almost 40 per cent of the total active population. The engineering and food processing industries, and in a secondary position, the chemical industry, are surviving rather than developing in the agglomeration.

One must look outside the agglomeration to find the most modern types of industry. Petroleum refineries and petrochemicals on the

---

* As opposed to its annexes on the Etang de Berre.

shores of the Etang de Berre and aircraft construction at Marignanne, employ 10,000 and 7,000 workers respectively. Shipbuilding at La Ciotat and Port-de-Bouc employs 5,000 workers but suffers from the general crisis of this sector of industry. The coalfield of Gardanne employs 5,000 workers in lignite mining, the Péchiney aluminium plant, the Lafarge cement works and various engineering and chemical factories.

It is significant that the most recent and enterprising industries result from the initiative of financial and industrial groups from outside Marseille, like Péchiney-Progil, the Lafarge cement company and the Banque de Paris et des Pays-Bas. At least 25,000 jobs created recently in the Marseille area are controlled by head offices away from Marseille.

The continuing tense situation in the labour market encouraged the launching of a large scale regional operation, the development of an industrial zone and a complex of new towns on the Gulf of Fos and on the eastern shore of the Etang de Berre. The industrial basis will be the new petroleum refinery fed directly from a terminal capable of receiving super-tankers, and an iron and steel works with an optimum output of from 6 to 8 million tons.

Some bold individuals have put forward the idea of an inter-regional complex on a European scale combining the Rhône-Alpes with its Mediterranean front in the framework of a major unit termed 'The Greater Delta', covering 112,000 square kilometres at present occupied by approximately 10 million people and accounting for almost a fifth of the French added value component. The first stage of the operation would be the creation of a powerful transport system.

V   THE SOUTH WEST, TOULOUSE AND BORDEAUX

The South West consists of thirteen *départements,* covering 86,000 square kilometres, 16 per cent of the French land area, but with only 4.5 million inhabitants, 9 per cent of the national total, of whom 440,000 live in the Toulouse agglomeration and a little over 550,000 in that of Bordeaux. This leaves scarcely more than 3.5 million inhabitants outside the two major agglomerations, 7 per cent of the national population.

In fifty years, the South West has lost a quarter of the population of

its rural areas and the secondary towns excluding Toulouse and
Bordeaux. Outside the two large urban areas, the region's income is
essentially provided by a few favoured areas which have retained or
developed their local activity. Examples are the Bordelais vineyards,
the market gardens and fruit growing of the Middle Garonne lowland,
the tourist centres of the Pyrenees and their foreland, and especially
Pau, with 104,000 inhabitants, which has acquired a distinctive industrial zone with its new town of Mourenx as a result of the discovery of the Lacq natural gas deposits. In spite of successive
attempts to convert agriculture and to renew the active population by
Italian and Spanish immigration and the resettlement of French
repatriates from Algeria, the rural economy with few exceptions is
stagnating or declining. The traditional industries, as in the Pyrenean
foothills for example, are disappearing or vegetating. Only Béarn and
the Basque country retain a high rural population density, but at the
price of a relatively low standard of living.

The two major agglomerations of Toulouse and Bordeaux have
gained respectively 265,000 and over 280,000 inhabitants, while the
countryside and small and medium-sized towns have lost a million inhabitants. The region's demographic balance sheet thus shows a
deficit. Moreover, the increased population of the two large
agglomerations should not be considered as a trouble free expansion.
As regards retailing, Toulouse plays the role of regional centre for
some of the *départements* constituting the Midi-Pyrénées region,*
without strictly speaking being a growth pole. Out of 140,000 people
in the work force, commercial and financial activities employ 31,500,
services and administration 40,000, and transport 5,300, making a
total of over half the work force. The building and public works industries employ 15,000 workers, leaving 42,000 jobs in the various
manufacturing industries, or only 30 per cent of the total labour force.
What is particularly significant, however, in the economic situation of
Toulouse is that, in most cases, the growth industries, with the highest
wage rates, most advanced technology and in a sound position, are
dependent on the State, even if they are not nationalised. By contrast,
the traditional industries are declining and the stimulus to growth from
public investment has so far been slight. The injection of government
capital has been made in several stages. Before and during the First
World War the arsenal, the State gunpowder factory, the O.N.I.A.
(the nationalised nitrates factory) and the Latécoère works were

* One of the twenty-two French planning regions, see Fig. 4.

located in Toulouse. On the eve of the Second World War, as part of the strategic decentralisation, came the Bréguet aircraft factory. In the course of the 1950s, with the development of the national aircraft industries, Sud-Aviation* was established, building the Caravelle jet airliner and now engaged on the Concorde supersonic airliner. The momentum is being kept up with the installation of the National Aerospace Studies Centre at Lespiret, the transfer to Toulouse of all the aeronautical colleges and the founding of research laboratories belonging to the university but oriented towards industry, for example the electronic optics laboratory at Rangeuil. Up until now the stimulus to growth has been weak. The nationalised firms find only a small number of supporting activities in the local industries, and must turn to industries in the North, the East and the Paris or Lyon regions. At present though, it appears that a real transformation is taking place. Important private firms are choosing Toulouse, the role of the university is becoming clearer, and one can envisage that from now on qualified workers will be recruited and will continue to be recruited increasingly on a regional basis, through the vast university facilities established by the State. The university had 35,000 students in 1970, three times the total in 1955. The fact remains that the region's under-industrialisation, both in the agglomeration's urban region and in the major region of Midi-Pyrénées, inevitably compels the advanced industries created by the State to turn to other industrial regions in order to safeguard their operations.

Of the traditional industries, shoe manufacturing is declining, the clothing industries seem very sensitive to market variations and are badly adapted to adjust to fluctuations in demand, but the hosiery industries seem better placed. These industries are important for the labour market above all because they complement the specialised chemical and aircraft industries most conveniently, by employing female labour especially. The same role is played by the food processing industries, making biscuits and rusks and treating milk. The paper and packaging industry only has a small employment capacity. The retention of important newspaper and book printing industries indicates a certain degree of regional cultural and political influence.

Professor Kayser, using objective criteria indicating permanent relationships, like use of services, distribution of consumer goods, the newspaper circulation areas and journey-to-work movements, has defined a small urban or suburban region, extending from Montauban

* Now regrouped with other aircraft companies under the name of 'Aérospatiale'.

to Pamiers and from Lombez to Mazamet, where local life is directly influenced by centres of control and service provision in Toulouse, and an economic and cultural region with a boundary passing through Albi, Cahors, Auch and Tarbes and coinciding to the south with the Spanish frontier. Beyond this boundary, in an area amounting to a third of the Midi-Pyrénées region, the influences from Toulouse are only partial and not dominant. Here one is in a border zone without urban domination where the influences of Toulouse, Bordeaux and above all Paris overlap.

Bordeaux seems well placed to benefit from the mass of investment made in the western part of the South West, in Aquitaine. The Lacq complex, important though it may be in the national economy, has created only a small number of jobs in the extraction and sulphur refining plants, the Artix power station and the aluminium and chemical industries; indeed it might be argued that housing demand has been over estimated in the building of Mourenx new town, which has been able to house several hundred repatriate families from Algeria. It is true that Pau draws off some of the stimulating effects of the new industrial plants. Nevertheless, a real industrial region has not been created on the Lacq gas field and it seems that there will not be one in the future, even if one could guarantee that the deposit currently being used would be replaced, when it is exhausted around 1980, by the exploitation of other reserves.

Bordeaux passed through a difficult period at the beginning of the twentieth century and up until the Second World War. The port had difficulty in maintaining its rank and its volume of traffic. The Landes timber and turpentine, which had been counted on to support the port, suffered a gradual loss of markets, and colonial trade declined. The wine trade was not enough to maintain the level of port activity. The urban economy was indirectly affected. The Bordeaux agglomeration lacked jobs to absorb the region's excess rural population which was forced to emigrate away from the region. Capital and talent found no opportunity to invest locally and also abandoned the region for Paris.

There has been a marked reversal of these trends since 1950. The discovery of petroleum and gas deposits created a psychological climate which tended to attract business attention to the region and to the city of Bordeaux as a growth centre. This involves a true process of substitution of activities rather than of conversion in the usual sense. The traditional industries, metallurgy, the forges and workshops of the Gironde, the wood and leather industries, are disappearing one after another. They no longer have economically viable operating conditions because their scale is too small, their structure is outdated or because their location involves excessive transport and operating costs. A few food processing industries, born of the historic functions of the port, like the chocolate industry, seem able to withstand the present trading conditions. Attention is now focused, however, on new industries belonging to the advanced sector of recent technology. Representative industries are the refinery and petrochemicals complex of Bec d'Ambés, capable of treating 4 million tons per annum and producing a range of secondary raw materials like carbon black and butane, and secondly the aero-space complex which includes the creation of a solid fuel plant for rocket propulsion on the site of the former gunpowder factory, a test centre for ballistic rockets at Biscarosse, the construction of aircraft factories for Dassualt and Aérospatiale together with an atomic research centre in the northern Landes.

As at Toulouse, growth was triggered by massive public investment, but one must see the outcome over the next decade before judging the stimulating effects of this investment. The size of the agglomeration and the existence of an industrial work force which has increasing difficulty in finding employment create favourable conditions. The success of the operation depends to a large extent on the attitude of private capital.

However, the revival of Bordeaux does not necessarily imply the setting up of a major region based on the city. At present public investment is located between the Gironde and Biscarosse, occupying available land in the Landes forest outside the areas of rural settlement. The Landes constitute a huge neutral zone between the *pays* of the lower Garonne and the Gironde, and especially the Bordelais vineyard area on the one hand, and on the other the highly active Béarn area, the Basque country with its chain of towns, Pau, Bayonne and the tourist zone of Biarritz (the Côte d'Argent). Commercially, Bordeaux dominates the lower valleys of the Garonne and the Dordogne as far as Agen and Bergerac and extends partially to Angoulême and Royan. Its university draws students from the Charente-Maritime, Dordogne, Lot-et-Garonne and Landes *départements,* as well as from Gironde, and continues to exercise an important influence in the French-speaking countries of Africa. It is in close contact with the overseas *départements* of the Antilles and with Latin America. On the other hand, the elevation of the university centre at Pau to full university status confirms the division between the

Garonne and Dordogne confluence region and that of the Pyrenean foreland. Pau has the functions of a regional metropole without having the title. It has direct contact with Paris as much as if not more than with Bordeaux. As around Toulouse, Aquitaine presents a picture outside the immediate zone of influence of Bordeaux, of *pays* with no regional organisation, living in a closed local economy and depending on the national network of services and commerce for any requirements out of the ordinary.

Bordeaux and Toulouse are handicapped by the negative economic significance of the Pyrenees. The mountains supply them with a tourist annexe, which provides sites for local investment and quite often for national investment too, but they are a boundary. Whereas Lyon has throughout history benefited and still benefits from its connections with Italy across the Alps, the economic vacuum of the northern regions of Spain, with the exception of Catalonia which is beyond Toulouse's area of contact and influence, frustrates all hopes for an expansion to the south.

The South West is a major geographical unit, defined in terms of morphological and climatic unity, agricultural structures and rural problems, demographic depression and the attraction exercised there by public sector employment which encourages people to seek teaching diplomas rather than technical training, but it lacks a regional structure in economic terms. The financial, commercial and cultural spheres of influence of Toulouse and Bordeaux form patches which are far from covering the entire regional area. Both cities have been raised to the rank of *métropoles d'equilibre,* giving them the task of organising, effectively dominating and stimulating their regions as defined administratively. The prospects in this respect are at variance with present reality and are still in the realm of future intentions.

VI THE WEST

The West accounts for a sixth of the national land area, 16 per cent of the French population, and has a high predominance of rural population and activities. Industries are concentrated in the port regions around Rouen, Le Havre, Caen, Brest and Nantes. In spite of strong historical traditions, the regional components are no more than inherited provincial structures. Within these regions – Normandy, Brittany, the Loire regions of Maine, Anjou and Touraine – there are active centres of from 100,000 to 300,000 inhabitants, together with small towns which have attracted decentralised firms because they are not too far from the Paris agglomeration. The control of Paris weighs heavily over much of these western regions, which for several generations have supplied labour to the industries and services of Paris, with the result that in the last twenty years there has been a certain demographic exhaustion, expressed in an appreciable ageing of the population structure, especially in Brittany. On the other hand, investment has scarcely penetrated beyond a 200 kilometre radius from Paris. The Lower Seine valley may be considered a technical annexe of the Paris agglomeration by virtue of its port role, and its industries function as refiners of imported products, especially petroleum. Various new or transferred activities have at different times stimulated the development of Le Mans, Orléans and Tours.

However, the most frequently mentioned problem is that facing Brittany. Neither agriculture nor maritime activities can guarantee employment for its population, which is still large. Industry is only found in a few towns with, moreover, a basis of State creations, like the arsenals of Brest and Lorient, or enforced transfers, like the Citroën factories in Rennes. Brest's position in France and its roadstead conditions make it suitable for the development of handling facilities for supertankers. The most diversified industrial zone is that of the Loire estuary, following on from its former function as an importing port for tropical and colonial produce, and linked with shipbuilding at Saint-Nazaire. With 370,000 inhabitants in 1968, the Nantes agglomeration is in the same size category as Rouen, but it has not benefited in the same way from interest on the part of Paris. The shipbuilding industry has been in a state of latent crisis for a long time and the effects of this crisis are felt throughout the metallurgical industries of the Loire estuary. The food industries also have their particular problems. The Loire estuary area has been classified as an area qualifying for government help for industrial conversion, and during the Fifth Plan Nantes was given the status of the *métropole d'équilibre* for the whole of Brittany and the lower Loire area. The creation of a metropolitan region is difficult, particularly as Rennes is the established trustee of Breton tradition and regionalism. Nantes is able to influence regions which still have a low level of activity, like the *pays* of the Poitou Threshold, and to help in the attempt at renewal being made in Anjou. To the present day, western France has remained a group of poorly defined regions, based on their towns at the level of *département* or *arrondissement*, far more than a group of economically structured regions. It is even less a major western region centred on its newly created metropolis.

It is generally accepted that Normandy and the Loire region are in Paris's direct sphere of influence. None of the towns is therefore called on to play the role of a regional metropolis, although a few service functions appropriate to a regional metropolis might be located in the area as a decentralisation exercise within a 100 to 200 kilometre radius of Paris. The possibility of regional autonomy is only recognised in Brittany, but the means of achieving it are still very vague, in spite of many well-documented plans made by the contentious Bretons. These, moreover, cannot help showing the internal diversity of Brittany's problems, since there are four clearly distinct economic units with different current trends: western Brittany incorporating northern and southern Finistère, northern and central Brittany, southern Brittany comprising the *département* of Morbihan, and the *pays* of the Loire-Atlantique *département*.

VII   THE CENTRE

Central France, including the Massif Central and the southern Paris Basin, covers 17 per cent of the national land area but has less than 9 per cent of France's population. The two natural units, the southern Paris Basin and the Massif Central, are subdivided into several historical regions, like Berry, Nivernais, Burgundy, Auvergne, Limousin and Velay. Certain parts of the Massif belonged to external provinces, such as Languedoc in the case of the southern *pays*, and the Lyon region for the massifs of the eastern margin. The pattern of the drainage network is symbolic, for central France is a zone of dispersion. The only natural unit is Auvergne, centred on the Limagne plains, but it is too small in size and too sparsely populated to act as a real magnet for the entire group of isolated mountain *pays*. They are attracted to neighbouring regions, with an easier way of life and with work opportunities, rather than inwards towards a mountain unit,* even a relatively privileged one. Clermont-Ferrand's appeal is limited spatially, although the town has a few high order services and a university. Contact is easier between Limoges and Paris or Le Puy and

* i.e. Auvergne, centred on Clermont-Ferrand.

Lyon than between Limoges and Le Puy and Le Puy and Clermont-Ferrand. Berry and Lower Burgundy are already within the sphere of influence of Paris. Dijon's status as a regional metropolis has not yet been recognised, even though the town is receiving a large amount of industrial investment and is growing at a rapid rate. At the outbreak of the Second World War, Dijon had 100,000 inhabitants, compared with 184,000 in the agglomeration in 1968. Clermont-Ferrand has 204,000 inhabitants and Limoges 150,000. The three towns may readily be considered as major centres relaying Paris's power of control. Each has its sphere of influence and its distribution area for funds and products and for service provision. Nevertheless, the flows converging on Paris are stronger than those which confirm their regional status. There is no regional structure in the broader sense of the term, merely an organisation at the level of secondary and subsidiary services under the control of Paris. It is tempting to propose the term sub-region or secondary region for the Lower Auvergne* area, taking into account the existence of a roughly outlined grouping and structure, but without confusing it with the clearly polarised regions described at the beginning of the chapter.

The Centre East region corresponds with the planning regions of Bourgogne and Franche-Comté, with 2.5 million inhabitants. It is an excellent example of an area without polarisation, although this by no means suggests that it is an economic vacuum or even economically weak. There are three distinct geographical units, defined by their physical character and individual economies; the Saône corridor and lowlands, the Burgundy or Alsace Gateway† and the Jura. The Saône corridor and the edge of the Burgundy plateau constitute an agricultural region dominated by the wealth of its vineyards, centred commercially on Beaune much more than on Dijon, and further south by the industrial activities of Chalon. The Belfort Gap has become an active industrial zone as a result both of the initiative of business families, like Peugeot and Japy, and the presence of manpower reserves of peasant workers. It has attracted outside investment, notably in the case of Alsthom at Belfort, and today is an important centre of mechanical and electrical engineering, from the manufacture of tools and precision machinery, to car building at Montbéliard, Sochaux, Valentigney and Audincourt, and even to very heavy elec-

---

* The effective core area of Auvergne, Clermont-Ferrand and the agricultural lowland of the Limagne, as opposed to the mountains of Haute-Auvergne.
† Usually referred to in English geographical texts as the Belfort Gap.

trical engineering at Belfort. The Jura has so far managed to maintain the combination of agriculture, based on a pastoral economy and cooperative cheese factories, with scattered industries constantly changing their products, best represented by the industries at Oyonnax. Urban functions are dispersed and scarcely play the role of regional organisation. Dijon has already been discussed. To the east, the largest town is Besançon with 116,000 inhabitants, followed very closely by the industrial conurbation of Montbéliard with 114,000, and much further behind by Belfort with 75,000 inhabitants. None of these towns acts as a polarising centre.

CHAPTER NINE

The Question of Paris

Paris's position in France and the problem of its expanding population and size present a fundamental paradox. Paris is not just the capital city of France. It is one of the great business centres, political meeting places and cultural capitals of the world. As national capital, Paris provides the French counterbalance to the concentrations of interests and activities which challenge France's authority in competition with Europe's major economic regions, especially the Rhinelands, in the wide or narrow sense. The inevitable consequence of this has been an expansion of all kinds of activities, attracting more population of all types. Only a romantic would imagine a Paris on the scale of the city under Napoleon III or even during the *belle époque,** given its current responsibilities. On the other hand the bitter reality is a sad picture of a city and agglomeration which only in terms of population size corresponds to the stimulus of its many functions, while its form, or rather lack of form, is unworthy of its function and risks creating a blighted urban development.

The positive elements are, in the first place, a heritage basic to an understanding of the essential character of the capital's present functions. Paris is an historic city with few equals in the world, rich in tradition and culture and with an inheritance of buildings and monuments which illustrate and punctuate the stages by which its tradition and culture were formed over two thousand years. On several occasions the winding paths of history have made it a European or imperial capital. From conflicting political relations and armed struggles were born organised contacts, common institutions and ways of thought, and cultural links which sometimes led to shared interests. It is easy but nonetheless relevant to think what Paris means for so many foreigners, according to their culture, age or occupation. It means everything that

* The period from the turn of the century to the First World War.

the visitors come for, several millions of them every year, staying for days or weeks.

This heritage has become more varied from century to century as administrative centralisation and Paris's function as capital city in the widest sense have encouraged an increasing proportion of the creative forces to take root there, at a time when these have become technical in character. Paris has become the technical capital of France, just as it was the 'capital of lights' in the eighteenth century. Its technical character implies industry, and vice versa. It is Paris that is expected to solve the problems arising from the development of an industry or the search for new markets. It is in Paris too that one is certain to find, in the shortest time possible, the invention or improvisation which guarantees the success of the latest innovation. Paris also provides the greatest variety of employment and the best chance of success in personal venture, and the possibility of changing functions is certainly greater there than anywhere else in France. In practice, this wealth of opportunities is expressed in a growing number of firms of all sizes and kinds, and this alone is a powerful factor of attraction.

Even more Paris has drawn together all kinds of national and international relations. It is a banking centre of the first rank with an influence extending to all continents. The Parisian business banks have interests not only in nations which were formerly French colonies but also in the East and in South America. The same applies to the commercial agencies in all specialised branches, insurance companies, consultants, market research offices and increasingly, development planning offices. In particular Paris is one of the capitals for technical cooperation with the developing countries. It is also a permanent exhibition centre, where industrial products acquire a world wide mark of quality.

Similarly, Paris still has an international cultural function, and has greatly expanded it in spite of the success of certain provincial initiatives in this respect. Individuals can develop their talent there. Diplomas acquired in Paris carry authority. Its university has more than 20,000 foreign students. Parisian theatrical companies make world tours. Its museums and art galleries exhibit all over the world and receive works and artists from all countries.

As a consequence, Paris is France's greatest tourist centre. A close-knit system provides air, sea and rail connections with foreign countries. The Parisian hotel business records over ten million clients every year. Diplomatic and commercial activities involve the permanent residence in Paris of several tens of thousands of administrators and business men from all nations. Representatives of over a hundred different nationalities have been counted in Paris. One cannot remain indifferent to anything that ever happens there.

In the circumstances, Paris crystallises all activities which to some degree concern the many different relationships with all the other countries of the world. The desire to be present where international affairs are dealt with and where it is possible to be involved in the activities inspired by these affairs and by the whole system of contacts dominated by Paris attracts a very large number of people and firms. The Parisian labour market is by far the largest and most varied in France. It offers the attraction of brilliant careers and professions, and a wide choice, together with an element of excitement. No more need be said than that nearly 100,000 provincials flock to Paris every year. It is no longer industry which absorbs most of this annual migration as it was during the first forty years of this century, but Paris is still France's largest industrial centre, in terms of the number of firms, the labour employed, the different manufactured goods marketed and the business turnover reached.

TABLE SIXTEEN

SELECTED INDICES OF THE STATUS OF PARIS IN THE NATIONAL ECONOMY

Percentages of the national total

Industrial workers	Industrial firms employing over 200 workers	Commercial firms with over 10 workers	Business turnover of industrial and commercial firms
20	25	33	48

The Paris agglomeration has firms representing the most enterprising and successful sectors of industrial production. Some of the most specialised products are prepared in Paris, even though they may be completed in factories outside the administrative limits of the Paris region. However, legislation controlling expansion *in situ* and the building of new factories has markedly slowed down the expansion of industry in Paris, particularly as regards the area occupied and the number of persons employed and this has exactly coincided with progress in productivity reducing manpower needs. Employment in Paris is increasingly in the tertiary sector, or, in the case of secondary

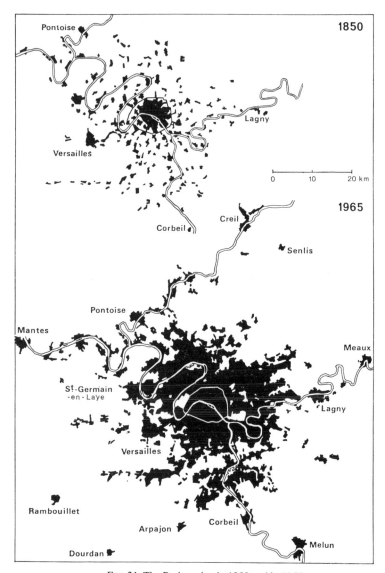

FIG. 21. The Paris region in 1850 and in 1965

employment, involves employment in the technical and managerial ranks. From an industrial city, Paris is becoming a city of services and business at a national and international level, and it is in this context that predictions of increased active and total population should be made.

I   THE PARIS AGGLOMERATION

There is very little point in trying to define the Paris agglomeration as lying within precise boundaries. By nature, the agglomeration is continually changing its shape, by increasing both its population and surface area. A spatial definition is needed for the administrative system to mark the limits of its service responsibilities. It must also take into account a deep-rooted heritage which, although now obsolete in terms of economic realities and not conducive to improving administrative activities, in the name of expressing the popular will and as a guarantee of freedom, is opposed to all attempts to change the political structure. This is why there are so many ways of enumerating the population and defining the limits of the urbanised area of Greater Paris. The study made in 1959 by the National Institute for Statistics and Economic Studies proposed, on the basis of many criteria such as population density, continuity of the built-up area, daily contact and commuting in particular, a distinction beyond the city of Paris,* between the 'restricted agglomeration', comprising the city of Paris and the inner suburban ring, and the 'greater agglomeration', combining the preceding area with a second ring of less completely urbanised suburbs, and a 'residential complex', encompassing in addition over a hundred communes subject to the attraction of Paris, as much in terms of the labour market as of daily and occasional movements as customers.

Whatever administrative limits or criteria are applied, the Paris agglomeration suffers from two fundamental difficulties which make its inevitable growth extremely dangerous. The first is a bad use of the urban land area inherited from the nineteenth century. The second, closely linked to the first, is the chronic crisis of urban traffic, which is deteriorating from year to year and is both a physical and psychological problem.

---

* Coinciding with the former Seine *département,* now the *département* of Paris, and approximately coinciding with the last fortified perimeter of 1840.

TABLE SEVENTEEN
THE AREA AND POPULATION OF THE PARIS AGGLOMERATION

	City	Restricted Agglomeration	Greater Agglomeration	Residential complex
Area in square kilometres	100	750	1,450	2,350
1954 population (thousands)	2,850	6,270	6,979	7,350
1962 population (thousands)	2,790	6,523	7,370	7,735
1968 population (thousands)	2,591	6,725	7,917	8,781

Paris in Napoleon III's time, before and after Haussman, was a town which was certainly large but which every inhabitant could know intimately from his personal acquaintance; a town of many aspects, full of secrets, the town of Victor Hugo and Eugène Sue.* Haussman, who has been made out to be a visionary of urbanism, simply organised what already existed, without foreseeing the expansion which would take place from this nucleus. Certainly, the annexation of suburban communes, extending the city limits to a boundary that, except for minor adjustments, no administration has dared to exceed for over a century, was a bold measure which made a unified development process possible. The opening up of wide boulevards made traffic jams less severe for several decades and contributed to the aesthetic quality of the capital. However, even before all Haussman's projects had been completed, the problem of Paris had assumed a larger scale. Even while Haussman's plans were being slowly implemented after his departure,† no further perspective or long term research was undertaken. Logical restrictions, which could scarcely be termed laws, were responsible for an empirical and spontaneous development. The building up of urban land was encouraged by the attraction of transport arteries, especially when they followed compact areas which were easy to develop. After filling the basin formed by the confluence zone of the Marne, Bièvre and Oise, and its annexes, like the Saint-Denis plain, the agglomeration reached out long antennae along the major transport axes, valleys and road and rail alignments. A certain degree of discrimination, guided by intuition and by financial reasoning which meant that the various parts of the area were valued differently, brought about specialised land use,

* The nineteenth century novelist, author of the popular *Les Mystères de Paris*.
† Haussman was dismissed as Prefect of Paris in 1870, because of the enormous cost of his planning schemes, as well as their aesthetic and social implications.

differentiating between industrial zones, the most extensive and oldest occupying the lowlands closest to the urban core to the north, west and south, and residential zones, the most sought after being scattered in the valleys and wooded slopes to the west, south and east. However, the distribution of urban terrain according to its land use pattern is far from having a logical structure. Detailed analysis of land use, both in the city of Paris and in the suburban rings and antennae, reveals an enormous waste of space, which, paradoxically, is very largely responsible for the traffic congestion and the shortage of public open spaces.

The main anomalies in the land use pattern are the excessive congestion of the original historical core, now known as the city centre, which cannot in anyway be described as inevitable in terms of function or evolution; the irrational under use of the nineteenth century districts, especially those in the suburban aureola annexed to the city by Haussman; the excessive industrialisation of the inner suburbs which in fact, as in all towns which grew during the second half of the nineteenth century, form a working class ring because they were proletarianised; and the lack of order in the development of the twentieth century urban antennae, which are partly industrial and partly lower and upper middle class residential districts. The hasty post-war decisions to take in part of the under used urban or suburban areas to build new kinds of districts, the *grands ensembles,* merely added another element to this empirical pattern of land use, and added to the incoherent urban development which now forms a mass thirty kilometres in diameter. Following other attempts to correct the situation, one wonders whether the master plan,* which for the first time is based on an administrative reorganisation of the entire urbanised area, will make a reconstruction of the city possible.

1   The Congestion of Paris, or the Problems of the Central Area

It is in the centre of the city and agglomeration that the idea of a changed image is most applicable, but the reality persists in spite of changes in the technology and methods of everyday life. There is a constant sense of almost total asphyxia. The 'city centre' of major capitals is easily but incorrectly confused with what is more appropriately termed the 'city'. However, the phenomenon of the 'city' is strictly localised, and the 'centre' as a whole is something very

* The *Schèma Directeur.*

different. In Paris, the 'city' might at most be identified as the assimilation of the Stock Exchange district with the head offices of the major banks and insurance companies, within the area defined by the Rue du Louvre, the Avenue de l'Opéra, the Rue de Châteaudun and the Seine. However, this perimeter includes the Palais-Royal, the Conseil d'Etat, the National Library and a mass of varied commercial activities and tourist and travel agencies, which are only in an accessory sense 'city' activities. On the other hand, the activities of the capital spread like a pool of oil around the 'city' as defined above, near the main line stations and to the south of Montmartre, where entertainment shows are combined with business activity. It is tempting to talk of 'parallel' activities, or even of a parasitic status in relation to the 'city' in the strict sense. In fact it is here that the phenomenon of the 'city centre' is really expressed, with its inflated land, building and property values. The Halles market area, immediately next to the Palais du Louvre and to Saint-Germain-l'Auxerrois, is a district which was originally aristocratic but which has declined continuously over the last three centuries, increasingly afflicted by the market for perishable foods extending from the Louvre to the Marais district and by the congestion and corruption characteristic of a neighbourhood which lives by night and has been largely recolonised by the outcasts of urban society. The area's future after the transfer of the Halles food market to Rungis has not yet been decided.* Further away the Marais, Saint-Gervais and Temple districts until recently seemed to be poor relations of the centre of Paris, in spite of their equally aristocratic orgins, but were closely integrated into the centre's life by all kinds of sub-contracting, artisan activity, home-based working and small services. Finally, the university district is linked to the city centre by function and geography. It was originally combined with the cathedral of Notre Dame and entered into international folk lore under the title of the Latin Quarter, extending from the slums of the Maubert district or the Rue Mouffetard to those, now renovated by the fashion for *caves*,† of Saint-Germain-des-Prés. A simple picture of the city centre as a depopulated urban section swarming with professional activities but deserted by the inhabitants seems adequate. Statistics seem to justify this picture, but statistics do not always convey the real situation. The

---

* This transfer has now been completed and the Halles demolished to make way for a renewal scheme and new metro station.

† Cafés and clubs, often in cellars, originally associated with the post-war Existentialist movement.

true 'city' is small. The city centre is increasingly the refuge of a more or less exactly numbered population and is more or less regularly controlled. The renovation of ailing enclaves which has been going on for thirty years moves the sickness without curing it. The dilapidated condition of districts which are old but not venerable is more and more in contrast with the functions which people want to maintain or extend there. It is also becoming increasingly difficult to preserve the dignity of archaeological monuments dating from the centuries when the present city centre was the whole city and a fine one. It is above all because of the constant congestion that the city centre is in an absurd situation, since its function is to be supplied and visited whereas in fact it is the opposite of accessible. Even the idea of prestige, inseparable from its function as a commercial, financial or administrative figurehead, changes and disappears in the crowd of vehicles and haze of exhaust fumes, in an urban mass which now seems an anachronism in comparison with the spectacular new achievements of big business. It probably lives on in the hearts of members of the old pre-war generations – but which war? – but it eludes the younger generation conditioned by other kinds of presentation from the world of business and public relations.

The city centre is changing rapidly. Although it still has its banks, head offices and insurance companies, which invested heavily in renovating their buildings between the two world wars, in the Boulevard Haussman and the Rue de Châteaudun for example, it is by no means certain that this will be so in the long term. The most stable elements are the more refined commercial activities, anxious not to make their business clients, used to old streets and the narrow alleys and squeaking staircases of the Rue du Sentier, Rue Richelieu or the Rue de Provence, feel out of place. This city centre, which is described as the site of activities characteristic of the capital, is tending to lose its functional meaning. It still has the old central activities, those which tend to be economically marginal; it is expanding its tourist function, but with very inadequate facilities more at the level of travel bureaux than accommodation. However, the true central activities, on the scale of a national and international metropolis at the close of the twentieth century, are tending to sprout up elsewhere. Of course an exception must be made for political and administrative activities, which, apart from the historic locations, like the Elysée, the Palais-Bourbon, the Senate, the Place Beavau or the Louvre,* are shared between the

* The site of the Finance Ministry.

ministerial district, dominated by the Quai d'Orsay,* and a crowd of scattered offices occupied on different occasions by public administration authorities according to their growth and need of space and according to chance circumstances. The city and *département* administration has remained loyal to the neighbourhood of the old Place de Grève. New administrative services look for impressive premises in the mansions of the Faubourg Saint-Germain, from the Rue Martignac to the Rue Barbet-de-Jouy and the Invalides. Others seek positions near rich residential districts, the first kind of escape from the city centre from which more and more of the central functions are fleeing. Sometimes the question of transferring these functions is raised. In fact each period has its own central functions, and locates them where they will prosper best and benefit most from the opportunities for display which are indispensable to them. As new activities have taken over from the former activities characteristic of the centre, they have been integrated into the centre or a breaking up of the centre takes place. Each time a new central function appears it is accompanied by related activities which give the impression of a process of fragmentation of the centre. The original centre of Paris pre-dated the motor car and world-wide interest in *haute couture.* When the car and fashion businesses became characteristic of activity in Paris and were located, after the First World War, in the Champs-Elysées and Etoile district, cinemas and luxury shops transformed the area. A similar evolution seems imminent today around the Maine-Montparnasse† development, and more certainly around the exhibition hall and business centre of La Défense,‡ even though this is a 'centre' placed outside the municipal boundary of Paris, with suburban addresses, and no one envisaged transforming the Champs-Elysées intersection into an American-style head office complex. The explosion of certain activities which were too constricted is a different matter, and the university is a revealing if not totally happy example. The lack of foresight on the part of generations which allowed property speculation to sterilise, from a university point of view, the district of the university faculties and Sorbonne, has had the effect of dispersing the university function. This began on modest lines with the creation of an

---

* The Ministerial district is predominantly in the Seventh arrondissement. The Quai d'Orsay houses the Foreign Ministry.

† A major urban renewal development and office complex adjoining the rebuilt Montparnasse railway station.

‡ A new suburban node begun in the 1960s to the west of the city centre.

annexe zone on the Rue Pierre Curie, still well placed between the Ecole Normale Supérieure and the Sorbonne, and with the building of student residences on the external boulevards, such as the Cité Universitaire on the Boulevard Jourdan. The process speeded up with the transfer of the science faculty to the former wine market, the building of the Cité Universitaire at Antony, the creation of new universities at Orsay, the Porte Dauphine, Nanterre, Créteil, Vincennes, Sceaux and Villetaneuse, the opening of the Centre for Higher Technical Education at Cachan and the transfer of the Grandes Ecoles* to the suburbs.

The evolution of the city centre recalls the classic way of solving problems by resorting to absurdity. The remedy for congestion is to disperse everything that is flourishing. It has been impossible to renew the centre because speculation has put building programmes beyond the means of both public and private funds. The most modern activities and even traditional ones abandon the centre, removing any reason for the inflation of land and building sites. There are many different reactions to this serious threat of decay.

A first set of reactions comes from the retailers, who are numerous in the central districts where they benefit from the very intense usage by a varied international clientele, and from artisans, generally working under contract for small or large concerns. These reactions have both negative and positive aspects. Shopkeepers and artisans are hostile to any radical change in the districts they occupy which would eliminate them by a change of buildings and functions which would mean they lost their clientele. However, they contribute to the search for solutions by conservation which might help to save important elements of the historical legacy. It would therefore seem possible to separate the function of business centre from that of retailing and tourism by banning car traffic in a certain number of streets during shopping hours, while keeping enough space or capacity for parking. A quiet commercial area, free from traffic and noise, becomes fit not only for visiting but also for living in. Living in the original traditional style in old renovated buildings only has to become fashionable for private investment to become involved in historical monuments or even in more modest dwellings several centuries old, thus ensuring their conservation and renovation. Initiatives so far have been cautious, particularly with respect to traffic control, but the commercial and tourist transformation of certain sections of the old centre is

* The specialised colleges for professional training, more strictly vocational than the university faculties and usually subject to highly competitive entry.

taking place, in Saint-Germain-des-Prés, the Marais district, around the Place Contrescarpe and the Saint-Médard Square for example, and perhaps, in future, in the Halles district.

A second type of reaction is that of the public administrations responsible for improvement. This is expressed in terms of renewal pure and simple by the destruction of unhealthy enclaves and a re-use of the freed area according to a new land use plan combining open spaces, buildings for public use and residential blocks. Until now these schemes have only nibbled at the city centre in the strict sense because of the high cost of the central enclaves. Nevertheless, there are several examples in the fourth and fifth arrondissements on the edge of the real city centre. Examples are the Saint-Gervais district, the Hôtel de Sens and the reconstruction of the administrative buildings of the Seine Préfecture.

2   The Remodelling of the Old Districts

Aerial photographs or detailed maps show the very bad urban land use pattern in the districts occupied in the second half of the nineteenth century. The critical cases are those of districts where early building speculation greedily crammed together housing and buildings for renting, leaving only a narrow gap between them for movement and inside the blocks a few shafts to pass as courtyards. The excessive density of the Montmartre districts, where some streets recall the names of the developers, like Rue Trézel, has rightly been denounced. There are other urban tracts in the twelfth, nineteenth and thirteenth arrondissements on streets now too narrow, which have been hemmed in by buildings on badly developed sites occupied by warehouses and by semi-derelict workshops. Often these empty sites adjoin low rise tenements, of three to five storeys at the most, which have become slums. In this case renewal is essential but by no means easy. It can be undertaken by public bodies, involved in both the demolition works and the construction of new groups of buildings, for example the municipal and *département* authorities, the housing agency of the National Savings Scheme, or the government-sponsored low rent housing agency, or it might be entrusted to private building companies, as in the case of the renewal of the Belleville area and the redevelopment of the Bercy warehouse zone.

Renewal means a fundamental transformation of the urban landscape as well as of the social and socio-professional structures of the districts concerned. The example of the operations completed in the thirteenth arrondissement is significant in this respect. In place of an enclosed pattern of lots hemmed in by old streets where small shops and artisan workshops huddled together, groups of flats have been built forming an open planned *cité*, with internal open pedestrian areas and commercial centres on supermarket lines. The district's former residents feel completely out of their element. Only a small number of them manage to settle there again, not because the density has been reduced (that is not always the case since it is possible to increase building heights compared with the former urban structure), but because the average level of rents is higher than in the former residences, and because the demand for artisan services and retail goods is no longer the same from the district's new clientele. The change in the building structure is accompanied by a change in its internal composition. Daily life, the rhythms and directions of circulation change and the resettling of the people who cannot adapt to the new structure poses problems. These are less urgent when the renewal concerns areas with former functions or industrial uses involving little or no housing, as in the case of land formerly used by the military, or the rebuilding of the Grenelle district and the Quai de Javel where the Parc des Sports and the cycle stadium were located, along with part of the Citroën factories, now dismantled. Gradually, but slowly, the urban structure of Paris as defined under the Second Empire is being changed, but the thoroughfares open to traffic are still inadequate. So far no major motorway has been built across the city of Paris. The approach motorways, the West, South and North motorways, end in bottlenecks in an overloaded road system. The only innovation is the construction of expressways on the banks of the Seine. The major problem is still that of intra-urban traffic, in spite of the transfer of the causes of congestion, like the wholesale market for perishable foodstuffs, from central Paris to the suburbs. Humourists have calculated as accurately as they can that to guarantee transport provision for central Paris and parking for the number of cars forecast in the next ten to fifteen years it would be necessary to demolish the whole of the centre. There are of course technical hypotheses for multi-storey or underground car parks which have difficulty in keeping up with the rate of increase in the number of vehicles in circulation, and for an intensified use of highly efficient public transport like the metro, the regional metro system* and the aerotrain. In any event, the future development of the city will be costly.

3   Decentralisation and Improvement in the Inner Suburbs

During the nineteenth century and the beginning of the twentieth century, above all between the two world wars, industry took root in the inner ring of suburban communes surrounding the territory allocated to the City of Paris by the imperial decree of 1860. Industries are closely interwoven with working class areas, built as cheaply as possible and usually as badly maintained by their occupants as by their owners. The firms are of all kinds, ranging from the large factory which has gradually taken over entire residential areas, like the Renault plant at Boulogne-Billancourt, to the artisan workshop at the back of a courtyard, and including small manufacturing firms inherited from the last decades of the nineteenth century. They alternate with warehouses, railway yards, wasteland, disused military installations, quarries and rubbish tips, in Ivry, the Bièvre valley, Saint-Denis, Aubervilliers, Bobigny and Bagnolet. Housing and traffic conditions have been bad there for a long time, in spite of the considerable efforts made by the municipal authorities. The changes which have been carried out there since the end of the Second World War affect three spheres, the renewal of the unhealthiest enclaves, the opening up of new roads and the reduction of the industrial areas.

The first act of renewal was the rebuilding of districts destroyed by bombing, especially near the railways and stations. This was followed by major shifts in the centre of gravity of settlement in each commune from the former municipal centre to land previously unbuilt on which new housing was erected. This had the double purpose of replacing destroyed housing and receiving the new inhabitants migrating from the provinces to the agglomeration. In fact, as in the case of renewal schemes and rehousing carried out in the city, it is difficult to achieve successfully the objective of a real transfer of population. A proportion of the former inhabitants of the old decayed districts, especially the elderly worse off classes, cannot bear the cost of new accommodation. To minimise this kind of distortion, investment was often cut to

---

* The regional metro system is an extension of the existing metro into the suburban tract, providing rapid transit along selected routes (see Fig. 24b). The aerotrain is as yet experimental and operates on the hovercraft principle.

the bone, and some of the *grands ensembles* of these inner suburbs cut a sorry figure. In this respect they have even been termed new slums.

Fortunately, the achievements have been very varied, and it would be wrong to see the whole picture in the least flattering light. It is obvious that, whatever their character, the renewal schemes have improved housing in a ring of suburbs which at present contain two million people. Far from having been completed, they will carry on throughout the period 1970–75 and will considerably alter the urban landscape of suburbs like Saint-Ouen, Saint-Denis, Pantin, Le Pré-Saint-Gervais and Aubervilliers to the north, and Ivry, Le Kremlin-Bicêtre, Villejuif, Arcueil, Gentilly, Montrouge and Clamart to the south. The principal result in the general pattern of urban land use in the inner suburbs is the spreading of the residential areas from the valleys, where settlement followed the road and rail communication lines, towards the intervening plateaux. Here, however, the expansion of the residential area runs into competition with services, which are also taking out options on the remaining unbuilt land.

The use of unbuilt land in the outer suburban ring has made it possible to rehouse part of the excess population of the suburbs closest to Paris, and at the same time has reduced the pressure exerted on the town and its oldest suburbs by the influx of new population. This is the context of massive building projects, like the urbanisation of the Pierrefitte, Sarcelles and Gonesse communes to the north and those of Massy and Antony to the south.

The opening of new routeways includes two kinds of schemes. The first concerns the development of access motorways, that is of roads of national importance linking the capital with the regional traffic flows of the regions situated around Paris and supplying the connection with the provincial growth poles. Three such specialised motorways have been completed so far, in chronological order of completion the West motorway, before the Second World War, the South motorway and the North motorway.* Other major exit roads have so far only been of local importance, for example the eastern exit.

The second group of schemes concerns traffic circulation within the suburbs and contact between suburbs and the municipal core area. It includes a very large number of realignments, widening and doubling of carriageways, which are difficult to summarise as a whole, and the preparation of expressways. The first ring of peripheral boulevards at the point of contact between the city and the suburbs, duplicating the

* To Rouen, Lyon and Marseille, and Lille respectively.

former boulévards along the fortification lines, called the Boulevards des Maréchaux,* is being completed. A second is represented in part by the main roads which function as components of a ring road system and which have been linked together administratively as the *route nationale* 186, which acts above all as a by-pass to the south of Paris, between the Pompadour intersection and Versailles. These roads have been improved by widening and the construction of intersections with the main radial routes from Paris. There is a need for much more civil engineering work, but this is made costly by the price of land and the changes required in the network of public utilities. They make only slow progress and with a serious delay in relation to demand.

The overloading of the traffic network, atmospheric pollution and the hindrance caused by renovation and modernisation works, are aggravated by the existence of a large number of small and large industrial firms, some of them obsolete from all points of view. Various measures are therefore directed towards evicting from this section of the suburbs these cumbersome industries with their unpleasant or dangerous surroundings. The planning laws requiring permission for all expansion or creation of industrial firms in the Paris region make possible a sifting operation and a gradual elimination. Some new factories, with the purpose of employing locally some of the active population in the new residential districts, are being built on industrial estates on land set aside for this purpose on the interfluve plateaux, as for example at Petit-Clamart. At the same time, the small firms which are more or less economically marginal, situated in the densest parts of the old suburbs, are disappearing or being absorbed by the mergers which accompany the creation of new factories outside Paris. The largest firms have caused major decentralisations affecting part of their plants, like the Renault and Citroën companies, and involving the transfer of their expansion schemes outside the agglomeration.

4 Industrial Decentralisation

The term 'industrial decentralisation' applies more to an intention than to an objective reality. In fact it is applied to every newly created industrial firm outside Paris whose head office or principal agency is in

* The external boulevards built on the lines of the last fortifications of Paris when these were dismantled.

Paris, as though *a priori* each one of these creations must have concerned the Paris region. As a result there is some confusion between the relocation of factories and workshops initially located in the Paris region, which are decentralisations in the strict sense of the word, and new creations made directly in the provinces.

From 1945 to 1962, 1,280 decentralisation* operations involving the creation of 114,500 jobs and a further 231,000 jobs forecast, were recorded. Of these 759 operations were located in the Paris Basin, with 71,200 jobs created and a further 129,000 anticipated. In a radius of 250 kilometres, encompassing eleven *départements*, 536 firms were located employing a little under 50,000 people and capable of expanding to nearly 100,000. The favourite region outside the Paris Basin is the Central South East, the Lyon city region extending from Geneva to Saint-Etienne, Grenoble and Valence.

Industrial decentralisation is a Parisian concern, in the sense that the firms which have their controlling interests in Paris do not plan to integrate into a provincial structural complex. They tend to avoid locating in the major provincial agglomerations or in provincial urbanised regions, unless they have previously eliminated any degree of autonomy which might have existed.† In the case of long distance decentralisations they prefer medium sized or small towns, where the power of decision is non-existent and which escape effective control from any regional metropole. In the case of short range decentralisations the firms use the infrastructures and labour pools of small and medium towns, which act as transit centres for internal migrations.

In a first wave of decentralisations firms were located in towns of from 15,000 to 50,000 inhabitants. More recent operations have affected smaller towns, provided that they have easy and rapid contacts with Paris. In the immediate periphery, within a radius of 250 kilometres, the west and the north have clearly been preferred, with respectively 31.2 per cent and 27.8 per cent of the operations, a total of 59 per cent. Evreux, Bernay, Vernon, Louviers, Fécamp, Barentin, Bolbec, Dieppe, Elbeuf, Rouen, Le Havre, Compiègne, Chauny, Noyon, Abbeville, Eu, Amiens, Creil, Albert, Doullens, Senlis, Saint-Quentin, Tergnier, Soissons, Laon and Hirson have been

* *Cahiers de l'Institut d'Amenagement et d'Urbanisme de la Region Parisienne,* fasc. 6, November 1966.

† In the case of provincial firms taken over by Parisian companies for example, and subsequently reorganised and expanded.

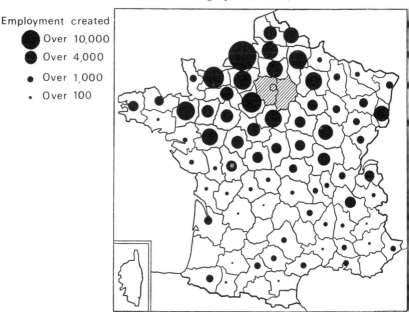

Employment created
- ⬤ Over 10,000
- ◕ Over 4,000
- • Over 1,000
- · Over 100

FIG. 22. Summary of industrial decentralisations completed between 1949 and 1963 (after O. Guichard, *Aménager la France,* p. 81)

major recipients of decentralised firms. Everything suggests that decentralisations have been attracted by the existence of small towns of from 15,000 to 50,000 inhabitants much more than by a handful of large towns like Le Havre, Rouen or Amiens. The East, which is less urbanised, has received less than a fifth of the decentralised factories, the majority being divided between the agglomerations of Reims and Troyes. The vast majority of the decentralisations concern the engineering industry and are dispersed, the electrical industries and precision engineering involving particularly the sector between Chartres and Dieppe, together with Amiens and Reims, and the chemical and chemical derivative industries, located in the same sector and in the South East.

5 The Increasing Area Devoted to Services

The area necessary for service installations in a large modern agglomeration is becoming gradually larger, and introduces a real element of competition for the use of available sites. These are now

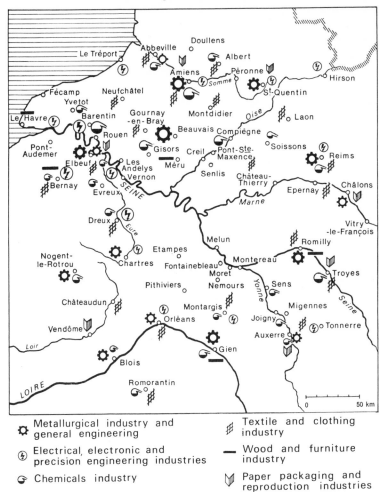

FIG. 23. Principal decentralisations carried out within a 250 km radius around Paris between 1950 and 1965. The largest symbols indicate the most important decentralisations (after J. L. Palierne and P. Riquet, *Cahiers de l'I.A.U.R.P.*, Vol. 6, Fasc. 1, 1966).

situated on the interfluves where until the Second World War military terrain and agricultural land persisted. This is where in the course of the 1920s and 1930s there were already extensive urban cemeteries. The airports have absorbed increasing areas as air traffic intensified and the technological requirements of flight evolved. Le Bourget has ceded first place to Orly, and in the near future a new airport will take over the handling of long range supersonic aircraft.* Ever larger areas are needed and, increasingly extensive areas are influenced by their proximity to the runways.

The new perishable food market, resulting from the transfer of the Halles from central Paris, near Orly airport at Rungis, covers an area of 286 hectares. It is now combined, at least as regards its position, with a huge retail market, the Belle-Epine supermarket, which boasts of being the largest in Europe.

For technical reasons power stations are distributed differently. The substitution of the use of transported coke oven and natural gas for town gas, has made it possible to reduce the area formerly occupied by sprawling gas works with unpleasant surroundings, although storage facilities have taken over some of the space abandoned by gas works. Electricity power stations line the river banks from Montereau to the Porcheville station near Mantes. One of the most modern has been built beside the Oise at Creil. The housing of a proportion of the atomic energy research effort in the Paris region has blocked out extensive areas at Fontenay-aux-Roses, Châtillon-sous-Bagneux and on the Saclay plateau.

However, more than the takeover of urban land by services, it is the growing difficulty in guaranteeing that these services will function on an increasingly large scale which poses both technical and economic problems. Water must be extracted from an increasingly wider perimeter, and the elimination of waste products and used water, especially water loaded with detergents resistant to biological breakdown, necessitates technical research and large scale investment.

Services are becoming increasingly costly and the use of expensive operation techniques is becoming more frequent and more necessary as the problems to be solved assume ever greater proportions. The most obvious example is that of transport services.

6 *The Daily Movement of the Urban Population and the Problem of Transport*

In 1968 approximately a million persons working in Paris were recorded as living in the city proper, making daily return journeys to

* The new airport of Paris Nord under construction at Roissy-en-France.

work from one district to another amounting to less than an hour on average. In addition, 850,000 persons also working in Paris came daily from the suburbs with an average daily return journey time exceeding an hour. As well as this commuting within the city of Paris and from the suburbs to Paris there were movements within the suburbs over relatively long distances, involving over a million inhabitants, and also rather less than 200,000 journeys made daily from the city of Paris to the suburbs.

Taking into account waiting time, the time lost changing from one means of transport to another and the time margin allowed by transport users to be sure of getting to work punctually, commuting wastes an amount of time equal to 15 to 20 per cent of the working day. It imposes fatigue and expense. The heavy burden of mass transit during the rush hours cannot be priced to cover operating costs. Suffering from heavy financial losses, supported by subsidies from local, *département* and even State public funds, the public transport system obtains only the indispensable minimum of investment; as a result the facilities always seem inadequate in relation to the needs, and modernisation and extension works are undertaken tardily and parsimoniously. However, the discomfort and the increasingly poor timekeeping of surface transport systems, choked by traffic jams, are insufficient reasons to explain the excessive, expensive and inconvenient use of private cars which increasingly congest the traffic and parking areas and are rapidly aggravating the difficulties of travelling within the entire agglomeration.

The movement by public transport of the Paris region's active population is in large measure accomplished by the railway stations which every day handle half a million suburban travellers in each direction. However, a proportion of the railway users have employed another means of transport to reach their departure station, and reach their workplace in Paris by metro or bus. The routes are often complicated and seem contradictory, especially when the worker, having arrived at a central station in Paris, retraces his steps by metro or bus to reach his workplace. Suburban bus services and the suburban metro are only involved to a lesser degree in commuting.

Two main types of movement may be distinguished; the simple radial movement of tertiary sector workers employed in the business, administrative and commercial districts of the city centre in its widest sense, and secondly the tangential movements, combined with complex radial movements and with both departure and terminal points in a suburb or peripheral district, as in the case of factory workers living in working class or residential suburbs.

The expansion of residential areas away from the arteries served by railways, as in the case of the *grands ensembles* with up to several thousand inhabitants, makes movement within the suburbs more and more complicated, and many radial migrations must begin with a tangential one to reach a station or motorway.

The transfer of certain activities of a central character to the suburbs, like administration, head offices, commercial and banking offices, university faculties and professional colleges, diverts the flows of daily movement towards new nuclei, while the transport network inherited from the preceding period and all the transport infrastructures were organised to serve a predominance of alternating centripetal and centrifugal movements.

The transport system must therefore be developed both as regards volume, with an increased capacity for movement along the major arteries and accessibility for an inexorably increasing number of private vehicles, and geographically, in the sense that new commuting patterns must be anticipated resulting both from the creation of residential zones and the location of employment in new situations. This is particularly the objective underlying the building of the regional express metro system which serves the recent relocation of central functions in the Défense redevelopment and permits more rapid mass transit in an east-west direction.

II THE DEVELOPMENT PLANS

Faced with inevitable urban expansion and the complex problems this poses, it is no longer possible to leave control of the Paris agglomeration's development to fragmented improvisation.

The cost of services is increasing more rapidly than the number of inhabitants. It is becoming increasingly difficult to guarantee a free flow of traffic within the agglomeration and especially in the city. The public transport systems are more and more overloaded, and their operating costs go up without the services becoming better and more regular. The idea of a remoulding of the agglomeration's structures has gradually become dominant, without so far bringing about a true technical revolution. The fear of the unknown means that people remain loyal to transport systems and an urban system which are patently inadequate and unsuited to present day conditions. The choice of structures is restricted to simple options, and even to an interchange between simple opposing formulas. The reluctance of private capital to invest in housing because of the policy of low rents after the First World War opened the way for a spreading out of settlement in detached houses along the main arteries and public transport routes. The awareness of the high cost of public services within a widespread and elongated settlement pattern encouraged a return after the Second World War to systems of concentrated settlement in groups of apartment blocks, the *grands ensembles*. The fact that these were, socially speaking, an unsuitable way of forming towns or districts quickly led to severe criticisms, with Sarcelles rather than Massy-Antony as the target, to such an extent that local authorities were led once again to view favourably the building of *cités* of detached houses. However, so far this has not led to a division of urban land and land to be developed into areas suitable for the building of *grands ensembles* because of their situation, the price of land and the character of service facilities, and, on the other hand, into land reserves to be devoted to various kinds of detached housing with individual gardens.

The pressure of numbers nevertheless forced the authorities to take decisions on the land to be developed, taking into account the best type of land use and the most effective use of public services, especially transport services. An initial development plan was prepared by the Paris region planning authority, the 'Plan d'Aménagement et d'Organisation de la Région Parisienne', (P.A.D.O.G.). The planners were overtaken by events. The administration of the Paris District, which is now the planning region of Paris, very quickly produced a master plan, designed to shape urban expansion over the next twenty to thirty years. A summary of the proposals is included below.

1   The Master Plan for the Paris Region

The master plan* stems from a choice between two options: a 'satellitisation' of the future agglomeration by creating a dozen new towns within a fifty kilometre radius of Notre-Dame, or an expansion of the agglomeration by a rational occupation of unbuilt land in contact with existing built-up areas and with easy links to their service

* The full title is the 'Schéma Directeur d'Aménagement et d'Urbanisme de la Région Parisienne'.

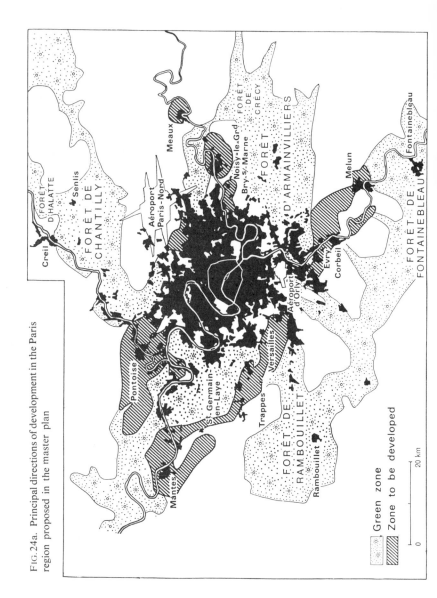

FIG. 24a. Principal directions of development in the Paris region proposed in the master plan

Green zone

Zone to be developed

0   20 km

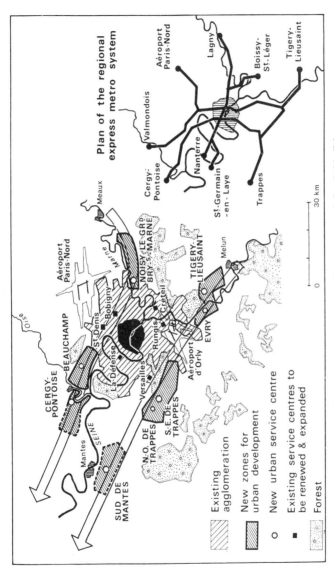

FIG. 24b. The major decisions of the master plan (after P. Merlin)

facilities. The second option, being more economical, appeared both more realistic and more practicable.

There are five distinct development areas. The first is to be reorganised rather than developed, and concerns the western inner suburbs of Paris which already have 1.2 million inhabitants and which must be restructured taking into account the transfer of head offices to the Défense scheme and the creation of the new préfecture at Nanterre.

The four others are more correctly regarded as zones for new urban development. The first is a southern zone, on the banks of the Seine upstream from Paris, centred on Evry, the préfecture of the Essonne *département,* Corbeil, Lieusaint and Melun. It is served by two railway lines, two main roads and the South motorway. It combines residential areas with industrial estates and tertiary employment complexes, penetrated by large open spaces, like the Forêt de Senart and the Seine waterside. It is planned to house 120,000 inhabitants on the left bank of the river around Evry and 400,000 on the right bank with Tigery as its geometric centre.

A second western zone utilises the flat surfaces of the plateau overlooking the small valleys of the Versailles region, the Yvette, Rû de Gally and Mauldre, between Orsay and Trappes, and at a later stage, the Seine valley downstream from Paris between Poissy and Rolleboise. Two new towns will act as poles for this development zone, Palaiseau-Bures-Orsay and Plaisir-les-Gâtines, capable of growing in less than thirty years from 35,000 to 400,000 inhabitants.

Thirdly, a northern zone is to be partly renewed and partly built between the Saint-Denis plain and Pontoise, with a broad outcropping onto the Oise valley. The Montmorency valley will house 600,000 inhabitants and the plateau to the west of Pontoise 300,000 inhabitants.

Finally, an eastern zone is to be centred on the Marne valley between the Ourcq canal and the Saint-Maur meander from Lagny to Vincennes, served by an eastern extension of the regional electrified rail network, with a cluster of industrial and residential *cités* housing from 300,000 to 500,000 inhabitants in all.

Choosing the option of a continuous urbanisation by no means excludes the possibility of a simultaneous expansion of the medium sized towns situated within a radius of fifty kilometres which for twenty years have shown a tendency to increase their populations and intensify their activities.

This organisation of the Paris region's area is accompanied by a comprehensive plan for restructuring both the road and transport plans; without dealing with technical innovations which are difficult to foresee at a distance of thirty years, this leaves the way open for experiments and the possibility of introducing new rapid transport systems, like fast electric trains, monorails and priority lanes for express bus services. In the context of the programme, only directions and intensities are suggested, taking into account the existing communications arteries and present operating techniques, but the possibilities of a technological revolution in transport are not excluded (Fig. 24b).

On the basis of this general plan, the administration of the Paris region has undertaken the construction of four new towns in comprehensive development zones at Noisy-le-Grand, Cergy-Pontoise, Evry and Trappes. At the same time, however, the opportunity of revising the Schéma Directeur is being considered, particularly to take into consideration the attraction of the north-south áxis and the new airport of Roissy-en-France. The particular quality of master plans is, after all, to stimulate new proposals, which of course have to take into account the impact of any scheme on the land market.

The development of the Paris region seems to be directed in the future towards multiplying the nuclei of urban life within a very large agglomeration, dominated by the symbol of Paris, but less and less by the core area of the old Paris alone.

This development has two levels, a regional level and a local level. The first level involves reanimating and expanding the towns restricted in their growth or even sterilised by the attraction of Paris. These are the towns situated within a radius of from 100 to 200 kilometres around the capital; Rouen, Amiens, Reims, Orléans, Tours and to a lesser degree, Beauvais, Troyes and Le Mans, and in its special situation as a major seaport, Le Havre. The driving force, which is expected to encourage growth, is public investment in school, university, cultural and hospital facilities, in housing construction, in transport infrastructures and in energy supply. In the context of the policy of industrial decentralisation, these towns have been favoured, since Parisian firms, or firms with a head office in Paris, are more willing to locate plant one or two hours away from Paris than to agree to a true decentralisation to the advantage of a more distant province. Their growth remains relatively slow, but is more rapid than the 12 per cent experienced by the Paris residential complex and this already indicates a reversal of the trend in the preceding period.

TABLE EIGHTEEN

POPULATION INCREASE, 1954–62 AND 1962–68, OF SEVERAL
TOWNS WITHIN A 100 TO 200 KILOMETRE RADIUS OF PARIS

	Change per cent	
	1954–62	1962–68
Rouen	16	12
Amiens	16	17.5
Reims	14	13
Orleans	22	29
Tours	18	23

The local level involves the proliferation around the existing agglomeration of urban centres which by virtue of their facilities and activities can retain a residential population distinct from the commuting population. In the debate which developed with the drafting of the master plan, those in favour of deliberately expanding small urban nuclei between thirty and eighty kilometres from Paris were opposed to those who wished to use the Parisian infrastructures to best advantage and who preferred to organise the urban tract of the suburban zone around new growth poles. The latter carried the day. The master plan calls for the provision of new towns on the edge of the former agglomeration, but does not disguise the risk of simply hastening the extension of the agglomeration and its internal mobility. A race has been started. The creation of jobs and the dispersion of services could determine the autonomy of the new towns, on a different scale from the autonomy of the old rural communes which are now suburban communes, within the structure of a great modern agglomeration, polarised by nuclei of over 100,000 inhabitants. However, equally the new towns might only be dormitory towns in an agglomeration animated each day by Brownian movements.* The geographers of the year 2000 will draw up the balance sheet.

* The irregular movement of microscopic particles in a fluid, named after Dr Robert Brown who first described the phenomenon in the nineteenth century.

Further Reading

The French edition contains an exhaustive bibliography of references exclusively in French, not all of which are readily accessible. It is considered more useful in the context of a translated work to include further reading in English and to restrict French references to works dealing with the geography of the entire country or of major regions. Most of the texts cited include very detailed bibliographies.

1 Texts devoted to the geography of the entire country

Chabot, G., *Géographie Régionale de la France*, Masson, 1966.
Clout, H., *The Geography of Post-War France*, Pergamon (Oxford), 1972.
Clozier, R., *Géographie de la France*, Presses Universitaires de France, 1967.
Evans, E., *France: A Geographical Introduction*, Christophers, 1960.
Harrison Church, R., *et al.*, Chapter 13 'France' in *An Advanced Geography of Northern and Western Europe*, Hulton, 1967.
Le Lannou, M., *Les Régions Géographiques de la France*, C.D.U., 1963.
Pinchemel, P., *France. A Geographical Survey*, Bell, 1969.
Scargill, I., *Economic Geography of France*, Macmillan, 1968.
Thompson, I., *Modern France. A Social and Economic Geography*, Butterworth, 1970.
Reader's Digest, *Grand Atlas de la France*, second edition, Paris, 1970.

2 Texts devoted to major regions of France

Blanc, A., *et al.*, *Les Régions de l'Est*, second edition, Presses Universitaires de France, 1970.
Bastié, J., *Paris en l'an 2000*, SEDIMO, 1964.
Carrère, P., and Dugrand, R., *La Région Méditerranéenne*, second edition, Presses Universitaires de France, 1967.
Clout, H., *The Massif Central*, Oxford University Press, 1973.
Derruau-Boniol, S., and Fel, A., *Le Massif Central*, Presses Universitaires de France, 1963.
Estienne, P., and Joly, R., *La Région du Centre*, Presses Universitaires de France, 1961.
Flatrès, P., *La Région de l'Ouest*, Presses Universitaires de France, 1964.
George, P., Randet, P., and Bastié, J., *La Région Parisienne*, second edition, Presses Universitaires de France, 1964.
Hall, P., Chapter 3 'Paris' in *The World Cities*, Weidenfeld and Nicolson, second edition to be published in 1973.

Heisch, R., and Lerat, S., *La Région du Sud-Ouest*, second edition, Presses Universitaires de France, 1968.

Labasse, J., and Laferrère, M., *La Région Lyonnaise*, second edition, Presses Universitaires de France, 1968.

Le Lannou, M., *Géographie de la Bretagne*, Plihon (Rennes), 1952.

Musset, R., *La Normandie*, Armand Colin, 1960.

Nistri, P., and Prêcheur, C., *La Région du Nord et du Nord-Est*, second edition, Presses Universitaires de France, 1964.

Phlipponneau, M., *Debout Bretagne*, Presses Universitaires de Bretagne (Saint-Brieuc), 1970.

Richardot, J.-P., *Rhône-Alpes, clef pour l'Europe*, Laffont, 1971.

Sutcliffe, A., *The Autumn of Central Paris*, Arnold, 1970.

Thompson, I., *The Saint-Malo Region, Brittany*, Geographical Field Group (Nottingham), 1968.

Thompson, I., *Corsica*, David and Charles (Newton Abbot), 1971.

Thompson, I., *The Paris Basin*, Oxford University Press, 1973.

Vaujour, J., *Le Plus Grand Paris*, Presses Universitaires de France, 1970.

3 Journals

The following journals contain articles on the major regions as indicated.

Bulletin de la Société Languedocienne de Géographie, Montpellier (Languedoc and the southern Massif Central).

Hommes et Terres du Nord, Lille (Northern France).

Méditerranée, Aix-en-Provence (Mediterranean France).

Norois, Caen, Poitiers and Rennes (Brittany, Normandy, the Loire regions, Poitou-Charente).

Revue de Géographie Alpine, Grenoble (Alpine France).

Revue Géographique de l'Est, Bescançon, Nancy and Strasbourg (Lorraine, Alsace, Burgundy, Franche-Comté).

Revue de Géographie de Lyon, Lyon (Alps, Massif Central, Rhône valley).

Revue Géographique des Pyrénées et du Sud-Ouest, Bordeaux and Toulouse (South West France).

Geographical Index

Subject Index